VIKING SOCIETY FOR NORTHERN RESEARCH
TEXT SERIES

GENERAL EDITORS
Anthony Faulkes and Richard Perkins

VOLUME XI

THEODORICUS MONACHUS

AN ACCOUNT OF
THE ANCIENT HISTORY OF THE NORWEGIAN KINGS

THEODORICUS MONACHUS

HISTORIA DE ANTIQUITATE
REGUM NORWAGIENSIUM

AN ACCOUNT OF THE ANCIENT HISTORY
OF THE NORWEGIAN KINGS

TRANSLATED AND ANNOTATED BY
DAVID AND IAN McDOUGALL

WITH AN INTRODUCTION BY
PETER FOOTE

VIKING SOCIETY FOR NORTHERN RESEARCH
UNIVERSITY COLLEGE LONDON
1998

© Viking Society for Northern Research 1998

Reprinted 2006 by Short Run Press Limited, Exeter
with corrections to the Notes and additional Bibliography
Reprinted by Short Run Press Limited, Exeter, 2016

ISBN-10: 0-903521-40-7
ISBN-13: 978-0-903521-40-6

Cover illustration: Munkeliv Abbey (Bergen)
Head of King Eysteinn (c. 1125)
© Bergen Museum
Photograph by Ann-Mari Olsen

CONTENTS

PREFACE	vi
INTRODUCTION	vii
1. The author	ix
2. The date of the *Historia*	xi
3. The *Historia* and other sources	xiii
4. Þórir munkr: man, monk and historian	xxiii
5. The text	xxx
THE ANCIENT HISTORY OF THE NORWEGIAN KINGS	1
NOTES	55
BIBLIOGRAPHY AND ABBREVIATIONS	116
MAPS OF NORWAY AND DENMARK	136
INDEX OF NAMES	139

PREFACE

The translators and the writer of the introduction have worked closely together, to their mutual benefit; it has been a pleasant collaboration. We are then jointly and severally grateful to numerous friends and colleagues for general advice, particular information and careful reading, most of all to these: Michael Barnes (London), Oren Falk (Toronto), Peter Fisher (Cambridge), Walter Goffart (Toronto), Lars Boje Mortensen (Bergen), Richard Perkins (London), George Rigg (Toronto), Svanhildur Óskarsdóttir (London), Michael Winterbottom (Oxford), Þorbjörg Helgadóttir (Copenhagen), and also to our General Editor, Anthony Faulkes, whose skill and patience have brought this book into print.

INTRODUCTION

THE WORK translated in this volume is a Latin account of the kings of Norway from Haraldr hárfagri, who became prime ruler of the country about the middle of the ninth century, to Sigurðr Magnússon, called the Jerusalem-farer, who died in 1130. Descent in the male line from Haraldr hárfagri was counted the chief justification for a claim to the Norwegian throne, but conferment of the kingly title by assemblies of local men was also essential. King Sigurðr had long been dead before churchmen succeeded in persuading the Norwegians that primogeniture and legitimate birth had anything to do with right of succession to the crown. Concubinage was commonplace—Haraldr hárfagri (died c. 930), for example, is thought to have had sons by six different women, Magnús berfœttr (died 1103) by five. Shared kingship was sometimes the outcome, occasionally amicable, more often leading to mistrust and strife. There was also a long spell, from about 965 to 995 and again from 1000 to 1015, when effective rule was in the hands of the Hlaðajarlar, a dynasty based in Trøndelag and Norway north of there. They were related to Haraldr hárfagri through female lines and never attempted to claim a kingly title. During their time the country was under the suzerainty, more or less nominal, of the king of Denmark and partially of the king of the Swedes; and for five years after the death of Óláfr Haraldsson in 1030 Norway was part of Knútr the Great's empire, with first a nephew of his and then a son as vice-regent.

The author tells us that he ends his history in 1130 because it is better to be silent about the disgraceful misdeeds of the following years (34.11–32). Other sources tell us about the faction fighting and virtual civil war of that period, when rival descendants of the royal dynasty struggled to gain or keep the crown. Two moments of particular importance need to be noticed. One was the creation in 1152 of the archdiocese of Niðaróss, whose large province included the Norwegian sees and those of the Western Isles, Orkney, Faroes, Iceland and Greenland. It gave an authoritative status to clergy willing to press for reform of church-state relations. Their aim was freedom from secular interference in every sphere and in the last resort they would assert the superiority of the power derived from God and embodied in the papal successors of St Peter over that of any mortal monarch. The other was the acceptance in 1161 of a boy of five, Magnús Erlingsson, as king. In effect this put rule into the hands of his father, Erlingr skakki, and his allies. It was also a break with tradition, for Magnús was of royal descent only through his mother, a daughter of the King Sigurðr with whom this history ends. Erlingr rapidly disposed of men who could be thought to have a closer claim and then sought acknowledgment of the legitimacy of young Magnús's reign from the archbishop. This was Eysteinn Erlendsson, a man of great family and an energetic reformer, consecrated as the second metropolitan of Niðaróss in 1161. A concordat which gave substantial concessions to the church resulted in the sanctification of Magnús's reign by a coronation ceremony in 1164. His kingship was thus doubly hedged about, but in the event secular and clerical powers combined could not prevent men who claimed kingly descent in the male line from finding threatening support here and there in the country. One unsuccessful claimant was Eysteinn meyla Eysteinsson, mentioned in this history (31.49). The one who was notably successful is not mentioned. He was Sverrir, who claimed to be a son of King Sigurðr munnr (died 1155), son of King Haraldr gilli (34.1–9; died 1136). After Eysteinn meyla's death in 1177 Sverrir inherited command of the insurgent band called the Birkibeinar. In a battle against him in 1179 Erlingr skakki was killed, in another in 1184 King Magnús fell. Sverrir, hated by the hierarchy, sat insecurely on the throne until his death in 1203 but was forefather of a dynasty which survived into the fourteenth century.

The tale of the kings of Norway is economically told in the *Historia*, with more expansive accounts in particular of Óláfr Tryggvason, the missionary king, who was lost in battle in 999/1000, and of the martyr Óláfr Haraldsson, who completed the conversion of the country and fell at Stiklastaðir, fighting his own people, in 1030. But the 270 years of the monarchy fill only half the book. The narrative sequence is interspersed with digressions, calculated, the author says, to delight the mind of the reader. These excurses, undoubtedly modelled on the practice of Paul the Deacon in his Langobardic history (cf. 17.9–12; notes 153–155),

Introduction

take us far afield, but they are often designed to guide our thoughts on various issues. They are, however, issues whose significance can only be gauged in the light of the history the author did not write, the history of Norway from 1130 on, the history of his own times. Extant twelfth-century writings by Icelanders and Norwegians are vastly exceeded in volume by the conflicting comment of modern scholars on them. Few topics in Norse–Icelandic studies have roused more controversy than these early works, and the substance of these introductory pages is more a rehearsal of problems than a statement of conclusions. The probabilities canvassed are however generally in line with suggestions or findings made by previous commentators. The credit, or discredit, for these views will be readily discovered by the reader who goes deeper into the study of the *Historia* with the translators' notes and the appended bibliography as guides.

1. The author

The prologue and *explicit* of the work refer to the author as Theodoricus monachus (Prol. 1; p. 54). There is nothing specific in the text itself to support the attribution but few scholars have doubted its authenticity. It is generally believed that Theodoricus is a latinisation of the name Þórir, and his Norwegian nationality is clear from numerous passages (e.g. Prol. 12; 1.6; 14.8, 19, 20; 15.17; 24.12–13; 31.39–40). In twelfth-century Norway the designation *monachus* could hardly imply anything but membership of a Benedictine community. We might compare this Þórir munkr with two of his Icelandic contemporaries, also known as authors and usually referred to in early sources as Gunnlaugr munkr (Leifsson) and Oddr munkr (Snorrason), who both belonged to the Benedictines of Þingeyrar. Since he dedicates his book to Eysteinn Erlendsson, archbishop of Niðaróss 1161–1188, it is generally assumed that Þórir munkr belonged to the Benedictines closest to his cathedral. Their abbey, founded (or refounded) about 1100, was on the islet called Niðarhólmr, just off shore from the township itself. The alternative house would be the St Michael monastery (often known as Munkalíf) in Bergen, founded by King Eysteinn Magnússon ten or fifteen years later than Niðarhólmr. A pointer to the former might be that Þórir munkr refers to the Niðaróss house as a 'renowned' monastery (31.32), but bestows no such accolade on the Bergen community (32.31–32). Unfortunately we are miserably ignorant of the state of these monasteries in the time of Þórir munkr. Although at some stage Niðarhólmr may have claimed to belong to the Cluny congregation, it appears not to have escaped episcopal jurisdiction, from which acknowledged Cluniac houses were exempt. There is no reason to think that the Rule was not decently observed. In Eysteinn Erlendsson's time the abbot was on the doorstep and under the eye of a zealous reforming archbishop, who might be trusted to keep him up to the mark.

Two members of the Norwegian hierarchy named Þórir have been suggested as the author of the *Historia*: Þórir, bishop of Hamar 1189/90–1196, and Þórir Guðmundarson, archbishop of Niðaróss 1206–1214. The grounds are entirely circumstantial: both were canons of the famous Augustinian monastery of St Victor in Paris and likely to be learned, and both can be counted protégés of Archbishop Eysteinn, a staunch promoter of the Augustinian order. On the other hand, given their Augustinian profession, there is no reason why either should ever have been referred to as Þórir munkr and not Þórir kanóki.

That Þórir munkr had been a pupil in a monastic or cathedral school is sufficiently demonstrated by his latinity and the biblical, Sallustian and hagiographic echoes in his prose. We have no idea whether he entered his order as an oblate, as a young novice or later in life. It has been forcefully argued that he must have studied abroad—that would be before he took his monastic vows—but he could just as well have become a competent latinist at home, like other monks who never left the cloisters that schooled them, and we simply do not know whether or not the numerous authors he cites were available in one form or another in Niðaróss, some in the monastic and cathedral libraries, some in private clerical possession. Although Þórir munkr very occasionally phrases a remark in such a way as to suggest that he was thinking of a reader who did not know Norway (e.g. Prol. 12; 4.36–37; 24.12–13), there is no doubt but that he had a Norwegian audience preeminently in mind. That presupposes that he knew a circle literate in Latin and likely to appreciate the form of his work and the learning with which he spiced his account of the kings. He does not say that his work was commissioned by a patron or was a task imposed on him by a superior. In a prologue which can hardly be called fulsome he presents it to the archbishop, saluting him with the obedience he owed him as a subject and trusting him to excise what is superfluous and approve what is worthy (Prol. 6, 49–52). That obedience could be said to be due from any inhabitant of the archdiocese, especially any cleric or religious, but it is possible that there was some closer connection. Þórir munkr might have been plucked out, by arrangement with his abbot, for some particular service in the archbishop's *familia*. This kind of special assignment was not unknown. Some fifty years later, for instance, Rita-Bjǫrn, monk of Niðarhólmr (and abbot there from 1232), was sent to Iceland as an emissary of Archbishop Pétr. Þórir munkr had certainly not been confined to his carol: he knew the Niðaróss township, and Þjálfahellir and Agðanes at the entrance to Trondheimsfjord (10.4–6; 32.37–38), and he had been in Bergen (32.31–37).

2. The date of the Historia

Þórir munkr completed his work in the time of Archbishop Eysteinn, who was back from his consecration in Rome by November 1161 and who died in January 1188. The time-span can be narrowed. He refers to the killing of Nikulás Sigurðarson in Niðaróss (31.49–50); that happened in September 1176. The associated description of Eysteinn meyla, the leader of his attackers, as *infelix tyrannus*, further suggests that this claimant to the throne was no longer alive: he is reported to have been killed while trying to escape after defeat in the battle of Ré in January 1177. By the following year Sverrir had established himself in Trøndelag, and from the late summer or early autumn of 1178 to about midsummer 1180 the archbishop was in Bergen, active with King Magnús and his father, Erlingr skakki, in combating the menace of Sverrir. Erlingr skakki fell in Niðaróss in June 1179, his son, Magnús, suffered a crushing defeat there in May 1180. Archbishop Eysteinn then left the country and retired to England, where Henry II's exchequer supported his maintenance, chiefly in the abbot's lodging at Bury St Edmund's and the bishop's lodging in Lincoln (both prelacies were vacant at the time). He returned to Norway in the early summer of 1183. Soon after his return Sverrir defeated the forces of King Magnús and the archbishop in a battle in Bergen. Eysteinn then made some sort of peace with Sverrir and returned to his cathedral.

There is nothing positive in the *Historia* to suggest that Archbishop Eysteinn was not at home in his see when the book was addressed to him. It has, it is true, been argued that the use of the verb *mitto* with reference to its presentation implies that he was not in Niðaróss at the time and that might especially favour the period 1178–1180 when he was in Bergen. But since *librum mittere* can have the particular sense of 'dedicate, present a book' ('submit' in the present translation, Prol. 48), the inference is far from certain.

The years 1177 and the first half of 1178 and the time between midsummer 1183 and December 1188 thus remain the most plausible dates for the completion of the *Historia*. Whether it was put together hastily or in fits and starts over a longer period cannot be told. The need to collect and select material, to reflect on it and turn it all into a decent Latin composition might certainly suggest some longer occupation. A vague limit for the inception of the work is suggested by the author's apparent knowledge of a papal letter of December 1169, in which Alexander III told Archbishop Eysteinn that ordeal by hot iron as a means of proof was *contra sacros canones* (cf. 34.7–8; n. 325). He probably knew another such letter to the archbishop, dated not later than 1172, in which papal belief in the baptism of Emperor Constantine by Pope Sylvester is firmly stated (cf. n. 106). Þórir munkr did not ignore this pronouncement but had good reasons of his own for not accepting it as unequivocally authoritative (cf. 13.31–39).

In uncertain favour of the earlier period, 1177–1178, for completion and presentation of the *Historia* is the fact that the reference to the death of Nikulás Sigurðarson is a unique intervention on the author's part. He is describing events that took place three-quarters of a century earlier and names three of the leading men who accompanied Magnús berfœttr on the campaign to Ireland where the king was killed in 1103. He then goes out of his way to say of one of them that his brother was the father of Nikulás killed in Niðaróss by Eysteinn meyla (31.48–50). Þórir munkr ends his account in 1130 because he is unwilling to describe the dismal events of the following period. Here he suddenly departs from his self-imposed limitation, following what must seem to us a rather remote association, and it might be that this event of 1176 was a recent blow and particularly shocking; it had not been driven out of the author's mind by Erlingr skakki's death in battle in 1179 or by King Magnús Erlingsson's in 1184. The description of Eysteinn meyla as *infelix tyrannus* in the same passage might also be read as intentionally ambiguous. To Archbishop Eysteinn it undoubtedly meant 'baleful tyrant'; it could also be glossed more neutrally as 'unfortunate monarch' (cf. n. 307). But if it was a cautiously chosen phrase, it is not a certain pointer. It could as well be appropriate to the years before 1184 when Sverrir and his enemies appeared to be still in equal contention as to the years between Sverrir's triumph in 1184 and Archbishop Eysteinn's death in 1188.

Whether such considerations are fully persuasive or not, the completion of the *Historia* can be dated to within the decade 1177–1187, and there is some indication that 1177–1178 was the likeliest time of its presentation to the archbishop. Before its delivery to him some longer period of preparation and composition may be assumed.

3. *The Historia and other sources*

In the prologue Þórir munkr says that his information had been gained by 'assiduous enquiry' among Icelanders: they are acknowledged memorialists and have ancient poetry as their warranty (Prol. 9–13). This statement does not, of course, imply that the author approached knowledgeable Icelanders with a blank mind and uncharged memory, rather that his enquiries enabled him to check and supplement his material. In ch. 1 he refers again to Icelanders as his guides to 'the count of years', but says he cannot guarantee the absolute date given for the beginning of

Haraldr hárfagri's reign, or other points of chronology, when 'written authority' is not to be had (1.4–14; cf. nn. 17, 21). This is taken to mean that he understood such dates to be the result of calculation, not validated by contemporary record, whether native or foreign in origin.

In his prologue and epilogue Þórir munkr also insists that he is retailing what he learnt from others, 'things not seen but heard' (Prol. 44; 34.35), and this is often backed up in the narrative by remarks like 'it is said', 'some say', 'as it is believed'. It is however generally agreed that the phrase *audita non visa*, frequently proffered by medieval historians, by no means precludes the use of written sources (cf. n. 11). Þórir munkr once notes something from such a source, a 'register' (*catalogus*) of Norwegian kings (20.53–54; cf. n. 214). That would certainly have been a sequence of names with regnal years, like the twelfth-century Danish lists called *Series regum Danie* and *Catalogus regum Danie*, but might also have included brief comment and anecdote, like early thirteenth-century lists from Västergötland, of lawmen, the Christian kings of Sweden, and the bishops of Skara. Elsewhere Þórir munkr declines to tell of the translation and early miracles of St Óláfr because it is matter already recorded (20.35–45; cf. n. 213). His failure to refer to written works relating to Norwegian history is in contrast to his frequent, and sometimes mistaken, citation of foreign authors. Some of these, like Pliny and Lucan, he did not know at first hand; others he seems certainly to have read for himself, Paul the Deacon, for example, and other more recent writers only one or two generations older than himself, Sigebert of Gembloux (died 1111) and Hugh of St Victor (died 1141).

We see that Þórir munkr frequently muddled the material that originally came from foreign writers, and even his biblical quotation is sometimes more like paraphrase than a literal repetition. He says, for instance, that he has read in the 'History of the Normans' that Óláfr Haraldsson was baptized in Rouen, but continues with some thoroughly confused remarks on Norman affairs (13.18–27; cf. n. 103): the result of hasty reading or faulty memory or jumbled notes, perhaps all three. Two other points may be borne in mind in thinking of his treatment of sources. One is that he aimed to be brief and this led him to simplify.

The other is that he had his own attitudes towards people and politics. Compression is evident in many places, but may be illustrated by a couple of examples. It is clear that various stories were current about Einarr þambaskelmir and the hostility between him and Haraldr harðráði. Þórir munkr encapsulates them in some words in indirect speech by Haraldr, which sound thoroughly in keeping with the character given to the king in other sources, and an implausible response in direct speech by Einarr, followed by the bald statement that this led to the death of Einarr and his son at the king's hands (25.31–39). Later he tells that Magnús berfœttr fled alone from a defeat in Götaland along with a solitary companion, Ǫgmundr Skoptason (31.22–24). This too seems an implausible reduction and Ǫgmundr appears to be a relic of some more elaborate account. The author does not mention him before or after this bare episode and presumably takes it for granted that he will be well enough known to his readers.

The particular views of Þórir munkr can be detected at various levels, from the pleasure he takes in attributing the miserable end of the wicked Queen Gunnhildr to the credulity and levity of females in general (6.15–17) to his implied admiration for Eiríkr jarl Hákonarson who left Norway for England rather than contend with an envious half-brother and co-regent, Sveinn (14.31–41). (Þórir munkr adds however that Eiríkr left his son behind in his place, an unavoidable historical fact which hardly lends convincing support to the overriding motive he imputes to him.) In this last distortion—Eiríkr was certainly invited, perhaps more likely summoned, by King Knútr to help consolidate his conquest of England—the author can only be seen to be reminding his readers of a better, more Christian, way of behaviour than was common in his own time: enmity of half-brothers as co-regents had led to the slaughter of Norwegian kings in 1136, 1155 and 1157; other kings had been victims of close kinsmen in 1139 and 1161.

Þórir munkr believed his book was the first history of his country ever written (Prol. 13–17, 40–41; 34.40–44). He obviously did not count anything in the nature of a 'register' as a history. Presumably the works of the Icelanders, Sæmundr Sigfússon (died

1133) and Ari Þorgilsson (died 1148), would have appeared to him in the same light (cf. n. 21). It is uncontroversially accepted that they wrote on the reigns of the kings of Norway; their books are lost but a notion of their content can be gained to some wavering extent. Each established a chronology which has left traces in subsequent Icelandic writings. Sæmundr may have done little more than work out a full regnal list. Ari was doubtless chiefly interested in synchronising the reigns of Norwegian kings with his other chronological coordinates, but we may conclude from his extant *Íslendingabók* that he probably found room for brief narrative, especially when it helped to substantiate a date or other statement. There is every reason to suppose that their writings would come promptly to Norway. Connections between the countries were close: family ties still existed, there was a thriving commerce, Icelanders found places as warriors and poets in royal retinues, pilgrimage was fashionable, and clerical links were many, especially after the metropolitan see was established in Niðaróss. We lack the sources to give a detailed account but a few suggestive examples may be mentioned. An Icelander, Óttarr, was bishop in Bergen in the 1130s. About 1150 Eiríkr Oddsson was in Norway; he was the Icelandic author of an account of the strife-torn history of the contemporary kings. At the same time his countryman, Einarr Skúlason, priest and poet, was marshal in the retinue of King Eysteinn Eysteinsson. In 1163 Brandr Sæmundarson came from Iceland to be consecrated in Niðaróss as bishop of Hólar and spent the following winter in Bergen. In 1164 Jón Loptsson, in his time the most prominent man in Iceland, was at the coronation of young King Magnús. Jón's kinship with the royal house was then acknowledged. His mother was an illegitimate daughter of Magnús berfœttr. His father's father was Sæmundr Sigfússon, the chronologist.

Þórir munkr could have known the works of Ari and Sæmundr but if he did, he did not follow either slavishly. His account of the discovery and settlement of Iceland in ch. 3 and of the acceptance of Christianity at the *alþingi* in ch. 12 bear marked resemblance to known Icelandic writings of early twelfth-century origin. Yet there remain numerous discrepancies which need explanation (cf. notes ad loc.). Similarly, he refers to the 'ancient poems' of the Icelanders as a respected source, and it has often been suggested that he made direct use of skaldic verse. There were obviously twelfth-century Norwegians who understood and even practised the skaldic art, but Icelanders were looked on as authoritative repositories. If old poetry had superior credentials it was because the makers of it were known or believed to have been eyewitnesses or at least close contemporary memorialists of the events they made their matter. This in turn must naturally imply that it would depend on the balance of interest whether in any given circumstance such verse was transmitted along with some shorter or longer explanatory narrative or whether some such anecdotal context was reported with verse quoted to substantiate it, as a flourish or on demand, or perhaps not quoted at all. There are, in fact, a number of similarities between the report of Þórir munkr and the matter found in verses in kings' sagas, but not of a kind to demonstrate that Þórir munkr certainly knew and sifted them independently. After all, the elicited facts were available to anyone who knew the verse and its setting. The Icelanders Þórir munkr says he consulted could have cited skaldic poetry either to corroborate what he already knew or to support what they told him.

Similar considerations must apply when it is noticed that statements by Þórir munkr also show some similarity to the poem *Geisli*, on St Óláfr and his miracles, composed about 1150, and *Rekstefja*, an epigon poem on Óláfr Tryggvason of uncertain twelfth-century date. Both were by Icelandic poets, the former specifically for a Norwegian audience. Both may well have existed in written form from the start, and they could have been read by Þórir munkr. On the other hand, we should expect him or his acquaintances to know that these were not 'ancient poems' but exercises which gave form to a selection of what currently passed for knowledge about the early Christian kings they celebrated. What was known to the poets was known to others, so there may be no essential need to postulate a literary connection between the verse and the *Historia*. Einarr Skúlason, the poet of *Geisli*, undoubtedly depended on a written collection for his rehearsal of St Óláfr's miracles.

In some cases use of a common source, now lost, may be posited to account for similarity between a passage in the *Historia* and a passage in known Icelandic recording. Otherwise we are left with the bare choice: either Þórir munkr had read the Icelandic matter or he had been told it. Here we should perhaps not forget the powerful part played by memorising in medieval schooling. Ari and Sæmundr did not write their opuscula to amuse but to instruct, and it was common enough in earlier times that such books were learnt, not merely learnt from. Þórir munkr refers to Hugh of St Victor's *Chronicon* (20.25–29). This includes long lists of names and dates (cf. n. 210). It would make a handy reference book but was in fact firmly intended for the classroom, for at the outset the author gives practical instructions to pupils on how best to get it all fixed in their minds. An educated twelfth-century Icelander, who might well have the Psalter by heart as well as a repertory of skaldic poetry, could conceivably have told what Ari said about the conversion of Iceland pretty much in Ari's own words, just as he might repeat a verse by Hallfreðr vandræðaskáld in reply to an enquiry about Óláfr Tryggvason's last battle.

When it is not evident that Þórir munkr was writing in compressed or tendentious fashion, we are reduced to conjecture in accounting for discrepancies between his work and sources he is supposed to have known, whether directly or indirectly. On occasion he may have misremembered what he had read or been told, or he may have thought he knew better either by inference or by following a source unknown to us. On occasion an informant may equally well have done the same. That the author allots St Óláfr a year in Sweden on his way from Russia to his death in Trøndelag may, for example, simply be because he, or someone, found the four months or so predicated by other accounts an implausibly short time to journey from the east, gather troops in Sweden, and move on into Norway. Even if we are probably justified in picturing Þórir munkr jotting notes of a useful conversation on the wax of his tablets, we have still to think of him subsequently transferring his information to a more permanent slip of vellum, and later, perhaps much later, rewriting it in suitable Latin as part of his whole composition. We cannot tell what oddities might result from such a process. It might at least explain why the notorious missionary priest, Þangbrandr, is given an otherwise unknown name, Theobrandus (cf. n. 65).

The sainthood of Óláfr Haraldsson was rapidly acknowledged after his death. His *dies natalis* was 29 July; the feast of his translation was celebrated on 3 August. (Hence the calculation of one year and five days between his death and his elevation, 20.38, was a given.) Material for liturgical use in Latin and for preaching in the vernacular certainly came into being in the 130 years or so between the saint's death and the monk's vows of Þórir. According to him, 'several' writers had left a record of the saint's first wonder-working and his translation (20.35–45), and in due course a consolidated record of miracles was kept at his shrine, as was the normal practice. Little of this early material relating to the cult can be identified, and what Latin breviary lections were once used were replaced by the eulogistic text of the *Passio Olavi*, composed by Eysteinn Erlendsson, Þórir munkr's archbishop. The *Passio* and the *Historia* show no decisive signs that either had influence on the other (cf. n. 188). It has, on the other hand, been argued that the heightened panegyric language of the passage on the saint in ch. 19 indicates that Þórir munkr was borrowing from earlier composition in service of the cult. It is hardly a necessary assumption. We might expect a Benedictine to find a 'humble' style suitable for his secular history, but it would come as no surprise if his experience of homiletic and hagiographic literature enabled him to adopt a 'high' style, exclamatory and hortatory, in celebrating a sublime subject. There are flashes of the same style in his fulminations on cupidity and ambition (18.5–11; 26.1–5).

This is not to say that he was uninfluenced by liturgy and legend related to St Óláfr. The earliest sources to tell of the king's order before the battle of Stiklastaðir, that the alms he provides should be spent for the good of his enemies' souls, are the *Historia* (19.29–33) and the so-called 'Oldest saga of St Óláfr', here represented by the 'Legendary saga' (see p. xx below). Both writers bring home its saintly significance, though in very different fashion. Þórir munkr quotes the command 'Love your enemies', and dilates wonderingly on this royal martyr's *imitatio Christi*. The vernacular author, in quite another style, quotes Óláfr's laconically confident reply to the man who questions his intention, assuring him that he means alms for the souls of his opponents and not for his own dead—'my men and I shall all be saved.' The anecdote is unlikely to be original in either text. It most probably came into being as a telling piece of hagiographic fiction introduced early in building up the saint's legend, like the tale of the king's dream before the battle which was already known to Adam of Bremen a century before Þórir munkr wrote his book (cf. n. 192). The passage in the *Historia* ends with a second parallel, that of St Stephen (19.59–65). The analogy of the Protomartyr and his words before his death, 'Domine, ne statuas illis hoc peccatum', would have been reinforced by the close liturgical bond between the two saints: Óláfr's translation on 3 August fell on the feast of the Invention of Stephen. In the liturgy of the Protomartyr much is naturally made of forgiveness of enemies, and his words just quoted recur in lection, response and antiphon, and this Christ-like merit is spelt out in prayer, ' . . . quia ejus Inventionem celebramus, qui novit etiam pro persecutoribus exorare . . . '. The coincidence of the festivals might have helped to prompt the anecdote about the alms-giving in the first place. Þórir munkr may have been the first to make the connection but it seems far more likely that he is drawing on earlier liturgy or legend.

Scholars have brought three works in particular into the discussion of the *Historia*: the so-called *Ágrip af Nóregskonunga sǫgum*, the *Óláfs saga Tryggvasonar* by Oddr munkr Snorrason, and the so-called 'Oldest saga of St Óláfr'. They are all believed to have been in existence by about 1200 but their precise dates of origin are uncertain. The first is extant but incomplete in an Icelandic manuscript probably written c. 1230; it covers the reigns of kings from Hálfdan, father of Haraldr hárfagri, down to about 1140 and had probably continued to 1177. The second was first composed in Latin but is now known in Icelandic in late thirteenth-century manuscripts. The third is known in a few fragments written about 1225 but is thought to be substantially preserved in the so-called 'Legendary saga', extant in a Norwegian manuscript of c. 1240. All these show various resemblances to the *Historia* of Þórir munkr. Unlike Þórir munkr himself, however, who sturdily says that he will avoid contention except in matters of faith, modern commentators have arrived at every permutation in their attempts to explain the similarities: all drew on a common stock of oral tradition; the *Historia* and this or that Icelandic–Norwegian text go back to a common written source; the vernacular texts are all in debt, directly or indirectly, to the *Historia*; Þórir munkr knew and made use of all the others. Connections more convoluted could doubtless be conceived. The following brief appraisal of possibilities and probabilities offers no hallmarked solutions.

Some passages in *Ágrip* are so close to the text of the *Historia* that it seems undeniable that one is a translation of the other. The answer usually accepted is that the writer of *Ágrip* was following the work of Þórir munkr, but only sometimes preferring it among several sources at his disposal. If we concluded that Þórir munkr made use of *Ágrip*, we should first have to ignore his stated belief that he was the first to write a history of the Norwegian kings (see p. xv above). Then, although we are aware that he was capable of compression, we are faced with disabling difficulty in finding plausible explanations of his large omissions and his divergences. But in historical circumstance there is nothing in the way of associating the *Historia* and *Ágrip*: the author of the first was most likely a monk of Niðarhólmr, of the second probably a resident of Niðaróss or the surrounding countryside.

The other two works concern individual kings and thus do not affect Þórir munkr's claim to be the first to write a whole history.

The notion of a connection between Þórir munkr and Oddr munkr is no more out of the way than connection between Þórir and the writer of *Ágrip*. Oddr was certainly a member of the oldest Benedictine house in Iceland and Þórir is presumed to have been a member of the oldest Benedictine house in Norway. We cannot document individual links but may remind ourselves that Karl Jónsson, abbot of Oddr's monastery from 1169, arrived in Norway in 1185 and soon found himself writing King Sverrir's biography under the king's own guidance. How long Abbot Karl stayed is uncertain, perhaps till 1189. King Sverrir wintered in Niðaróss those years—it would be his only time for more leisurely dictation—and it is hardly conceivable that Abbot Karl had no contact with his fellow-monks on Niðarhólmr, just a boat-ride from the city. It would have been by no means exceptional if he had lodged with them. No evidence can show that Abbot Karl introduced the *Historia* to Oddr, or Oddr's Latin work on Óláfr Tryggvason to Þórir munkr. But his stay in Niðaróss certainly confirms the possibility of bookish traffic between the two monasteries.

The problem is bedevilled by the fact that we do not know just how closely the Icelandic versions of Oddr's *vita* correspond to his Latin. As it stands, however, a good deal of matter on Óláfr Tryggvason in the *Historia* reads like an abstract of a text similar to that found in the Icelandic, but we have no straightforward philological means of deciding priority. Sometimes a common source might be posited. It has been suggested, for instance, that Ari Þorgilsson could well have first written an account of the death of Hákon jarl with just the detail given by Þórir munkr (10.25–34) and Oddr. On the other hand, the details are few and anybody who had read or heard that story more than once could tell it in essentially the same way.

The closest resemblance between the *Historia* and the 'Oldest saga of St Óláfr' (here represented by the 'Legendary saga'; see p. xx above) is found in the passage on the king's return to Norway from England (15.12–41). They have the details that he sailed with two cargo-ships (cf. n. 122), that he had 120 men notably well armed, and that he met Hákon jarl Eiríksson in Sauðungssund. There is also some similarity, less striking, in the *Dagshríð* episode at Stiklastaðir (19.76–84). The author of the 'Oldest saga' was knitting together a great many pieces of information relating to King Óláfr Haraldsson, and he could have pillaged the *Historia* for these descriptions, while it may seem less likely that Þórir munkr would cull only these sparse items from the much more elaborate narrative of the saga. On the other hand, when he writes, 'they are said to have numbered 120, all of them in coats of mail,' he is evidently sticking to his last as a retailer of what others report. The writer of the 'Oldest saga' could have been one of them (that of course begs the question of where he got his details from). In our ignorance we cannot dismiss the possibility that both had the details from a common written source. It should be noted that the passages in question have some content in common with early skaldic strophes referring to the Sauðungssund affair and apparently mentioning the *Dagshríð*. If the verse was accompanied by some narrative, as we are bound to suppose it was, there may be less reason to think that the combination of detail found in the *Historia* and the 'Oldest saga' was peculiar to these texts alone and necessarily indicates a literary connection between them. It is apparent, too, that Þórir munkr is compressing, for though he sets the scene for Óláfr Haraldsson's ruse in capturing Hákon jarl Eiríksson, he does not describe its operation, as though he relied on the comprehension of his readers. Perhaps he counted on their familiarity with the 'Oldest saga'. Perhaps he thought it was common knowledge.

In sum, we may say that *Ágrip* almost certainly derived material from the *Historia*. Direct connection between the *Historia* and the 'Oldest saga of St Óláfr' need not necessarily be posited. A fair case can be made for believing that Þórir munkr knew the work of Oddr munkr Snorrason on Óláfr Tryggvason, presumably in its Latin form. This must then have come into his hands before the 1177–1187 decade in which the *Historia* was completed. It would not be unreasonable to date Oddr's composition to c. 1170–1175. (One Icelandic version—the other is defective—refers to the 1170 translation of St Sunnifa's relics to Bergen, but we cannot be certain that this reference was in Oddr's Latin.) It was put into Icelandic within the next thirty years or so, but we can only guess whether that happened sooner or later in the period.

4. Þórir munkr: man, monk and historian

In the vernacular narratives of kings' sagas and sagas of Icelanders the author's ego is more or less rigorously suppressed. Not so in the *Historia* of Þórir munkr. Prologue and epilogue are thoroughly personal in expression, and throughout the work the writer constantly lets the reader know that he is in command with interjections like 'as I have said', 'as I mentioned just now', 'as I said at the outset'. He occasionally permits himself a sigh of regretful dismay, 'Alas!' (5.20; 8.45; 14.4; 18.86; 26.110). He adds a touch of concern in one or two not very profound generalisations about the response of human nature in a given predicament (10.12–13, 29–30; 19.41–42; 24.24–25), and shows fellow-feeling even toward Chosroes, who deserved to die but not cruelly at the hands of his own son (26.93–96), and the Irish who killed Magnús berfœttr—they were prepared to die for their country (32.9). He inserts a disparaging comment on the 'fickleness and inconstancy' of the men of Trøndelag (15.49); and when a man he calls a pseudo-king is put forward as a claimant to the throne, he mordantly remarks that this is a Norwegian habit (31.5–6). He is free with references to monuments of the past which still exist in his own time: St Óláfr's laws are upheld 'to this day' (16.11) and his merits are 'demonstrated daily' (16.19–21; cf. 19.54–59); his broken battle-axe is 'now preserved in the cathedral of Niðaróss' (24.35); his body now rests in the Holy Trinity church built by Óláfr kyrri (29.14–17); St Mary's church, built by Haraldr harðráði, 'may be seen to this day' (29.17–19); and much the same is said of the monastery and palace built by King Eysteinn Magnússon in Bergen (32.31–37).

There may be a conventional element in the author's refusal to guarantee dates and make decisions between conflicting reports, but since he is willing enough in general to make his voice heard, the diffidence he expresses so frequently and personally may impose itself as a genuine characteristic of the man or the monk. Clauses like 'but since I do not know I neither affirm nor deny the truth of the matter' (3.6–7) and 'who has written more truthfully is "a matter still before the court"' (13.38–39) may be counted typical; for others see 1.10–14; 14.15–16; 19.73–75, 90–91; 20.4–6; 33.22–24.

Þórir munkr's narrative sequence is for the most part tidy, though not without minor repetition (e.g. 5.9–12 and 6.24–28) and instances where abrupt introduction appears to show that the writer presumes a reader's prior acquaintance with the person in question (e.g. 4.27–28; 31.10–11, 23–24). Chs 2 and 3 might have come reversed on chronological grounds, and mention of Haraldr harðráði's exploits in the east before he returned to be king in Norway come in retrospect after his reign and death have been described (28.38–47). The chief divagation otherwise is in ch. 13 where the alleged baptism of the three-year-old Óláfr Haraldsson in the presence of Óláfr Tryggvason leads to a discussion of sources and includes a comment on the age of the saint when he met his death. This may be said to interrupt the history of the first Óláfr and to forestall the account of the battle of Stiklastaðir. On the other hand, it allows Þórir munkr to stress the foreordained sanctity of the martyr king, which remains an enveloping theme. It may be, too, that the author was willing to sustain some suspense at this point before moving on to the death of Óláfr Tryggvason, just as he introduces two digressions in his account of Óláfr Haraldsson's reign before moving on to his last battle.

The author makes a firm effort to give his work a sturdy backbone in the count of years. He offers only three absolute dates, two with reservation, the third without: 858/862 for Haraldr hárfagri's accession (1.1; cf. n. 17), 1029 for the death of Óláfr Haraldsson (19.89), 1066 for the death of Haraldr harðráði (28.34). In between he notes the regnal years and is not much at odds with accepted chronology (cf. the notes *passim*). His account of each ruler, very spare in the case of Haraldr hárfagri, most expansive in the case of the two Óláfrs, is chiefly concerned to indicate how far a king matched given ideals. Apart from the two Óláfrs, who can do no wrong, the most favoured are the popular Hákon Aðalsteinsfóstri and Magnús the Good (chs 4 and 27), and the peaceful and public-spirited Óláfr kyrri and Eysteinn Magnússon (chs 29 and 32). Eiríkr Haraldsson, who killed his brothers, and his queen, Gunnhildr, are rejected for their cruelty, and the kingdom suffered under their son, Haraldr gráfeldr, who followed the counsels of his bloodthirsty mother (chs 2 and 4). Hákon Hlaðajarl is a wicked idolater (ch. 6). Grandfather and grandson, Haraldr harðráði and Magnús berfœttr, are alike, the one grasping, the other restless, both aggressive and both killed fighting on foreign soil (chs 28, 30–32). The personal engagement of Þórir munkr comes out most clearly in his portrait of Óláfr kyrri: 'And I would be at a loss to name another of the Norwegian kings, from the time of Haraldr Fair-hair down to the present day, who enjoyed a happier reign than he' (29.19–22).

The author does not refer to the religion of the kings before

Óláfr Tryggvason, but Hákon Hlaðajarl, who was ousted and killed on Óláfr's arrival, is an arch-pagan who met a suitably despicable end (6.20–22; 10.25–31). Hákon's son, Eiríkr jarl, is said to have vowed to become Christian if he was victorious in the battle of Svǫlðr but made no attempt to impose the new faith during his rule. Otherwise, pagans in confrontation with Christianity are savage, barbarous, obdurate, whether Orcadians, Icelanders, Saxons or Wends, and the author finds no fault with the harsh methods of conversion employed by Óláfr Tryggvason (ch. 9 and 11.4–15) and Charlemagne, the emperor who is held up as an ardently admired example (30.44–53, 59–65). Those who defeated and killed St Óláfr have the same adjectives applied to them as the heathen. The root of their rebellion, however, lay in the bribery of Knútr the Great, whose greed Þórir munkr vehemently denounces (18.5–15) and who is finally dismissed by him with a note of disdain (20.51–52). In contrast, Ingi Steinkelsson, king of the Swedes, is described as 'an excellent man': the author seems to have thought so because of the peace Ingi contrived to make with the bellicose Magnús berfœttr (31.24–28).

As we have seen, Þórir munkr protests more than once that he wishes to avoid contention and at various points will not commit himself to a decision between varying reports. In 19.75–76 he adds a further personal comment: 'nor do I wish to soothe the ears of others with an obliging lie'. This seems uncalled for in the context, but apparently gives us to understand that dispute was alive over the identity of those who inflicted wounds on St Óláfr, the 'Lord's anointed'. Such dispute would be most likely among the descendants of Óláfr Haraldsson's chief opponents at Stiklastaðir, the kindred of the Arnmœðlingar and Bjarkeyingar, for example, who were still great men in the kingdom in the author's day. Þórir munkr is not prepared to curry favour by absolving anyone; on the other hand, if challenged by proponents of one side, he could perhaps absolve himself by saying that, of course, his sly comment was not meant to refer to them. He could similarly hedge on the relevance of his remark, noted earlier, on the 'fickleness and inconstancy' of the men of Trøndelag. He could argue that in its context it referred to their treatment of St Óláfr, though it could also be read, and was very probably intended to be read, as a comment on their current switch of allegiance from Magnús Erlingsson to Sverrir (cf. n. 128).

A degree of contemporary caution may be seen in yet another remark, again not strictly necessary in its setting. King Sigurðr allowed Haraldr gilli to undergo ordeal to prove he was a son of Magnús berfœttr (34.3–9). Here Þórir munkr interposes, apparently with reference to the nature of the ordeal imposed, 'more harshly than fairly as it seemed to some', and he concludes in confirmatory fashion, 'But assisted by God, as it is believed, he showed himself unburnt.' He evidently accepted the legitimacy of a claim to the kingship by Haraldr gilli, notorious as a disastrous character but still in the male line from Haraldr hárfagri. By implication he would also accept the claims by Haraldr gilli's own descendants, including Eysteinn meyla, his grandson, and Sverrir too, if his own account of his parentage was believed. Here and there Þórir munkr refers to 'ancestral succession' and 'hereditary right' (18.14–15; 25.22). When he used the phrase as part of Tostig's persuasion of Haraldr harðráði to invade England (28.11–12), he was presumably unaware that heredity played no part in the accession of Harold Godwineson, Tostig's brother, to the English throne. But when Magnús the Good, his death impending, restored the Danish throne to Sveinn Úlfsson because of the latter's 'hereditary right' (27.41), he must have known that Sveinn's claim lay only through his mother, a king's daughter. This was precisely the same claim as Magnús Erlingsson had. Þórir munkr might be thought to be reserving his position. Succession in the male line was the natural tradition to which he held, but he did not deny that there were circumstances in which descent from a king's daughter could also confer a valid right to rule.

The desirability of Christian peace is a main theme in the author's view of the Norwegian past and is clearly intended as a lesson for the Norwegian present. He repeatedly warns of the dangers of divided rule and the misery of civil war, the perilous results of envy, greed and ambition. The digression in ch. 26 is a series of examples of kinsman's cruelty to kinsman, dwelling particularly on the bloodcurdling story of Chosroes and his son. Other digressions lead a reader's thoughts to another kind of divided kingdom, also firmly indicative of the author's stance in the face of contemporary problems. In speaking of Emperor Otto's pressure on Haraldr of Denmark to accept Christianity, Þórir munkr takes time to tell of the emperor's error in giving churchmen rule over lay lords: 'You have poisoned the church', Otto was told in an angelic visitation. This led to opulence which bred insolence—'as can be seen to this very day'—and the truth of the utterance is proved daily by the perpetual discords between rulers and pontiffs (5.12–25). Þórir munkr muddles his imperial history but his message is unequivocal: it is one thing to put down wickedness 'with the sword of secular might', another to correct souls with 'the rod of pastoral care'. The message is reinforced by the digression in ch. 23, which is prompted by notice of the treaty between Magnús Óláfsson and Hǫrðaknútr, reminiscent of the pact made by Charlemagne and Carloman. This allows Þórir munkr to go on to tell, again with a good many mistaken details, of Charlemagne's liberation of the pope from Langobard tyranny. In such a case it was proper for the emperor to obey the supreme pontiff, but when the rescue is complete and Charlemagne asks what is to be done with the captive king of the Langobards, the pope's response (quoted in direct speech, which Þórir munkr uses sparingly), uncompromisingly begins: 'I bear a spiritual sword, not a physical one' (23.46). Þórir munkr was clearly thinking of contention between the greatest men of his own day, Pope Alexander III and Emperor Frederick Barbarossa, Archbishop Thomas Becket and King Henry II—and perhaps Archbishop Eysteinn and King Sverrir. He appears to see the enrichment of the church and the involvement of churchmen in the exercise of secular authority as the tap-root of the trouble. His view may be counted that of a plain and principled Benedictine. That he points instead to the primitive ideal is no less in natural keeping with his monastic renunciation than his vivid condemnation of greed and ambition for glory in this world elsewhere in his moralised history. It was not for him to criticise the archbishop to whom he owed obedience as a subject, but he could regret his embroilment in affairs of state and in armed conflict within the realm and bring to mind the better alternative.

Þórir munkr's digressions do more than convey his personal

Introduction xxix

attitude and lessons for his contemporaries. They broaden and deepen the background and give the Norwegian past a place in universal history, the history of salvation and the history of imperial Rome, whose conversion and continuation, personified in Charlemagne and Otto, led to the inclusion in Christendom of even the remotest peoples. The wonders of a Charybdis can be seen in the Pentland Firth (ch. 17). There is an implied analogy to be drawn between Hákon the Evil and Julian the Apostate (ch. 8). That Norwegian men of old were far bigger and stronger than nowadays is proved by the cyclic cosmology of classical authors, by Jerome's biblical exegesis and eyewitness report, and by recent Roman archaeology (ch. 18). Divine intervention was shown when the Huns suddenly withdrew from Cologne (ch. 17). It was shown no less when, against all odds, the violence of the heathen was restrained at the Icelandic *alþing* (ch. 12) and Magnús Óláfsson defeated the Wends (ch. 24). The dates offered with due caution in the *Historia* are from the birth of our Lord but beyond that are the years to be told since Creation, variously calculated by the most eminent authorities (ch. 20). We are put in touch with a wider world of learning, reminded of the Gelasian decree and the faults of Origen, and these are matched elsewhere by the quoted wisdom of classical poets, not always correctly attributed. The material is derivative and the composition lopsided but the generously ambitious scope of the *Historia* reveals a mind which in the twelfth-century Norwegian context as we know it must seem of a distinctly original cast.

In the absence of other sources we would have been glad to have the *Historia*, its chronology, character assessments and anecdotes. As it is, Þórir munkr adds little to our knowledge of Norway's early history, and the significance of what he adds must remain dubious. As a commentator on the past, however, and by implication on the present too, he is revelatory. In his interest in times gone by, in his firm belief in a national Norwegian identity and in his respect for kingship he is doubtless representative of his age. In his attitude to contemporary affairs he appears or skilfully contrives to appear non-partisan, and in this he may well typify many who were weary of the atrocities of civil war and longed for a settled peace. His view of ideal church–

state relations seems to be that of an honest individual and monk reflecting on gospel truth, historical precedent and social need. Throughout we are aware of the author's own voice. If his work repays study it is in the end not because it introduces us to a factual history of dead Norwegian kings but because it introduces us to a live twelfth-century Norwegian historian who is a consistent upholder of a moral order. For all the lingering questions we cannot answer, Þórir munkr imposes himself convincingly upon us, an author sophisticated in his way, even devious, but vocal and sincere, with aims very different from those of the more copious and conventionally self-effacing vernacular historians of the kings of Norway. He thus becomes a notable addition to our sparse portrait gallery of early medieval Scandinavians. Any picture we may have of Norway in the latter part of the twelfth-century must be complex enough to accommodate this thoughtful monk.

5. The text

Early in the 1620s Jakob Kirchmann (1575–1643), schoolmaster and librarian in Lübeck, found in the city library there a codex, of uncertain medieval date, containing four Latin works. Since three of them were to do with Danish–Norwegian matters, it is thought that the volume, since lost, was most probably of Danish or Norwegian provenance. One of them was the *Historia* of Þórir munkr. Kirchmann made efforts to interest Danish authorities in publishing an edition of this and he appears to have made at least three transcripts of it. Of the known manuscripts those with the sigla A, B, M and S (see Bibliography, pp. 123–124 below), all written in the seventeenth century, and the *editio princeps* of 1684, descend from copies by Kirchmann that are no longer extant. The manuscript denoted L, however, is a transcript in Kirchmann's own hand and since its discovery in 1936 it has been accorded some special status. Its existence does not solve every problem, since due account must be taken of the fact that Kirchmann himself apparently showed it no special preference; at least, it was a different copy which he left with annotation and was finally published by his grandson in 1684. The L text may thus contain readings or improvements which another perusal of the codex led him to reject.

The edition in *MHN* was prepared by Gustav Storm from the sources available to him, viz. A, B, S and the 1684 edition. Little material is available from the manuscript M, which was not known to Storm; it seems unlikely to have much independent value as a witness to the text of the *Historia*. Manuscript L is naturally of greater interest. An inadequate collation of it with Storm's text was provided in Lehmann 1937 (120–122; rpt 1959–1962, 427–429), and more readings from L are cited in Lange 1989 (184 n. 21). The present translation follows Storm but adopts a few significant readings from L (see nn. 17, 19, 104, 241, 277, 311).

There has been argument—perhaps there always will be—on points of detail in the text of the *Historia*. Fortunately, a new edition, doubtless definitive as far as the materials permit, is in preparation by Professor Egil Kraggerud of Oslo, as part of a project launched under the joint auspices of the classics departments of the Norwegian universities and signalled in *Symbolae Osloenses* 72 (1997), 195. In general, however, the style and structure of the work are coherent enough to persuade us that, whatever imperfections may be demonstrated, there are no serious grounds for thinking it was much altered in its transmission from its origin in the late twelfth century to the copies made by Kirchmann in the 1620s.

HERE BEGINS THE PROLOGUE OF THE MONK Theodoricus to his account of the ancient history of the Norwegian kings[1]

To his lord and father, the most reverend Eysteinn, archbishop of Niðaróss,[2] the humble sinner Theodoricus pledges the obedience owed by a subject, and the support of prayers.

I have deemed it worthwhile, noble sir, to write down in brief these few details concerning the ancient history of the Norwegian kings, as I have been able to learn by assiduous inquiry from the people among whom in particular the remembrance of these matters is believed to thrive—namely those whom we call Icelanders,[3] who preserve them as much celebrated themes in their ancient poems.[4] And because almost no people is so rude and uncivilized that it has not passed on some monuments of its predecessors to later generations,[5] I have thought it proper to record for posterity these relics of our forefathers, few though they are. Because it is clear that no established succession of the royal line existed in this land before the time of Haraldr Fair-hair,[6] I have begun with him; and I have not done this because I doubted that before his day there were in this land men who, by the standards of the present age, were distinguished by their prowess, since certainly, as Boethius says, 'reputation without authors has effaced those men who were very famous in their own times'.[7] To prove this, I shall summon suitable witnesses. Hugh of blessed memory, canon of Saint Victor in Paris, a man most skilled in every branch of learning,[8] made mention of our people in his chronicle as follows: 'The Northmen,' he says, 'departed from Nether Scythia' (by which he doubtless means Upper Scythia, which we call Sweden), 'and sailed in their fleet to Gaul, and entering the country by the river Seine, they laid everything waste with iron and flame.'[9] Sigebert the monk of

Gembloux likewise writes as follows in his chronicle: 'The Northmen,' he says, 'a most horrible Nordic people, sailed to Gaul in their longships, entered the river Loire and penetrated as far as Tours, devastating everything.'[10] It is therefore clear from these accounts, O best of men, that before the days of Haraldr there were in this land men mighty in war, but that, as I have said, a dearth of writers has effaced any remembrance of them. However, the degree of pure truth in my present narrative must be placed entirely at the door of those by whose report I have written these things down, because I have recorded things not seen but heard.[11] Moreover, in the manner of ancient chroniclers, I have added digressions in appropriate places which, in my opinion, are not without value[12] in serving to delight the mind of the reader. I have therefore submitted the little document[13] before you to your excellency for examination, since I know that you lack neither the very sound[14] understanding to cut away what is superfluous, nor the good will to approve of what has been set forth correctly.

May almighty God long keep safe your holiness for His holy Church. Fare well.

Here ends the prologue

Here begin the chapter headings of the work which follows

1. On Haraldr Fair-hair.
2. On his son Eiríkr.
3. On the discoverers of Iceland.
4. On Hákon and Haraldr gráfeldr.
5. On Hákon the evil.
6. On the murder of Gunnhildr through the treachery of Hákon.
7. On the same man's deceitful scheming against Óláfr Tryggvason.
8. How on returning to his native land Óláfr brought with him a certain bishop and other churchmen to preach the word of God to the Norwegians.
9. How at his instance the earl of Orkney became a Christian along with all his people.
10. How the plots and deceptions of Hákon were revealed to Óláfr.
11. On his steadfastness in the word of God.
12. How Iceland received the Christian faith through his instigation.
13. What some people say about the baptism of the blessed Óláfr.
14. On the death of Óláfr Tryggvason.
15. On the return of the blessed Óláfr from England to Norway.
16. On the flight of the blessed Óláfr to Russia.
17. On the nature of Charybdis and concerning the Langobards[15] and the Huns.
18. How the blessed Óláfr returned to his country; and on the decrease in size of the bodies of men.
19. How the blessed Óláfr died a martyr in battle.
20. On the lack of agreement in calculating the number of years from the beginning of the world.

21. On Magnús, son of the blessed Óláfr.
22. On the peace treaty between Magnús and the king of Denmark.
23. On the pact which was made between Charles the Great and his brother.
24. How the same Magnús, made king of the Danes, waged war against the Wends.
25. On the return of Haraldr harðráði from Greece.
26. The author's diatribe against the ambitious, and how Chosroes ended his life.
27. How King Magnús shared the throne of Norway with his paternal uncle; and on Magnús's death.
28. How King Haraldr led an expedition against England, was defeated in battle and died.
29. On his son Óláfr.
30. On Magnús berfœttr,[16] and a brief account of the portents which preceded the death of Charles.
31. On the deeds of Magnús berfœttr.
32. On the death of the same Magnús, and on his sons.
33. On King Sigurðr and his deeds.
34. On Haraldr of Ireland.

Here end the chapter headings

Here begins Theodoricus's account of the ancient history of the Norwegian kings

Chapter 1. On Haraldr Fair-hair

In the year 862[17] after the birth of our Lord, Haraldr Fair-hair, son of Halfdan the Black, became king. He first drove out all the petty kings, and alone ruled all Norway for seventy years[18] before he died. In this book[19] I have set down the count of years which I ascertained by making the most diligent inquiries I could among those whom we in our language call Icelanders. It is well known that they without doubt have always been more knowledgeable and more inquisitive[20] in matters of this kind than all the other northern peoples, but because it is exceedingly difficult to arrive at the pure truth in such matters, especially where no written authority[21] provides assistance, I by no means wish to pronounce in favour of this date rather than a more certain one, if one can be found, since I keep in mind the words of the apostle to Timothy: 'Shun genealogies and endless questions';[22] and elsewhere: 'If any man seem to be contentious, we have no such custom.'[23]

Chapter 2. On his son Eiríkr

Haraldr was succeeded by his son whose name was Eiríkr. Because he killed his brothers, Eiríkr earned the nickname 'brothers' bane'.[24] The aforementioned Haraldr had, however, sent one of his sons, whose name was Hákon, to Æthelstan the king of the English, to be fostered there and to learn the customs of the people. On account of the cruelty of his brother and especially of his wife Gunnhildr, the Norwegians recalled Hákon and made him their king. As for Eiríkr, he sailed to England, where he was received with honour by the king; and he lived there until the day of his death.[25] He ruled Norway for three years—two years on his own, and the third jointly with his brother.[26]

Chapter 3. On the discoverers of Iceland

In the ninth or, as some believe, the tenth year[27] of Haraldr's reign, certain traders sailed to the islands which we call the Faroes, where they were caught in a storm and suffered a long and hard ordeal at sea. Finally they were driven to an exceedingly remote land, which some believe was the island of Thule; but since I do not know I neither affirm nor deny the truth of the matter. They accordingly disembarked and explored round about and even scaled some mountains, but found no trace at all of human habitation. So they returned to Norway and told of the land which they had found; and by praising it greatly they emboldened many others to go in search of it.[28] Prominent among these was a man of noble blood by the name of Ingólfr, from the province which is called Hǫrðaland. He made ready a ship and had with him his brother-in-law,[29] Hjǫrleifr, along with many others. He set out in search of the aforementioned land, found it, and in about the tenth year of Haraldr's reign he and his people began to settle it.[30] And it was then that that land which we now call Iceland began to be settled for the first time, save that a very few people from the island of Ireland, that is Lesser Britain,[31] are believed to have been there in ancient times because of certain pieces of evidence—namely books and several utensils of theirs which have been found.[32] However, the aforesaid Ingólfr certainly had two predecessors in such an enterprise. The first of these was called Garðarr and the land was at first known as Garðarshólmr after him. The second was called Flóki.[33] But that will do concerning this subject.

Chapter 4. On Hákon and Haraldr gráfeldr

Hákon, fosterson of Æthelstan[34] and son of Haraldr, ruled for twenty-five years.[35] He was handsome in appearance, vigorous in bodily strength, pre-eminent in fortitude of heart and mind, and greatly in favour with all the people. He ruled in peace for nineteen years. After that the sons of his brother rose up against him, in the words of Lucan: 'That is a fight for a poor kingdom,'[36] and as the same author says in another passage: 'All power will be impatient of a consort.'[37] That war between them lasted five years. But in the end they fought a battle at the place called Fitjar on an island which is named Storð. Here Hákon gained the upper hand in the first encounter, but as he pursued his enemies he was unexpectedly struck by an arrow; and some impute this to the evil-doing[38] of Gunnhildr, who had been the wife of his brother Eiríkr.

Once Hákon had met his death in this way, Haraldr gráfeldr succeeded to the throne together with his brothers. He followed the counsels of his bloodthirsty mother, and for twelve years[39] was a severe affliction to the people of Norway. After that, he was killed in Denmark by a certain Haraldr[40] who was the nephew of the king of Denmark. That king had the same name, Haraldr, and he was son of Gormr.[41] He later became a Christian, the first of all the kings of Denmark. Haraldr gráfeldr was, in fact, killed as part of a plot of the Danish king who had fostered him. The king was incited to do this, and Haraldr likewise betrayed, by Hákon jarl Sigurðarson, who was nicknamed 'the evil'.[42] After the slaying of Tryggvi, father of Óláfr, Haraldr gráfeldr along with his mother and brothers had done many injuries to Hákon, and forced him to search for the infant Óláfr.[43] After the death of his father Tryggvi, Óláfr could scarcely find a safe hiding-place on account of the traps set for him by Gunnhildr, who feared that he would succeed to the kingdom in place of her sons. For his father Tryggvi was of royal lineage—he was the son of Óláfr, son of Haraldr Fair-hair—and he had ruled over the inland province which the Norwegians call Upplǫnd.[44]

Chapter 5. On Hákon the evil

Because Hákon, of whom I spoke earlier, received help from the above-mentioned King Haraldr of Denmark, they made a pact between them that every year twenty falcons were to be paid to Haraldr;[45] and that Hákon with his army should immediately come to his aid should any exigency of war ever assail the Danish king. Hákon then returned to Norway with a powerful force, and put to flight Guðrøðr, the son of Gunnhildr. He ruled Norway alone for thirty years,[46] but without the title of king.[47] At that time King Haraldr of Denmark greatly feared the most Christian emperor Otto, whose plan it was to place on him the gentle yoke of Christ—which, in fact, he did.[48] It was that same Otto, a most upright man, pre-eminent even among the most illustrious, who conferred more honours and almost more riches on the Church and all the clergy than was expedient, making dukes and earls subject to the Church as her vassals.[49] For after that, opulence gave birth to insolence, as can be seen to this very day. For that reason, as one discovers in the *Roman History*, an angel said to him: 'You have given poison to the Church.'[50] Alas, the perpetual discords between rulers and pontiffs offer daily proofs of the truth of that pronouncement. For it is one thing to keep at bay the wickedness of evil men with the sword of secular might, another to correct souls with the rod of pastoral care. That Otto, nicknamed Rufus, was the son of the Otto who was called 'the pious'.[51] From the very best of parents came an almost better offspring. But let me return to my subject.

Chapter 6. On the murder of Gunnhildr through the treachery of Hákon

After Hákon returned to Norway, he and Gunnhildr became embroiled in various conflicts and plots against each other, for neither of them was short of cunning malice. She always appeared to yield by feigning flight; he followed in pursuit. In the meanwhile the country was laid waste and many hardships were inflicted upon the whole population. Finally Hákon devised the following scheme. He sent[52] a message to the king of Denmark (who at that time was still a pagan, and so on very friendly terms with him), and asked him to send a letter to Gunnhildr in secret, asking for her hand in marriage. He was to say that Denmark would be fortunate to have such a queen, and that while she had no intention of seeking young men to marry, he was getting on in years himself, and they might well make a good match. Thus, the woman received the king's letter; and transported with joy, and with the credulity that is characteristic of female caprice, she hastened to Denmark. The king had her seized forthwith and drowned in a bog.[53] And that was the end of the crimes and evil deeds of Gunnhildr.[54]

Once secure in his control of the kingdom, Hákon soon became pre-eminent as a slave of demons and constantly made sacrifices to call upon them for help. Ten years after this he cancelled the treaty which he had made with King Haraldr.[55] As an excuse for this breach, he seized upon the fact that the most Christian emperor Otto was exerting strong pressure on the king of the Danes to make him and his entire country submit to Christ—an objective which, with the help of that same Saviour, he fully achieved.[56]

Chapter 7. On the same man's deceitful scheming against Óláfr Tryggvason

In the twenty-ninth year of his reign Hákon learned that Óláfr Tryggvason was in England. He was a promising youth, who on his return from Russia, where he had been fostered and assisted by King Valdemar,[57] engaged in a viking expedition in Denmark. But after leaving his ships, his enemies cut him off to keep him from returning to them. Forced in this predicament to call upon divine aid, he vowed that he would become a Christian if he were rescued from his present danger. Accordingly, he was set free by divine intervention,[58] and having regained his ships, he left for Ireland. He proceeded from there to the Scilly Isles, which are situated beside Greater Britain,[59] and there he and all his men were baptized by a venerable man, the abbot Bernard.[60] From there he moved into England, where he remained for several years. He changed his name, however, and called himself Ole, because he did not wish it to be known who he was.[61]

Now when Hákon learned that he was definitely staying there, he racked his brain to find some way of depriving him of life, because he feared him as almost the sole threat to himself and his heirs. And since he was altogether deceitful he brooded long and hard over what he should do. In the end, he summoned before him Óláfr's own uncles, Jósteinn and Karlshǫfuð, the brothers of his mother Ástríðr, and threatened them with death unless they obeyed his commands.[62] So he sent them to England along with a certain inveterate traitor named Þórir klakka,[63] who had formerly kept company with Óláfr for a time. Not daring to oppose his authority, they promised that they would go, but only on the condition that they might reveal the earl's treacherous plan, though not until Óláfr had come beyond Agðanes to the place called Þjálfahellir.[63a] This was of little concern to Hákon, who trusted that his usual stratagems would succeed and that he would as good as have Óláfr in his hands, if he once ventured as far as that, still ignorant of any treachery. And since he was perfectly aware that Óláfr would believe no one but them, he granted them what they asked. So Hákon ordered them to announce to Óláfr that he was dead, that the whole country anxiously awaited Óláfr's return, and that he ought to make haste, lest any unforeseen development should pose an obstacle.

Chapter 8. How on returning to his native land Óláfr brought with him a certain bishop and other churchmen to preach the word of God to the Norwegians

When Óláfr heard what these messengers had to say, he believed them, since they were his own uncles. He hastened to make ready his ships and took with him churchmen— Bishop Sigeweard,[64] who was ordained for the specific purpose of preaching the word of God to the heathen, and several others whom he was able to have with him—Theobrand, a priest from Flanders,[65] and another priest named Thermo;[66] and he also brought some deacons. For that virtuous man had resolved in advance to strive in every way to make that land subject to Christ, or else not to rule a people utterly heathen. In this he followed the example of the very wise Jovian.[67] When the Roman army at war against the Persians found itself in great peril, he was besought by the soldiers to assume the imperial title, but replied without hesitation that in no circumstances did he wish to rule over heathens.[68] By contrast, Julian, that renegade from Christ who from a subdeacon and Christian became a most heinous apostate and persecutor of the Christian name, in the course of the same campaign against the Parthians, according to the testimony of the blessed Jerome, vomited forth six books against Christ.[69] This Julian was led astray by evil spirits, who promised him certain victory in that battle; and to these he sacrificed almost daily not only dumb animals, but also that which is much more agreeable to them— his own body and soul. He had ordered all the ships in which he had sailed there to be burnt in order to incite the hearts of his soldiers to battle, now that hope of withdrawal was removed. But the Lord returned the wickedness of the blasphemer upon his own head,[70] for by divine intervention he was pierced through in that same battle, it is not known by whom; and he placed his hand under the wound as the blood gushed forth and made it spurt into the air with this blasphemous cry: 'Thou hast conquered, Galilean' (for this is what he was in the habit of calling our Lord). And with that blasphemous utterance he crossed from temporal death to death eternal.[71] Therefore, the Roman army, as I have said, left in an utterly dire predicament, elevated to the emperorship the aforementioned Jovian, a most Christian man and adorned with the noblest virtues, and vowed with one voice that they would become Christians. For Julian had turned many away from the true faith. Once he had assumed power, Jovian managed by dint of the utmost assiduity to lead his army to safety after concluding such a treaty with the Persians as he could in so desperate a situation. He himself, alas, died far too premature a death, for he was not emperor for half a year. But let me return to my subject.

Chapter 9. How at his instance the earl of Orkney became a Christian along with all his people[72]

Now when Óláfr left England he set a straight course for the Orkney islands, and because they are subject to the Norwegian king, he urged Sigurðr jarl, who governed those islands at that time, to become a Christian. And when he prevaricated and voiced objections, Óláfr pressed him still harder. Sigurðr even vowed that he would submit to him as king, if he would not force him to adopt the Christian faith. When he continued to resist for some time, it is said that Óláfr abducted his son, a small boy of three named Þorfinnr,[73] from the place where he was being fostered. He swore that he would slay him in his father's sight, and threatened Sigurðr moreover with eternal enmity, if he would not give in. Just as it is written: 'Fill their faces with shame, and they will seek thy name, O Lord,'[74] so the earl feared both the righteous wrath of Óláfr and that his son would die. So by believing or, rather, by consenting, he was baptized along with all the people who were subject to him. And once he had been confirmed in the faith, he remained from then on a faithful Christian, as were all his successors.

Chapter 10. How the plots and deceptions of Hákon were revealed to Óláfr

From here Óláfr hastened on his journey to Norway, and put in first at the island which is called Mostr.[75] He later built a church there, the first of all those erected in Norway.[76] After this, when he had come beyond Agðanes to the place called Þjálfahellir, he stayed there for one night, although there is almost no harbour there. As yet he knew nothing of the deception and plots of Hákon. But that very night, his uncles came to him and laid bare Hákon's treachery, since they were now freed from the oath which they had sworn to Hákon. They implored him to look without delay to his own good and theirs, and indeed to the good of the whole country. He was troubled, as one usually is in such a plight, but committed his whole cause to almighty God, that with His help he might have the strength to carry out what God had already inspired him to undertake. Then that inveterate traitor Þórir klakka, who had gone to England to ensnare him, was put to death there. And the very next day, with the help of God, Óláfr proceeded to the place called Niðaróss. At that time there were only a few huts belonging to various traders there, though now it is the capital of the entire realm[77]—a city gloriously distinguished not only by its metropolitan seat, but also by the relics of the most blessed martyr Óláfr. There a multitude of people flocked to him.[78] He was then proclaimed king, and at once set out against Hákon. Hákon, meanwhile, had been abandoned by his own men and, setting hope on flight alone, came to a small farmstead named Rimull.[79] There his concubine Þóra hid him and his only remaining slave, whose name was Karkr,[80] in a pigsty. When, as often happens to one sad at heart, sleep had stolen upon him, he was stabbed in the throat by that same servant, and died. Afterwards, however, when the slave brought the head of his lord to Óláfr, the king ordered him to be hanged as a reward for the crime he had perpetrated against his lord.[81]

Chapter 11. On his steadfastness in the word of God

After this, the king set his mind, with all his strength and the help of heaven, to the task of driving idolatry and demon-worship from the entire country. He was a tireless husbandman in the vineyard of his Lord.[82] He pressed his cause with prayers and sermons, reinforcing these at times with threats and intimidation. For he saw that the hearts of the heathens were savage, and that only a strong hand could free them from the age-old, ingrained filth of faithlessness and the more or less inborn devil-worship which they had practically imbibed with their mother's milk. And since they were little moved, he often reinforced words with blows,[83] following the example of his Lord, who poured oil and wine into the wounds of the injured man,[84] and following too those words of the Gospel: 'Force them to come in, that my house may be filled.'[85]

There is a place in the diocese of Niðarós which is called Mærin. There, it is said, oracular responses were uttered by demons; and Hákon had brought together there a multitude of idols. Therefore, when the king came there, he called before him all those who had been ensnared even more tightly in the fetter of the devil's falsehoods and who in the vernacular are called *seiðmenn*.[86] And because he saw that they were past curing, and lest they do harm to his new plantation, he ordered that they be gathered into the building dedicated to demons and burnt together with the images.[87] And people say that they numbered eighty altogether, both men and women.

Chapter 12. How Iceland received the Christian faith through his instigation

When a year had passed,[88] the king sent the priest Theobrand to Iceland to preach the word of God. I mentioned above that Iceland is thought by some to be the island of Thule, because of certain similarities between the two places, in particular since daylight is continuous there around the summer solstice, as is night around the winter solstice.[89] When he arrived there, he began to preach Christ to them, and although he was assiduous in his efforts, in the space of almost two years[90] he was able to make only a tiny number of converts, on account of the innate obduracy and savage natures of the inhabitants. Foremost, however, among those who accepted the yoke of Christ, were the following:[91] Hallr of Síða and all his household, and Gizurr of Skálaholt (he was the father of Bishop Ísleifr, who was the first to establish an episcopal seat in that country, in the church which he himself built and consecrated to the blessed apostle Peter, bestowing on it his entire patrimony);[92] the third was Hjalti from Þjórsárdalr; and the fourth Þorgils of Ǫlfus.[93] Two of these men, namely Gizurr and Hjalti, accompanied Theobrand when he returned to the king. But when Theobrand came before the king, he was rebuked by him for having failed to complete his task. The following summer, therefore, the king sent the priest Thermo, whom they called Þormóðr in their mother tongue. The two men already mentioned also went with him,[94] and promised the king that they would work together for the gospel of Christ with all their strength. The grace of the Holy Spirit attended the preaching of this priest to such good effect that in a short time he converted all that barbarous nation to Christ. For they arrived in the country at the time when the public gathering which they call the *Alþing* was being held there. And when the host of heathens became aware of their arrival, the whole populace ran to arms, because they were of one mind in wishing to take their lives. However, by divine intervention they were so restrained that although it was only a tiny band of Christians who opposed them, they neither could nor dared do them any harm.[95] But let what has now been said about these things suffice.

Chapter 13. What some people say about the baptism of the blessed Óláfr

That he might the more easily make the whole country submit to Christ, King Óláfr therefore married his three sisters to men of high standing.[96] He married one, whose name was Ástríðr, to Erlingr Skjálgsson; the second to Þorgeirr, a powerful man from the Vík who later burnt Guðrøðr Gunnhildarson to death in a house because he intended to seize control of the kingdom from Óláfr;[97] the third to Hyrningr, the brother of Þorgeirr. And when he had made all of them accept baptism, he made his way inland, to Upplǫnd.[98] There he came upon Óláfr, who was then a little boy of three, but who later became a faithful martyr of Christ. He was staying with his mother Ásta, for his father Haraldr was then already dead. (Haraldr was the son of Guðrøðr sýr,[99] whose father was Bjǫrn, who was nicknamed 'the trader' and was the son of Haraldr Fair-hair.) That Óláfr was the future propitious hope and glory of the Norwegian people. According to some, the king had him and his mother baptized then and there;[100] others maintain that he was baptized in England.[101] But I, for my part, have read in the 'History of the Normans' that he was baptized in Normandy by Robert, archbishop of Rouen.[102] For it is certain that Duke William of Normandy took him with him to help him in his fight against King Robert of France, whose by-name was Capet (he was the son of the most noble duke Hugh Capet), when together with the count of Flanders Robert was preparing to wage war against Duke William. In fact, he was trying to drive William out of Normandy, because his ancestors had wrested that province from the king of France by force.[103] But whether Óláfr was baptized in Rouen or in England, it is clear that he was rather advanced in age when he was crowned with martyrdom, as those whom one should trust most in matters of this sort maintain.[104] Nor is it any wonder that this could have happened with regard to Óláfr in that land where there has never been a chronicler of ancient events,[105] when the blessed Jerome writes the same thing concerning Constantine the Great, son of Constantius and Helena. He notes that some say that he was baptized in Bithynia in advanced old age, others at Constantinople, some at Rome by the blessed pope Sylvester.[106] Who has written more truthfully is 'a matter still before the court'.[107]

Chapter 14. On the death of Óláfr Tryggvason

In the fifth year of Óláfr Tryggvason's reign, which was also his last, King Sveinn of Denmark, King Óláfr of Sweden, and Eiríkr the son of Hákon 'the evil' went to war against him, and caught him, alas, too unprepared. For it is said that with only eleven ships he engaged in battle against seventy.[108] In the end, because the enemy could constantly relieve one another and put in fresh men for those who were wounded,[109] our king's army was not so much defeated as worn away.[110] His opponents, however, by no means carried off an unbloody victory, for every one of their doughtiest warriors had either fallen in the battle or come away severely wounded.[111] Some say that the king then escaped from there in a skiff, and made his way to foreign parts to seek salvation for his soul. Some, on the other hand, say that he plunged headlong into the sea in full armour. I dare not say which of these accounts is the truer. I like to believe only this: that he now enjoys perpetual peace with Christ.[112] This battle was fought beside the island which is called Svǫldr; and it lies near Slavia, which we in our mother tongue call Vindland.[113] In the same battle, Eiríkr swore that he would become a Christian if he obtained victory.[114] And he fulfilled his vow.

Now a pact had been made between the kings and Eiríkr to the effect that, if they were able to take the kingdom from Óláfr, each would get a third. Eiríkr accordingly received two-thirds of the kingdom (though, like his father before him, he dispensed with the title of king), because King Sveinn of Denmark conceded his share to Eiríkr for the sake of his daughter, whom he had promised to him in marriage. King Óláfr of Sweden gave his share in fief to Eiríkr's brother Sveinn. Then, after a few years had passed, Sveinn began to envy his brother, because Eiríkr had two-thirds of Norway, while he had but one, and that only as a fief. Eiríkr, however, was determined to be just towards his brother, and had no desire to pollute his kingdom with a fratricide. And he reflected at the same time that Sveinn would scarcely be guided by brotherly love in dealing with him in other matters either, as those verses of Lucan put it:

> There is no faith between sharers in sovereignty;
> and all power will be impatient of a consort.[115]

So he departed from his homeland and sailed to England, leaving behind his son Hákon as successor to his realm. Eiríkr ruled with his brother Sveinn for fifteen years. He neither diminished nor extended Christianity, but allowed each man, at least in this respect, to live according to the creed he preferred. He ended his life when he arranged to have his uvula[116] removed by surgery, and died as a result of excessive loss of blood. After he left his homeland, his brother and son ruled for two years.

Chapter 15. On the return of the blessed Óláfr from England to Norway

At that time Óláfr Haraldsson, later to become a martyr of Christ, was in England; and there he reconciled Æthelred with his brothers, and achieved his elevation to the throne.[117] King Knútr of Denmark, who was called 'the mighty',[118] afterwards deprived the same Æthelred of his kingdom and forced him to live in perpetual exile.[119]

It is said that while in England Óláfr visited a certain hermit,[120] a man of great holiness, who foretold him many things—that the Lord would lavish on him the abundance of His grace, and also by what sort of death he would pass from the light of this world to Christ.

In the following year[121] Óláfr prepared to make his way to Norway, with two cargo-ships[122] and well-armed followers—they are said to have numbered 120, all of them in coats of mail. Having made a favourable voyage across the ocean, as a kind of divine omen he put in first at an island which in our mother tongue is called Sæla, and which rendered into Latin is *felicitas*, 'happiness',[123] without doubt a portent of the king's future sanctity, and a sign that through the good omen of his coming, he brought the hope of eternal happiness to his whole country. From here he sailed to a place which is called Sauðungssund,[124] where he remained for a few days. A report then reached him there that Hákon Eiríksson was approaching with two ships, one a small vessel of the type we call *skúta*, the other a longship,[125] of the type the ancients called 'a Liburnian'; whence Horace says:

> You will go, my friend, in Liburnian galleys
> amid ships like towering fortresses.[126]

On hearing this news, Óláfr devised the following trap. Since he was at a very narrow point in the sound, he had his ships stationed one on either side, and ropes stretched between them in such a way that they would be covered by water and the enemy would not detect the stratagem. In this way, the earl and his men could be ensnared there when they least expected it, and might be taken prisoner unharmed and, if possible, without bloodshed. And that is how it turned out. When Hákon arrived, he did not suspect that they were anything other than merchants, and was immediately taken prisoner by the king.[127] He renounced then and there his claim to all that part of Norway over which he had had control; and then he went to England.

When Sveinn, Hákon's uncle, heard of the arrival of the blessed Óláfr, he gathered an army and soon set out against him. But King Óláfr—he had, in fact, already received this title from his men, in the manner of the ancient Romans, for among them it was also customary for the army to create the commander-in-chief and bestow the regal title—

did not count on help from the men of Þrándheimr, for he knew their fickleness and inconstancy,[128] so he withdrew to Upplǫnd,[129] and spent the winter there with his stepfather Sigurðr and his mother Ásta.[130] When spring came, they both set out for the Vík, and there gathered an army and hastened to confront Sveinn. At the same time, Sveinn moved quickly to attack them; and they joined in a naval battle at the place called Nesjar.[131] When Sveinn was vanquished, he disdained flight and resolved to fall with his men. And he would have done so, had he not been prevented and his ship withdrawn from battle against his will by one of his chieftains, a kinsman by marriage—Einarr þambaskelmir,[132] a man of immense vigour, who had married Sveinn's sister Bergljót.[133] He advised him to flee and more or less forced him[134] to make his way to Russia,[135] where he lived until his death.

Chapter 16. On the flight of the blessed Óláfr to Russia

During the time of Eiríkr's reign, many Christians had turned aside from the true faith. King Óláfr strove by all the means at his disposal to lead these people back to the right path and to show them the way of salvation, to establish churches in those places where there were none, and to endow those which were established.[136] In this he strove to appear as the collaborator of that best of men, Óláfr Tryggvason, so that he, as one taught by the spirit of God, might prudently water what his predecessor had gloriously planted. He had laws replete with justice and equity committed to writing in the native language; and to this day these are upheld and venerated by all good men.[137] Dogged in his pursuit of justice for all, he persecuted no one, oppressed no one, condemned no one except, to be sure, those whose own wickedness and persistence in evil had already condemned them. In short, in ruling over mortal men his sole aim was to lead them, insofar as it was in his power, to the glory of everlasting life. This was both manifestly confirmed then by the outcome of events, and is no less amply demonstrated daily by the blessings of almighty God which, we believe, are bestowed for the sake of his merits.

The king then married Ástríðr, the daughter of King Óláfr of Sweden. He had formerly been betrothed to the Swedish king's eldest daughter, but when her father's anger became an obstacle, neither of them was able to enjoy the marriage they had hoped for.[138] By Ástríðr Óláfr had a daughter named Úlfhildr, whom he later gave in marriage to Duke Otto of Saxony.[139]

After this, Knútr, king of Denmark and England, a man who hungered after the possessions of others, called to mind that his father Sveinn had possessed a third of Norway, and at the same time took note that his sister's son Hákon, who was then staying with him, had been driven out of his own country.[140] So he began to incite the chieftains of Norway against the king, and to bribe them in secret.[141] Among these were Erlingr Skjálgsson of Sóli, Kálfr Árnason, Þórir hundr and numerous others;[142] and because Erlingr was the foremost man among them, he assembled an army and closed with King Óláfr in a naval battle, in which he himself fell. And this happened in a place which is called Tunga.[143] Erlingr was killed there, though not at the king's will, by one of his own kinsmen, Áslákr fitjaskalli.[144]

Afterwards, when the king learned that King Knútr was at hand with an immense force (indeed, his fleet is said to have numbered 1200 ships),[145] realizing that he was not equal to such an encounter, he abandoned his ships and withdrew to the court of his father-in-law,[146] King Óláfr of Sweden. From there he travelled to Russia, to King Jaroslav.[147] He had married Ingigerðr, to whom Óláfr had been betrothed but whom he was unable to wed, as I mentioned just now. He remained there for one year, and was treated with honour and the utmost courtesy by King Jaroslav. Óláfr committed to his care his son Magnús, a boy of five, born to him by a concubine.

Meanwhile, King Knútr lured to himself all the chieftains of Norway by giving many gifts and promising more if they would be loyal to his nephew Hákon, whom he had brought with him. And after he had taken hostages from those he thought less trustworthy,[148] he returned to England. Then, a year later, Hákon proceeded to England to fetch his wife; but on his way back he was caught in a storm and driven into the mouth of Charybdis in that part of the sea which is called Petlandsfjǫrðr,[149] off the Orkney Isles. And there he and all his people were sucked down into that bottomless whirlpool.[150]

Chapter 17. On the nature of Charybdis and concerning the Langobards and the Huns

Since I have had cause to mention Charybdis, ancient authors give the following account of its nature. Pliny the Elder (the author of the *Natural History* and a sage and most learned man), the philosopher Chrysippus, and many others say that the place is a passage-way to the mother-abyss from which the entire torrent of the seas is thought to flow, and therefore no bottom is to be found in it.[151] Concerning this abyss it is written in Genesis: 'And all the fountains of the great abyss burst forth.'[152] Likewise, Paul the Deacon, a monk of the community of Monte Cassino, who wrote a brilliant history of the province of Pannonia in which he made many useful and no less delightful digressions, gives almost the same explanation of the nature of Charybdis.[153]

The same author, as a matter of fact, informs us that it

was from out of Pannonia that that savage and ungodly people who invaded Italy with the permission of the patrician Narses spread forth.[154] At that time they were called 'Longobarbs', from *longa barba* 'long beard', but now their name has been corrupted to 'Langobards', through substitution of the letter *d* for *b*.[155] Pannonia, however, has been called Hungary since the time when the Huns wrested it, more or less by force, from the emperor of Constantinople. In order to induce them to cease their pillaging and ravaging of his realm, he gave them the province, though unwillingly, once the previous inhabitants had been moved elsewhere.[156] Those Huns, as Jornandes writes in his history,[157] burst forth from the Maeotic swamps,[158] where Alexander the Great, son of Philip, is said to have confined them.[159] They were a half-bestial and utterly godless race, and extremely repulsive in appearance, for in their heads instead of eyes they had, as it were, two holes which seemed to have been filled with the blackest pitch. While still very small children, their cheeks were cut so that even while drinking their mother's milk they might learn to endure wounds.[160] When they found an opening in their place of confinement, where a stag had passed through,[161] they spread like locusts across the face of the entire earth,[162] led by their king Attila. Overrunning every Gaulish province, they filled everywhere they went with pillaging, burning and atrocities, desecrating holy places and laying them waste. It was they who butchered the blessed Nicasius, archbishop of Rheims, and his sister the blessed virgin Eutropia,[163] and put the city of Rheims to the torch. Later, when they laid siege to Agrippina, which is now called Cologne, the blessed Ursula, daughter of the king of the Britons, suffered martyrdom at their hands, along with all her companions—an almost unbelievable number of both men and women.[164] After they had perpetrated this crime, through divine intervention they were immediately put to flight and the city was liberated through the merits of those most blessed virgins. And the words of Scripture were fulfilled in them: 'The impious man flees though none pursue him;'[165] and likewise in what the Psalmist says: 'There fell those who did evil' (that is, in their hearts); 'they were driven out and could not stand.'[166]

Chapter 18. How the blessed Óláfr returned to his country; and on the decrease in size of the bodies of men

Thus, when Knútr, king of England, learned of the death of his nephew Hákon, he immediately sent his son Sveinn to govern the kingdom of Norway[167] and at the same time to oppose Óláfr should he decide to return to his homeland. O, the calamitous and insatiable greed of mortal men! O, the very wretched human soul! The more it has dissipated itself on visible things and spreads over 'the figure of this world which will pass away',[168] the more difficult it is for it to be made whole again after this life; and it becomes all the more estranged from God, who is the true sufficiency.[169] This is abundantly, even overabundantly, clear in the case of Knútr who, although he possessed two kingdoms, still strove to wrest yet a third from the most just king Óláfr, one moreover to which Óláfr was entitled by ancestral succession.

And when, as it is reported, Óláfr was urged in dreams that it behoved him to return to Norway,[170] he bade farewell to Jaroslav and Ingigerðr, and left his own son Magnús there with them.[171] He then returned to his father-in-law King Óláfr in Sweden; and he remained there over that year.[172] When spring came, with the help of his father-in-law he assembled an army made up in great part of heathens, and he led it through the northern regions into Norway. When the king pressed the heathens to accept baptism and they refused to take on the yoke of our Lord, Óláfr said that he had no need of heathens and godless men, especially when fighting against Christians, and that for him any victory won with the help of evil men would be base. The heathens answered that they were ready to engage in battle and to do anything else which the king might command, but that they would not set this new doctrine above their ancient custom, and would sooner return home. When the king heard this, he allowed them all to depart.[173] After this, Óláfr's kinsmen flocked to his support, and with them his brother Haraldr, who was then a youth of fifteen years, as well as certain other noblemen. Among these were Hringr Dagsson, with his son Dagr, and Finnr jarl Árnason, the brother of Kálfr, who was one of the king's leading adversaries. The king was also followed in every danger by his inseparable companion, Rǫgnvaldr Brúsason.[174] His father Brúsi was the son of Sigurðr, whom I mentioned earlier,[175] the first of all the earls of the Orkney Islands to become Christian.

These were men of vigour and strength, much more powerful in body and spirit than people are in these wretched times, although they were still greatly inferior to their predecessors. Pliny the Elder offers the following explanation of this general decline in his *Natural History*. I cite his own words. 'On the whole,' he says, 'it is more or less plain to see that the entire human race is becoming smaller daily, and that few people are taller than their fathers, as seminal fertility is becoming exhausted by conflagration, the fate to which the age now inclines.'[176] Thus Pliny; and this was certainly not unknown to philosophers, for they were aware that earlier there had been a flood and that the present world would end in a conflagration. Lucan, too, no less a philosopher than a poet, says this in addressing

Julius Caesar because he forbade the cremation of the dead in war:

> If, Caesar, fire should not consume these multitudes now,
> It will consume them with the earth, and burn them with the waters of the deep;
> There remains for the world a common funeral pyre,
> Which will mix stars with mortal bones.[177]

For all things on earth are generated through heat and moisture. Those things in which there is an abundance of heat tend to be frailer, thinner and more delicate; and those things in which moisture prevails are thicker, taller and more fleshy. Plato draws attention to this alternation of periods of fire and flood; for he says that at the end of every fifteen thousand years alternately one or the other of these takes place, and that all mankind dies save for a tiny few who escape by some chance, through whom the human race is afterwards restored. This has always been the case and always will be.[178] Plato did not, however, mean to suggest that the world is coeval with God; but just as the footprint comes from the foot, not the foot from the footprint, so both the foot and the footprint come from the same source. Likewise the world, through *eimarmene*[179] (that is the unbroken sequence of time), may indeed imitate eternity, but it can never attain it. Indeed, God is the most absolute eternity, infinite in form, who looks upon everything as present, whereas the world is made varied by alternations and times. That worthy commentator on the holy scriptures, Origen, fell into this error regarding the alternations of the ages. This is, alas, readily apparent in that book which he entitled $\pi\epsilon\rho\grave{\iota}\ \grave{\alpha}\rho\chi\tilde{\omega}\nu$ (that is, 'Concerning the first things'),[180] in which he intermingled many worthless passages from the books of the philosophers which conflict with sound doctrine.

Saint Jerome, also speaking of the decrease in size of

the human body, makes mention of the twelve stones which the sons of Israel carried up out of the bed of the river Jordan, when they crossed it dry-shod, just as they had crossed the Red Sea before[181]—whence the Psalmist sings:

> What ailed thee, O thou sea, that thou didst flee:
> and thou, O Jordan, that thou wast turned back?[182]

For the Lord bade that one man from each of the tribes should carry up onto the river-bank a stone which he could easily lift, as testimony of so great a miracle. And Saint Jerome attests that he had seen these same stones himself, and that one of them was broken by some accident and then bound together again with iron. He says that each of them was of such size that it could scarcely be carried by two men, not because the stones had grown bigger, but because men had grown smaller.[183] And indeed it is now almost eight hundred years since the blessed Jerome passed over into the kingdom of heaven.[184]

About seventy years ago, the body of Pallas, son of Evander, whom Turnus killed, was discovered at Rome.[185] The blessed Augustine says that when Pallas died an image of Apollo wept, through the astonishing cunning of that demon, as if it lamented the fall of this most excellent man.[186] A silver vessel was also discovered, placed upon his chest, in which there was a very costly mixture of myrrh and balm. Protruding from this vessel were two golden reeds, the ends of which were fixed into the nostrils of the corpse so that, by virtue of this ointment, the body would remain undecayed no less inside than out. Two engraved lines of verse were also found:

> Pallas, son of Evander, whom the spear of Turnus
> the warrior killed, lies here in accordance with his wish.[187]

When the body was afterwards raised up, with the huge wound under the chest exposed, its height almost equalled that of the city walls. The corpse stood there until, after the balm had been washed away by the rains, it caved in and the bones were committed once again to the earth.

Chapter 19. How the blessed Óláfr died a martyr in battle

And so, after he had assembled what force he could muster in Upplǫnd, Óláfr turned toward Þrándheimr, for he had heard that Sveinn Knútsson lay in wait for him in the Vík with a powerful army, and for that reason Óláfr gave him a wide berth. But when the people of Þrándheimr had heard of the king's approach, they assembled in the city of Niðaróss as one man against the Lord and against his anointed, young together with old in one wretched faction, that they might attack God's saint.[188] Among them were the leaders who mounted the greatest opposition against the king, Þórir hundr and Kálfr Árnason.[189] When the king heard that a great host was assembled against him, he sent to meet them Finnr, the brother of Kálfr, whom I mentioned earlier.[190] He was to offer the people peace, and make known that the king's mind was favourably disposed and that, forgetful of past offences, he was ready to forgive each person for whatever he had hitherto done unlawfully. He abhorred the shedding of human blood, especially in civil wars, and by no means wished to engage them in battle, if they would acquiesce to his sound admonitions. But the savage temperament of those barbarous men unanimously rejected peace; and rather by far than accept his salutary admonitions, the wretches chose to attack God's saint in hostility. They all therefore hastened to oppose the king and advanced with all speed to the place which is called Stiklastaðir.[191] Finnr the king's messenger preceded them, however, and informed the king that they were obstinate in their evil intent.

Then the blessed Óláfr, warned by a divine revelation, had a presentiment of his death,[192] and it is said that, summoning his steward to him,[193] he ordered special alms to be faithfully distributed out of the royal treasury for all those who should fall while bearing arms against him in this battle. For Óláfr was not unmindful of his Lord's commandment:

Love your enemies, do good to them that hate you.[194]

Here one may behold with wonder the spirit of our martyr. The fury of his persecutors raged and, struck with a deplorable blindness, they railed against God's saint with savage invective;[195] yet he remained unmoved and firmly rooted in Christ, and took pains to provide for the salvation of his persecutors—and this when so hard pressed that anyone might have forgotten even those most dear to him. People throughout the world, I beg you, hear what I have to say. This man, born in almost the remotest parts of the North, among barbarians and savages, see how he shone forth like a star, how humble he was and how sublime, and this not in a slave's condition, but in the exalted rank of king. Consider in what frame of mind he made ready for war, to what he directed his thoughts. His purpose was manifest beyond all doubt and free from any uncertainty— to keep wicked men and criminals from persecuting those who were good; to confirm the things which had been ordained by Christ and, if it could be done, 'of the hardest stones to raise up children to Abraham'.[196] That this was most certainly the case is demonstrated by the daily benefactions and the miracles, as frequent as they are extraordinary, which almighty God deigns to perform for the sake of his merits, not only in our part of the world, but wherever anyone faithfully prays for the help of the blessed martyr. Indeed, one can see how devoutly and diligently this blessed man followed in the footsteps of that first standard-bearer of our Saviour, namely the most blessed protomartyr Stephen. Stephen, amid a hail of cascading stones, prayed for those who stoned him;[197] Óláfr ordered that alms be distributed on behalf of his own murderers. But in all these things He is to be acknowledged, He praised, He glorified, who at the first calling gave faith, and at the last steadfastness.

When the troops were drawn up, a bold man by the name of Bjǫrn bore the standard before the king.[198] He was killed at once in the first engagement by Þórir hundr, who led the van against the king.[199] This was followed immediately by the fall of the king who, it is said, had received a great wound. Who struck him down, or whether he received one wound or more, I will not be so bold as to affirm, since different reports are given by different people;[200] nor do I wish to soothe the ears of others with an obliging lie. But when Dagr, one of the king's captains and his kinsman, saw that the standard had fallen with the king, he manfully raised the banner up, exhorting and entreating his comrades not to let the king's death go unavenged,[201] lest their enemies should have dual cause for jubilation—both the slaying of the king and a bloodless victory. Thereupon they all rushed headlong into the fray, breaking two or three times through the enemy line and cutting down a great many men. The battle dragged on until evening, when night separated the combatants.[202] At last both sides withdrew, not so much vanquished as exhausted and crippled by wounds.[203]

The blessed Óláfr went to his rest on the twenty-ninth day of July, which was then a Wednesday, in the year 1029 after the birth of our Lord, as far as I have been able to ascertain with some degree of certainty.[204]

Chapter 20. On the lack of agreement in calculating the number of years from the beginning of the world

It should be understood that in books nothing is as garbled as the calculation of numbers, especially through the fault of scribes, but also through lack of diligence on the part of those doing the reckoning. Therefore, as I stated at the outset, I do not wish to present this count of years as preferable to one which may be more certain. For always and everywhere I seek to avoid strife, especially in such matters as are not at odds with faith. But I should like to relate a few details from the books of ancient authors and their own opinions about the reckoning of years from the beginning of the world until the advent of Christ, and to set forth the diverse calculations of diverse writers.

Bishop Eusebius of Caesarea, the first of all those whose writings have come down to us, deduced from the Hebrew verity[205] that the time from the beginning of the world until the birth of our Saviour was 3971 years. Because, however, the same Eusebius was unwilling to disregard altogether the authority of the Septuagint translators (if indeed this was their calculation), he observed that according to them the same period spanned 5199 years.[206] Bishop Isidore of Seville posits a figure of 5154 years.[207] Bede follows the Hebrew verity, but reckons 19 years fewer than Eusebius, that is, 3952 years.[208] Bishop Remigius of Auxerre, a man of profound book-learning, follows Bede, and does not disagree with him by so much as one year.[209] Hugh, canon of Paris, however, in everyone's opinion and without any contradiction a most careful commentator, follows in the footsteps of Saint Jerome (as is abundantly apparent in his chronicle) and prefers in all respects the Hebrew verity. According to Jerome, therefore, and the verity which Hugh gleaned with the utmost diligence from Hebrew sources, the number of years from Adam to Christ was 3952.[210] But let these remarks concerning the range of opinion among time-reckoners suffice.

It has been related by several how almighty God soon made known the merits of his martyr Óláfr, by restoring sight to the blind and bestowing manifold comforts on the infirm;²¹¹ and how, after a year and five days, Bishop Grímkell (who was the nephew of Bishop Sigeweard, whom Óláfr Tryggvason had brought with him from England²¹²) had Óláfr's body exhumed and laid in a fitly adorned place in the metropolitan city of Niðaróss, where it had been conveyed immediately after the battle was finished. But because all these things have been recorded by several,²¹³ I regard it as unnecessary to dwell on matters which are already known.

The blessed Óláfr reigned for fifteen years, for thirteen of which he had sole possession of the realm. For during the first year of his reign he warred against Sveinn, son of Hákon the Evil, and drove him out of the country, as I recounted earlier; and during the last year he endured a revolt led by Sveinn, son of Knútr king of both England and Denmark (about whom enough has been said), and the kingdom was in turmoil. But in the register of Norwegian kings, five years of rule are ascribed to this same Knútr and his son Sveinn and his nephew Hákon.²¹⁴

Chapter 21. On Magnús, son of the blessed Óláfr

Scarcely had three years passed after this²¹⁵ when the Norwegians, moved by belated repentance of the crime which they had committed against the blessed Óláfr, and at the same time unable to bear the tyranny of Sveinn's mother, Álfífa,²¹⁶ decided to send for the blessed Óláfr's son Magnús, then a boy of ten—seeking at least to restore to the son what they had brutally snatched away from the father. For this mission they chose four men: Rǫgnvaldr jarl (who, as I mentioned earlier, was a very close friend of the blessed Óláfr), Einarr þambaskelmir,²¹⁷ Sveinn bryggjufótr,²¹⁸ and Kálfr Árnason, who had formerly committed acts of great enmity against Óláfr, but then, moved to repentance, strove in every way to restore the king's son to the throne.[219] And when these men had come to the court of Jaroslav and Ingigerðr in Russia, where the boy was being fostered, they made known to the king the decision which they and everyone in Norway had made. Queen Ingigerðr was unwilling, and declared that she would by no means give up the boy unless they promised on oath that he would be made king. For she had greatly loved the blessed Óláfr and for that reason had fostered his son most conscientiously. They in turn promised everything demanded of them and more and made ready to depart. And when they returned to Norway they were received with great joy by the entire country; and the boy Magnús was immediately made king with the approval of the whole population.

Chapter 22. On the peace treaty between Magnús and the king of Denmark

And so, when Sveinn Knútsson heard of the people's devotion to King Magnús, uneasy about his own position, he returned to Denmark and in the same year ended this present life.[220] And his father Knútr, king of England, also departed from the affairs of this world in that same year. Not much time had passed after this when King Magnús, mindful of the wrongs which the Danes had perpetrated against the kings of Norway, assembled a fleet and sailed for Denmark. He reached the islands which we call Brenneyjar,[221] where he was confronted by Hǫrðaknútr,[222] the son of Knútr and brother of Sveinn. Whereupon the leading men, seeing that the two kings, still immature, could easily be swayed in any direction, and that they themselves would more likely bear the blame for anything the kings might do amiss, fell back on the more sensible plan of negotiating peace. They entered into a pact in which the following condition was stipulated: that whichever of the kings should first depart from this world without an obvious heir (that is, a child of his own body) the one remaining should gain both kingdoms without any opposition. And thus they parted from one another not only in agreement, but actually as the best of friends.[223]

Chapter 23. On the pact which was made between Charles the Great and his brother

This treaty was not unlike that concluded by Charles (who on account of his glorious victories and exemplary character was afterwards called 'the Great') with his elder brother Carloman. Two years later, however, this Carloman put off his mortal form, leaving behind his two sons, and his widow took them and with female inconstancy fled to King Liutprand[224] of Italy—which greatly displeased Charles. This king of the Langobards did great harm to the Roman Church, going so far as to besiege our lord the pope, confining him in Pavia. Placed in such a desperate situation, our lord the pope sent a written appeal to Charles, the king of Francia, for he had heard that he was a youth of noble disposition. He appealed to the king to come to the aid of the Church in its hour of need, and wrote that one could have no greater obligation than to support one's mother when she was in distress; that it behoved him as a Christian king to obey the supreme pontiff who, placed in the greatest danger, awaited his coming day and night; and that he should attend to the matter with all haste, for their stores of food would soon be exhausted. Although Charles had at that time been planning an expedition against Saxony (which was then still devoted to idolatry), on receiving this letter, he assembled an army with astonishing speed, for all his nobles were threatened with a grisly penalty should anyone stay behind after the king's departure.[225]

With unbelievable and unexpected speed he crossed the Alps—so that that line of Lucan's might very fittingly apply to him:

Now with rapid course had Caesar crossed the Alps.[226]

He appeared without warning; no report at all of his approach had preceded him; and with his troops in battle array he encircled the king of the Langobards, so that by a strange and extraordinary turn of events, no escape route was left open to the very man who had previously confined others. When this became known in the city, it was filled with the greatest rejoicing; the gates were thrown open and the citizens boldly attacked their enemies. With Charles hemming the enemy in from without while the townspeople attacked from within, the entire army of the Langobards was overcome and subjugated. The king himself was led in chains before the feet of our lord the pope. He was handed over not to a tribunal but, as he had so often deserved, to the vilification of the mob.

King Charles asked of our lord the pope what he commanded to be done with the prisoner. The pope answered simply: 'I bear a spiritual sword, not a physical one;[227] it is enough for me if the Church is given back her authority and patronal rights, and those things which are Saint Peter's are restored to him. It is up to you', he continued, 'my most dear son, to decide whether the title of "king" should continue to exist in Italy; for Constantine the son of Helena renounced that title in honour of our Lord Jesus Christ and bestowed it as a perpetual right on Saint Peter and the Roman pontiff.'[228] And so King Charles deposed the king of the Langobards, and banished him to Vienne—restoring to him, however, his wife and children and an adequate amount of money, and treating him mercifully and with kindness. And so from that time on the Roman Church was freed from the tyranny of the Langobards through the perseverance and assistance of the most Christian king, Charles, some three hundred years after the Langobards first invaded Italy.[229] But let us return to Norway.

Chapter 24. How the same Magnús, made king of the Danes, waged war against the Wends[230]

Not long after the agreement mentioned above had been concluded between the two kings, Magnús and Knútr, this same Knútr died without an heir.[231] When he learned of this, King Magnús assembled a fleet and sailed to Denmark. There he was received with honour by the leading men of the kingdom, who had been party to the aforementioned treaty; and he was raised to the throne. When news of this reached the ears of Sveinn, the son of Úlfr and Ástríðr (the sister of King Knútr of England),[232] he gathered an army and met Magnús in a naval battle.[233] But he was soon defeated by Magnús and fled.

While these events were taking place, the Wends, whom we in our mother tongue call *Vindir*, descended upon Denmark in unbelievable numbers,[234] covering the face of the earth like locusts.[235] That race is pagan and hostile to God, savage men of the wild who live by pillage. Indeed, they made it their custom to harry Denmark constantly with plundering raids; but on this occasion they met with an especially good opportunity for attack, because there was unrest in the realm. When King Magnús learned of this he was alarmed, for he neither had time to assemble an army nor thought it safe to contend with a few men against such a multitude. Yet it seemed intolerable that the country should be ravaged under his very nose. While the king was in this anguished state of mind, it is said that the blessed Óláfr, his father, appeared to him the following night and told him to put his faith in God, for it was as easy for Him to give a victory to few as to many. He said that Magnús should go into battle the next day, and that victory, through God's mercy, would not be denied.[236] And so, strengthened by this vision, the following day King Magnús proceeded bravely into combat. He marched under the standard which had been his father's, and carried in his hand Óláfr's double-bladed battle-axe, which was broken in the fight which followed, and is now preserved in the cathedral of Niðaróss.[237] And so, all the mightier, he fell upon the enemy and laid most of them low. The rest, with the help of God, he put shamefully to flight. This battle was fought in the place called Hlýrskógsheiðr.[238]

After this, there were various clashes between Sveinn and Magnús, and they fought several battles in different places, of which these were the greatest: one at Helganes,[239] another at Áróss,[240] and there were a good many[241] besides, but since it is tedious to dwell on each of these in turn, let us move on to other matters.

Chapter 25. On the return of Haraldr harðráði[242] from Greece

Realizing that he could not stand up to Magnús's forces, Sveinn withdrew from the country. But the king pursued him with his fleet, and put in at the place called the Eyrarsund.[243] One day while they were waiting there, they saw a ship approaching, more beautifully fitted out than is usual, for the entire sail was of gleaming purple.[244] The king, amazed at this unusual sight, immediately sent messengers to ask who they were and where they were coming from. The king's messengers received the reply that this was Haraldr, brother of King Óláfr of Norway, on his way from Greece. Haraldr's crew, in turn, asked who was the commander of the fleet which they saw in the harbour. They answered that he was the blessed Óláfr's son Magnús, king of Denmark and Norway. When Haraldr heard this, he went immediately to visit his nephew, by whom he was received with honour, as was fitting; and he stayed there for some days. But when Magnús asked Haraldr whether he would help him to bring the kingdom of Denmark under his rule, to which he was entitled on just grounds, Haraldr is said to have answered that he would rather ask Magnús to share with him the kingdom of Norway, to which he was entitled by hereditary right. When King Magnús had given him an amicable reply (for he had a peaceable and good-natured disposition), one of the king's counsellors, Einarr þambaskelmir,[245] thinking to himself that the words of each party did not issue from a wellspring of equal goodwill, remarked that it seemed just that, if King Magnús were to grant half of Norway to Haraldr, then he should likewise share with Magnús the money which he had brought back from Greece; for Magnús was in dire need of money, having spent huge sums on his continual military campaigns. Haraldr took this answer badly and retorted that he had not exposed himself to perils in foreign lands to amass wealth in order to enrich the retainers of his nephew Magnús. Einarr answered him, 'You should know, then, that wherever I can, I shall stand in the way of your gaining the throne.' This remark, as the outcome of events proved, caused the death in this world of Einarr and his son, for both were afterwards killed by Haraldr.

Enraged by this answer, Haraldr left the king and set out for Norway.[246] When the reason for Haraldr's departure from Magnús became known to Sveinn, he immediately followed after him, promising him half of Denmark if they could get Magnús out of the way.

Chapter 26. The author's diatribe against the ambitious, and how Chosroes ended his life

O truly wretched longing for glory! O pitiable and pitiful and, as it is described by the philosophers, truly blind ambition, which tramples things divine and human, which dishonours nature and renders devoid of self-control anyone whose mind it has once invaded. It was this which armed Absalom for the murder of his father, that he might obtain the kingdom through parricide.[247] And, to mention a pagan example, it was ambition which drove Pharnaces, son of King Mithridates of Pontus (who for forty years had waged war against the Romans) to besiege his own father, confined in a city.[248] When Mithridates had addressed his son for a long while from the highest wall of the city, desiring to move him to mercy, and he saw that Pharnaces was inexorable, he is said to have cried out: 'O ancestral gods, if you exist at all, grant that Pharnaces too may implore his own sons with the same entreaty as I have made, and not be heard.' After this he descended from the battlement and gave poison to all his concubines and sons and daughters. Then he also swallowed poison; but its force had no effect upon him, because of the countless potions with which he had frequently strengthened his internal organs against the same contagion, as a safeguard against murder at anyone's hands. In the end, when the wall was broken down, he stretched out his neck to his executioner.[249] As Lucan says of this:

> . . . scarcely ended by barbarous poison.[250]

Pliny the Elder writes about this king in these words: 'Mithridates,' he says, 'king of Pontus, was a very powerful and rich man. He went on waging war against us for forty years with varying results. He was king over twenty-two nations, and gave judicial decisions in as many languages, addressing each group in turn at its assembly without the aid of an interpreter.'[251]

This same wretched ambition armed Syrois to murder his father Chosroes. And since I have made mention of this king, I pray that it will not seem burdensome to the reader if a few selections from the *Roman History*[252] are added here as they are found in the work which is called 'On the exaltation of the Holy Cross',[253] a book in which many streaks of falsehood appear among some true details and which, for that reason, is not accepted by the holy Roman Church. For Pope Gelasius, a man of great learning and authority in God's Church, distinguishes in a brief sermon the apocryphal writings from the sacred canon,[254] saying that God's Church has no need of support from falsehood, for it is founded by God, who is truth itself. The blessed Augustine corroborates this in several places with the same sentiment and in almost the same words.[255] This same Gelasius includes among the apocrypha the passions of the apostles (except that of Andrew alone), the book of the infancy of Jesus, the book about the birth of the blessed Mary, the itinerary of Clement, the gospel according to Thomas, the gospel according to Bartholomew, and many other texts which it would take a long time to enumerate.[256]

But now let us see how this treatise, 'On the exaltation of the Holy Cross', accords with the truth of the *Roman History*.[257] Heraclius (son of Heraclius, the governor of Africa), a very bold military man, was elected as Roman emperor by his soldiers. For six years in succession he marauded through all Persia, and razed to the ground countless cities, and even the most venerable buildings of the ancient kings. He fought a Persian giant on a bridge in single combat, defeated him and hurled him into the river below. And he forced Chosroes himself to flee to the remotest hiding-places in his kingdom. When he had surrendered to complete despair,

Chosroes named his son Mardasa king. On learning of this, Syrois, Chosroes' first-born son, bore it exceedingly ill that he should be rejected, since he was entitled to the throne by order of birth; and having won over the military commander Gundabunda, he brought the entire army over to his side. At once he set out in pursuit of his father Chosroes, caught him and, after fettering his feet and neck with massive chains, shut him up in an underground chamber which the king himself had built in a well-concealed spot as a hiding-place for his treasure. Then Syrois gave his commands and said: 'Let him eat gold and silver, for which he impiously slaughtered many and laid waste all the world.'[258] And then Syrois committed a crime unparalleled throughout all time, but so it was ordained by divine judgment. For he summoned the viceroys who he knew particularly hated his father, and handed Chosroes over to them for five days, to be maltreated and spat upon and subjected to various outrages. And then at last he ordered the king to be shot to death with arrows, but not before five of his sons were put to death before their father's own eyes. So this was the end of that impious man, the violator of the temple of the Lord and proud beyond human limits. For he had answered Heraclius's envoys, who had come to him to sue for peace, with great pride, saying that either the Christians should relinquish their own religion and join him in worshipping the sun, or else their kingdom would be completely destroyed.[259] But God let this arrogance recoil upon the blasphemer's own head. And yet, although Chosroes paid a fitting penalty for his crimes, it was nevertheless abominable before both God and men that what he suffered was at the hands of a child of his own body.

And did not this same wretched ambition drive Domitian, a thoroughly wicked man and practically another Nero, to plot against the life of his brother Titus? This Titus, because of his benign character and innate goodness, was called the delight of the human race. One day, when it was drawing toward evening, he recalled that on that day he had done no one a service, for no one had asked anything of him; and he is reported to have said to his comrades: 'Today I have squandered a day, for I have done no one a service.'[260] Titus tried to mollify his brother Domitian with kind words, begging him not to defile himself with the blood of his own brother, for in a short time the supreme rule would be his, and it was not fitting that he should obtain it through such a crime. But these words were, alas, too true, for Titus survived on the throne for only two years, and Domitian succeeded him. And the latter also added this to his crimes, that he instigated the next persecution of Christians after Nero. But let us now pursue our own subject.[261]

Chapter 27. How King Magnús shared the throne of Norway with his father's brother; and on Magnús's death

When King Magnús heard that Haraldr his uncle and Sveinn had left for Norway and had entered into an alliance against him, he at once set out after them. But when they heard that the king was on his way, they were afraid to confront him and turned back to Denmark. And so King Magnús, deciding that he could scarcely defend both kingdoms against their aggression, sent a legation to recall his uncle Haraldr. Magnús yielded one half of the kingdom of Norway to him, demanding nothing in return, save that Haraldr should be obliged to join him in defending both kingdoms, while Magnús should nevertheless have sole rule over the kingdom of Denmark.

This agreement between nephew and uncle was settled by a lake in Upplǫnd[262] in the presence of Bishop Grímkell, Einarr þambaskelmir[263] and many other leading men, who declared absolutely that they were on no condition willing to serve under two kings unless they were bound together by a treaty of peace. They knew perfectly well that any kingdom divided within itself would go to ruin;[264] and therefore they made a firm agreement among themselves that whoever would not abide by the peace treaty should be put to death. Concerning this sort of insane dissension Virgil exclaims:

> That rulers have for long enough defiled the honourable bonds of peace,
> Wretches whom a hideous longing for power has held prisoner—
> This I confess I have written of.
> It is enough to remember such evils![265]

Lucan, likewise, says of the same subject:

> The frenzy of arms hangs over us; and the power of the sword will overturn all justice by force;
> And execrable crime shall have the name of valour;
> And this madness will take many years to pass away.[266]

And so, when this peace was settled between uncle and nephew, King Magnús sailed to Denmark and drove out Sveinn, who in the meantime had now subjugated the entire country to his rule. Magnús lived on for only one year after the expulsion of Sveinn.[267] And when he sensed that the day of his death was at hand, Magnús sent to Sveinn a man named Þórir, Magnús's half-brother on his mother's side, and restored the throne of Denmark to Sveinn because he was entitled to it by hereditary right.[268]

This Magnús, son of the blessed martyr Óláfr, was a man distinguished by goodness, endowed with gentleness, vigorous in warfare, and marvellously skilful in the conduct of public affairs. For these reasons he almost always emerged the victor in any contest; and because of his pleasant nature and generosity he was very popular with all his subjects. Magnús reigned for eleven years, for five of which he ruled over both kingdoms.

Chapter 28. How King Haraldr led an expedition against England, was defeated in battle and died

After him Haraldr, the brother of the blessed Óláfr, reigned for twenty years. He ruled nineteen years on his own, and one year with his nephew Magnús. Haraldr was a vigorous man, far-sighted in his decision-making, quick to take up arms, jealous of what was his and covetous of what was another's; and so he waged many wars against Sveinn, in the hope of wresting from him the kingdom of Denmark.[269] But when this met with little success, he prepared an expedition against England, urged on by Tostig, the brother of King Harold of England.[270] Tostig promised Haraldr half the kingdom if he drove out his brother, for by hereditary right Tostig was no less entitled to the throne.[271]

When Haraldr arrived in England together with the aforementioned Tostig, they made the territory of Northumbria subject to their rule. King Harold of England had at that time gone to Normandy;[272] but when he heard of the arrival of enemies, he made a speedy return to England, assembled a huge army and took the invaders unawares. When Harold drew near, most of the Norwegian forces, laden with booty, made for their ships. The remainder, though few, with steadfast courage prepared for battle. 'But what can a few brave men do against so many thousands?'[273] And as King Haraldr himself, mounted on horseback, endeavoured to draw up his battle line, his horse stumbled and he was thrown to the ground; whereupon he is reported to have said: 'Seldom is a sign of this sort an omen of victory.'[274] Nor was he mistaken in this unlucky omen, for he fell in that same battle. Tostig, the brother of King Harold of England, who had lured Haraldr there, was also killed, and almost all their army was annihilated. This battle took place in the year 1066 after the birth of Christ. For several days a comet appeared with a glowing red tail; and this prefigured the defeat of the English, which followed immediately afterwards.[275]

This Haraldr had performed many bold deeds in his youth, overthrowing many heathen cities and carrying off great riches in Russia and in Ethiopia (which we call *Bláland* in our mother tongue).[276] From there he travelled to Jerusalem and was everywhere greatly renowned and victorious. After he had travelled through Sicily and taken much wealth by force there,[277] he came to Constantinople. And there he was arraigned before the emperor; but he inflicted an amply shameful disgrace upon that same emperor and, making an unexpected escape, he slipped away.[278]

Chapter 29. On his son Óláfr

After Haraldr was killed in England, his son Óláfr returned to Norway with the remains of his army. This Óláfr had a brother by the name of Magnús, who ruled alone for one year, while his brother was away on the expedition against England which I have just described. After that, Magnús lived on for only a few years, and left after him one son whose name was Hákon, whom a worthy man named Steigar-Þórir, born to high station among his own people, undertook to foster.[279]

After this, Óláfr reigned for twenty-seven years. He was a man dear to both God and men, who made every effort to achieve a state of peace and concord.[280] He allowed everyone to enjoy what was his own, but restrained the base behaviour of wicked men by authority alone. He built a basilica in honour of the Holy Trinity in the metropolitan city of Niðaróss, where the body of the blessed martyr Óláfr now rests, just as in the same city his father Haraldr had built a church dedicated to the Blessed Virgin Mary, which may be seen to this day.[281] And I would be at a loss

to name another of the Norwegian kings, from the time of
Haraldr Fair-hair down to the present day, who enjoyed a
happier reign than he.²⁸² He died in the Vík, but is said to
have been buried in the aforementioned church of Niðaróss
which he himself had built.²⁸³

Chapter 30. On Magnús berfœttr, and a brief account of
the portents which preceded the death of Charles

Óláfr was succeeded by Magnús, his son by a concubine.
His nickname was 'barefoot'.²⁸⁴ He reigned for ten years,
one of them together with his uncle's son, Hákon. This Hákon
was a promising youth; and he is praised for having removed the taxes hitherto unjustly laid upon the necks of
the people of his part of the country.²⁸⁵ When he was subsequently removed from the light of this world by an untimely death,²⁸⁶ Hákon left the throne to his cousin Magnús,
who ruled after that for nine years. This Magnús was very
unlike his father in character, and resembled more his grandfather, Haraldr.²⁸⁷

And since I mentioned a little earlier that this same Haraldr
had tumbled from his horse and that his death was prefigured in that fall, I should like to recount briefly the portents which preceded the death of the most victorious and
most outstanding of all exceptional men, Charles the Great.²⁸⁸
The first portent involved the bridge over the Rhine at Mainz,
constructed over a period of eight years,²⁸⁹ and so firmly
built that it was thought it would last for ever. But on the
very day that it was completed, a cloud gathered over the
bridge and a thunderbolt suddenly fell and burnt up the
whole structure, so that not so much as a splinter was left
standing above the water. The second portent involved the
massive portico in Aachen, between the basilica and the
palace. One Sunday when the emperor himself wanted to

enter the upper church, the entire structure fell to the ground before his feet.[290] The third portent involved the ruler's own name, written along the top of a wall in golden letters so large that anyone standing on the floor below could read them with great ease. In the last year of his life, however, this inscription was so effaced that it could not be read at all. The fourth sign which prefigured his death was that while he was riding on a calm day, carrying his lance in his hand, a thunderbolt fell right in front of his horse's feet, throwing it down and the king with it. His lance was also knocked from his hand and thrown a long way off and the saddle-girths were torn apart, but the emperor himself remained uninjured. This happened during Charles's last campaign, which he waged against King Hemming of Denmark.[291] Hemming had spoken disdainfully against his imperial majesty, and crossed through the middle of Saxony, a region which after thirty years of continual rebellion Charles had barely, by dint of much sweat and untiring persistence, managed to bend to the gentle yoke of Christ. For the Saxons had on three occasions cruelly put to death the bishops and priests who had been sent to them. So finally, the most merciful emperor, disgusted by their wicked behaviour, sent and had killed all parents, both men and women, who were taller than his sword.[292] And when there were only boys remaining, he had bishops and priests ordained for them, who were to teach them the way of eternal salvation, since 'a jar will long keep the scent of what it was once steeped in when new'.[293] But when Hemming heard that the emperor was approaching, he went humbly to meet him and received forgiveness.

And although Charles most certainly knew that these signs in some way foretold his death, nevertheless he dismissed them all with manly steadfastness and strength of mind. For the mark of indomitable virtue shone in him, and with that superiority of spirit he disdained both good fortune and bad. And lest any trace of virtue be omitted from this description of his most perfect character, let me add that in making and maintaining friendships he surpassed almost all mortal men; for he made friends readily and took the utmost pains to nurture their friendship. But let us return to our own affairs.

Chapter 31. On the deeds of Magnús berfœttr

And so, after Hákon, the son of Óláfr's brother Magnús, had died, Steigar-Þórir, who had fostered Hákon, was disgruntled that the entire kingdom of Norway should be under the rule of Magnús; so he set up a certain Sveinn Haraldsson as a pseudo-king in opposition to Magnús[294]—as is common practice among the Norwegians. When Magnús learned of this, he immediately set off in pursuit of the fugitive Þórir, and captured him on a small island in the province of Hálogaland. The name of the island was Vambarhólmr[295] and there Magnús hanged him together with another chieftain by the name of Egill, an upright and very eloquent man.[296] But the Sveinn just mentioned escaped.

After this, Magnús prepared an expedition against Gautland, where he wished to re-take three territories, the names of which are Dalr, Hǫfuð, and Véar.[297] He said that these territories had anciently belonged to the kings of Norway, but had been seized by violence by the kings of the Gautar; and so he wanted to reclaim them by force of arms if no alternative was offered. As Lucan says:

. . . to the man bearing weapons he grants everything.[298]

And yet Magnús accomplished little in this first campaign. In the second, he did in fact engage in battle; but he was beaten and fled alone, accompanied only by his companion, Ǫgmundr Skoptason.[299] Peace was, however, negotiated through the good offices of the king of the Gautar Ingi Steinkelsson,[300] a most excellent man, who also gave his daughter Margareta to Magnús in marriage, and made the aforementioned territories over to him, calling them a dowry.[301] At that time there were many noble men in Magnús's army, among whom Sigurðr ullstrengr[302] was the foremost no less for his prowess than for his nobility. He afterwards built a renowned cloister in honour of both the blessed Benedict and the most precious and invincible martyr of Christ, Laurence, on a tiny island which lies off the metropolitan city of Niðaróss.[303] After that, Magnús went to the Orkney Islands, which were part of his kingdom. Magnús was a restless man who coveted the property of others and set little value on his own. He harried Scotland and Cornwall (which we call *Bretland*) with pillaging and carried out viking raids. In the latter place he killed Earl Hugh of Cornwall (whose nickname was 'the stout') when he offered resistance.[304] With the king at that time was Erlendr, earl of Orkney, along with his most excellent son Magnús, a promising youth of eighteen. Frequent miracles bear witness to the greatness of his merit in the eyes of God.[305] There were also many others: Dagr, the father of Gregorius, Viðkunnr[306] Jóansson, Úlfr Hranason (the brother of Sigurðr, who was the father of Nikulás whom the baleful tyrant Eysteinn killed in the city of Niðaróss),[307] and many more.

Chapter 32. On the death of the same Magnús and his son[308]

With his ships laden with much booty, King Magnús returned to Norway. Then after an interval of a few years, he again made ready a fleet, and with his usual restlessness of spirit returned to Ireland in the hope of conquering the whole island. However, after winning control over part of the island, hoping that the rest might be conquered with ease, he began to lead his army with less caution, and fell into the same trap as his grandfather Haraldr in England. For when the Irish, prepared to die for their country, had gathered a whole host, they cut off any avenue of retreat to the ships, attacked the enemy fiercely, and brought down King Magnús.[309] Part of his army fell there with him; the rest made their way back to the ships as best they could.

Magnús left three sons—Eysteinn, Sigurðr and Óláfr.[310] On his way to Ireland, he had brought Sigurðr with him[311] to the Orkneys. After his father died he returned to Norway and was elevated to the throne along with his brothers. Óláfr, cut off by a premature death, was removed from the light of this world in the third year after the death of his father.[312] And all Norway mourned him, because he had been well liked by all on account of his gracious manners and agreeable speech. After his death, his two brothers divided the kingdom between them. After he had ruled the kingdom for twenty years, however, Eysteinn departed from human affairs;[313] and his brother Sigurðr alone ruled all Norway for seven years.

Eysteinn was a paragon of honesty who governed himself no less than his subjects with moderation and wisdom. He was a king who loved peace, an assiduous manager of public affairs, and above all a fosterer of the Christian religion. For this reason he built a monastery in honour of Saint Michael the Archangel beside the city of Bergen, as one can still see to this day.[314] In fact, he built buildings which were of great benefit to the kingdom in very many places— for example, the palace at Bergen, which was a beautiful piece of craftsmanship, though made of wood, and which has now almost collapsed from excessive age. He also built the port at Agðanes, to the great benefit of sailors;[315] and in this he imitated Augustus Caesar,[316] who built the port of Brundisium, which was destined to benefit almost the whole world. Likewise, the same Augustus ordered public roads to be laid out at vast expense for the benefit of the entire empire, through places which had previously been impassable and full of swamps. On that public highway he wished there to be such general peace in honour of the emperor, that if any thief, murderer, or sorcerer were caught on it, he should suffer no injury whatsoever, so long as he remained there.[317] That this was an established practice is amply corroborated by the writings of the ancients.

Chapter 33. On King Sigurðr and his deeds

Among the many outstanding deeds which King Sigurðr performed, one thing in particular is remembered with words of praise: that he voyaged to Jerusalem with his fleet in the seventh year after that city had been freed from the tyranny of the Persians by the grace of God.[318] He is praised for having razed to the ground many cities of the heathens on that expedition. Among these, he even took from the heathens Sidon, the most renowned city of the province of Phoenicia, and restored it to the Christians.[319] He also captured, through cunning no less than force, a mountainside cave which was full of robbers who plagued the entire region, and so freed the country from their depredations.[320] He performed many bold deeds, and was honoured by King Baldwin[321] with numerous gifts, the foremost of which, and the one rightly to be placed before all the rest, was a piece of wood from the Lord's cross.[322] And so Sigurðr returned home with great glory from this expedition, while his brother Eysteinn was still alive.

At that time Sigurðr was deservedly counted among the best of rulers, but later only among those who were middling. Some say that his mind became deranged because he drank some poisonous concoction.[323] But let those who maintain this answer for their own words. I, for my part, leave it an open question.

Chapter 34. On Haraldr of Ireland

At this time a certain Haraldr came to King Sigurðr from Scotland,[324] and said that he was his brother, that is to say the son of King Magnús nicknamed 'barefoot'. And he was stubborn in requesting that he be permitted, according to the laws of the land, to prove what he said. So King Sigurðr ordered him (more harshly than fairly as it seemed to some) to walk over nine red-hot ploughshares, contrary to ecclesiastical decision.[325] But assisted by God, as it is believed, he showed himself unburnt.

A few years after that, King Sigurðr put off his human form.[326] And here I too shall end this little document of mine, since I deem it utterly unfitting to record for posterity the crimes, killings, perjuries, parricides, desecrations of holy places, the contempt for God, the plundering no less of the clergy than of the whole people, the abductions of women, and other abominations which it would take long to enumerate. All these things so flooded in, as if in one cesspit, after the death of King Sigurðr that the satirist may seem to have alluded to our nation in particular when he said:

> Straightway, all evil burst forth into this age of baser vein;
> Modesty and truth and faith fled the earth,
> And in their place came tricks and plots and snares,
> Violence and cursed love of gain.[327]

Indeed, Lucan advises that one should conceal the crimes of one's own people, when he says:

> Turn away, my mind, from this phase of the war
>   and leave it to the shades;
> Let no age learn from me in my poetry of evils such as these,
>   nor of the full licence of civil war.[328]

and elsewhere:
> Rome, about what you did in this battle,
> I shall be silent.[329]

I have touched upon these few details concerning our forefathers to the best of my ability, though with an inexpert pen, and treated not what I have seen, but what I have heard.[330] For this reason, if anyone should condescend to read this, and should perhaps be displeased that I have arranged this account as I have, I beg that he should not accuse me of falsehood, because I have learned what I have written from the report of others. And let him know that I would assuredly have rather seen someone other than myself act as the chronicler of these events, but since to date this has not happened, I preferred that it should be me rather than no one.[331]

Here ends Theodoricus the monk's account of the ancient history of the Norwegian kings

NOTES

1. *in historiam de antiquitate regum Norwagiensium*: Cf. *DMLBS*, s.v. *antiquitas*, d., 'ancient history'; *OED*, s.v. *antiquity*, 6: '(Now *pl.* or *collect.*, formerly often *sing.*). Matters, customs, precedents, or events of earlier times; ancient records.'—The title here in B and S, *historia de antiquitate* . . . , agrees with the opening sentence of the Prologue and the *incipit* before ch. 1 below. AKL, however, begin here with *Incipit prologus* . . . *in ecclesiasticam historiam Norwagiensium*.
2. Eysteinn Erlendsson, archbishop of Niðaróss 1161–1188.
3. Cf. Theodoricus's further remarks on his Icelandic informants in ch. 1. Sven Aggesen (*Brevis Historia Regum Dacie* i, 1917–1922, I, 96; Christiansen 1992, 49) and Saxo Grammaticus (*Gesta Danorum*, praef. i.4; Fisher–Davidson 1979–1980, I, 5) likewise acknowledge their debt to Icelanders for information about early Scandinavian history. On Theodoricus's possible or probable use of written as well as oral Icelandic sources, see Introd. pp. xiii–xviii, xx–xxiii; Bjarni Guðnason 1977; Lange 1989, 97 ff. Theodoricus's remark, 'those whom we call Icelanders', was meant to be pointed. It contrasts with the usage of some learned men, the author of *Hist. Norw.* and Saxo Grammaticus, for example, who called Icelanders Tilenses, implying the identification of Iceland with the Thule of the ancients, an identification of which Theodoricus is not convinced: see ch. 3.
4. Cf. remarks on poetical sources by Saxo (*Gesta Danorum*, praef. i.3; Fisher–Davidson 1979–1980, I, 5), and Snorri (*Hkr[prologus]*). For discussion of cases where Theodoricus may have drawn on scaldic poetry as source material, see Lange 1989, 55–97; cf. Introd. pp. xvii–xviii.
5. A similarly nationalistic motive for writing history is expressed by, for example, Saxo (*Gesta Danorum* praef. i.1; Fisher–Davidson 1979–1980, I, 4) and William of Malmesbury (*Gesta regum* ii. prol.; 1998, 150; cf. Richter 1938, 57). See Hanssen 1949, 74.
6. *Haraldi pulchre-comati*: on Haraldr's by-name, *hárfagri*, see Lind 1920–1921, 136; Fidjestøl 1997a, 9–12. We have translated into English all Norse nicknames which Theodoricus renders into Latin. Cf., for example, chs 30, 34, where Theodoricus's

rendering of *berfœttr* ('bare-leg') as *nudipes* is translated 'barefoot'. Where Theodoricus introduces a vernacular term, we have retained the standard Old West Norse form of the word in our translation. Thus, for example, in the heading to ch. 30, *De Magno berfort*, the Norse nickname *berfœttr* is retained. Cf. nn. 16 and 284 below.
7. Cf. Boethius, *Cons. Phil.* II, pr. 7, 13 (*scriptorum inops . . . obliuio* for Theodoricus's *scriptorum inops . . . opinio*).
8. Hugh of St Victor (†1141). Hanssen (1949, 123) notes that the phrase *vir undecunque doctissimus* was originally applied to Varro in a verse by the grammarian Terentianus Maurus (*De metris* 2846: *Vir doctissimus undecumque Varro*). Augustine's quotation of the verse in *De civitate Dei* VI.ii ensured the popularity of the formula.
9. Storm (1880, ad 3.21) identifies a parallel passage in the synopsis of world history included in the *Liber exceptionum*, a compilation formerly thought to be the work of Hugh of St Victor (printed by Migne under the title *Exceptiones priores*, PL 177, 191–284), but now attributed to Richard of St Victor (†1173; see Chatillon 1948; Goy 1976, 492–493 and n. 25). Cf. *Liber exceptionum* I.x.10 'De gente Normannorum', 1–8.
10. Cf. Sigebert of Gembloux († 1112), *Chronica*, s.a. 853 (1844, 340).
11. *non visa sed audita*: cf. the same phrase at 34.35 (Storm 1880, 68.2). Hanssen (1945, 172–173, and 1949, 75–76) cites examples of this formula from hagiographic texts, and compares in particular Gregory the Great's invocation of the example of the evangelists Mark and Luke to justify his use of secondary informants in writing of past events (*Dialogi* I. prol. 10): 'quia Marcus et Lucas euangelium quod scripserunt, *non uisu sed auditu* didicerunt.' The opposition of 'things seen' and 'things heard' was a commonplace of medieval historiography which distinguished between chronicling the events of one's own time as an eyewitness, and writing history based on information gathered from secondary (written or oral) sources. A clear sense of the greater authority of history recorded by an eyewitness is reflected in Isidore's derivation of the word *historia* (*Etym.* I.xli.1): 'Dicta autem Graece historia ἀπὸ τοῦ ἱστορεῖν, id est

a videre vel cognoscere. Apud veteres enim nemo conscribebat historiam, nisi is qui interfuisset, et ea quae conscribenda essent vidisset.' For further examples and discussion, see Schulz 1909, 17–20, 28–31; Momigliano 1961–1962; Guenée 1980, 77–78; Goffart 1988, 118–119; Lange 1989, 35, 43–47, 102–105, and refs.

12. *non inutiles*: Hanssen (1949, 176) suggests that the phrase has a contextual sense, 'not uninteresting'.

13. Theodoricus's use of the deprecatory *schedula* (originally 'a loose leaf') to refer to his history both here and in ch. 34 (Storm 1880, 67.7) is a conventional 'modesty formula' (see Hanssen 1949, 76–78; Lange 1989, 34 and refs).

14. *certissimae*: or perhaps for *certissime* (adv.): 'since I know *for a certainty* that you lack neither the understanding . . . nor the good will . . .' Cf. Skard 1941, 268; Hanssen 1949, 71.

15. *de Longobardis*: translated 'Langobards', rather than 'Lombards', to allow for Theodoricus's remarks on the derivation of the name in ch. 17.

16. *De Magno berfort*: for *berfotr*, i.e. *berfœttr*. Cf. nn. 6 and 284.

17. Storm prints 858, the reading in S, and points out that the same year is given for the beginning of Haraldr's reign in *Annales regii* (ed. Storm 1888, 98; cf. Ólafia Einarsdóttir 1964, 184–191). Suhm (1783, 314 n.) suggested that the 1052 date in A, M, and K was an error for 852 (cf. Ellehøj 1965, 183, n. 35; Skånland 1966; Salvesen 1969, 51 and 89, n. 4). Lange argues in favour of the L reading, 862 (Lehmann 1937, 121; rpt 1959–1962, 428 [6.3]), which agrees with the date given for Haraldr's accession in *Annales Reseniani* (ed. Storm 1888, 13). It is a date for which a comparative reckoning in *Íslendingabók* makes Ari a not improbable source (cf. Lange 1989, 115–118; Stefán Karlsson 1977, 694). But behind the 858/862 difficulty there presumably lies the fact that at some stage 'lviii' (58) was read as 'lxii' (62), or 'lxii' was read as 'lviii'. We have no way of deciding which stood in the manuscript from which Kirchmann took his copies.

18. Ari, *Íslendingabók*, prologus and ch. 1, offers a close but not precise verbal parallel: '[Haraldr enn hárfagri] es *fyrstr varð þess kyns einn konungr at ǫllum Norvegi* . . . En svá es sagt at Haraldr *væri sjau tegu vetra* konungr ok yrði áttrœðr.'

(Cf. Andersson 1979, 16.) *Ágrip*, ch. 4 fin., likewise gives 70 years as the length of Haraldr's reign. Other sources record that Haraldr ruled for 73 years (*Nóregs konunga tal* st. 9 [*Skjd.* A I, 580], *Hist. Norw.* 104.4, *Fsk* ch. 5, *Ólhelg[Sep]* ch. 1, 'Konungatal i Noregi', *Flat.* I, 583), probably on the assumption that the two years Haraldr lived after transferring power to Eiríkr blóðøx were a period of joint rule between father and son. Cf. Bjarni Aðalbjarnarson 1937, 31–32; *idem* 1941–1951, I, lxxi–lxxvi; Ólafia Einarsdóttir 1964, 177; Ellehøj 1965, 69–70, 248 and 252–253; Lange 1989, 216–217, n. 386.
19. L has *in hoc libro* (see Lange 1989, 184, n. 21). Cf. Storm 1880, 6.8: *in hoc loco*.
20. *curiosiores*: or perhaps 'more careful'.
21. This need not imply that Theodoricus was unfamiliar with written sources of information about the reign of Haraldr Fairhair, only that sources such as the historical writings of Sæmundr or Ari were too recent to be regarded as *auctoritates* (cf. Bjarni Guðnason 1977, 109; Lange 1989, 105 and n. 313; Introd. pp. xv–xvi). Lange (1989, 105) suggests that Theodoricus may simply mean that he has been forced to work out the year of Haraldr's accession himself, by relative chronology from other dates given in a written source, and that the year as such was not specified in any history or chronicle known to him. Andersson (1979, 12–13) argues that, while Theodoricus probably made good use of Icelandic written sources, in this passage he expresses his awareness that there are uncertainties when such sources are ultimately based on oral tradition. Cf. Introd. p. xiv.
22. Cf. 1 Tim. 1:4 [*vet. lat.*]. Lehmann 1937 (1959–1962, 384) suggests that the citation is coloured by a reminiscence of Titus 3:9. Old Latin (*vet. lat.*) readings are from Sabatier 1743–1749.
23. Cf. 1 Cor. 11:16.
24. Storm (1880, ad loc.) and Bjarni Aðalbjarnarson (1941–1951, I, 119, n.1) suggest that *fratrum interfector* may be substituted for Eiríkr's more familiar vernacular by-name *blóðøx* (rendered *sanguinea securis* in *Hist. Norw.* 105.4–5). Cf. *Ágrip* ch. 5: 'Hann réð Óláf digrbein bróður sinn ok Bjǫrn ok fleiri brœðr sína; því var hann kallaðr blóðøx, at maðrinn var ofstopamaðr ok greypr.' Beyschlag (1950, 136) and Lange (1989, 56–57)

suggest that Theodoricus may recall the epithet *brœðra søkkvi* ('sinker/destroyer of brothers') applied to Eiríkr in a verse by Egill Skallagrímsson (*lausavísa* 20, *Skjd.* A I, 53; Turville-Petre 1976, 22–23). According to *Fsk* ch. 8, Eiríkr earned the *blóðøx* nickname for his viking raids *um ǫll Vestrlǫnd*.

25. According to the D and E versions of the *Anglo-Saxon Chronicle*, Eiríkr was accepted as king of Northumbria in 948, but was driven out the same year. He returned in 952 and was expelled again in 954 (*ASC* 1892–1899, I, 112–113; *EHD* I, 223–224). A later English tradition recorded by Roger of Wendover has it that Eiríkr 'was treacherously killed by Earl Maccus in a certain lonely place which is called Stainmore' (in Westmorland; *Flores Historiarum* I, 402–403; *EHD* I, 284; copied in Matthew Paris, *Chronica Maiora* I, 458; cf. Steenstrup, III, 88–89). According to *Ágrip* ch. 7 and *Hist. Norw.* 106.4–6, Eiríkr died on a viking expedition in Spain after being forced out of Northumbria (a detail which Finnur Jónsson, 1920–1924, II, 614, n. 2, suggests may be due to a confusion of *Stan-* with *Span-*). *Fsk* ch. 8 and *Hkr(Hákgóð)* ch. 4 say that he and five other kings died together in battle in an unnamed place in England; see Seeberg 1978–1981.

26. Cf. *Nóregs konunga tal*, st. 11 (*Skjd.* A I, 580): 'var vigfímr / vetr at landi / eírekr allz / einn ok fíora', i.e. five years in all (probably including three years of joint rule with Haraldr; cf. *Fsk* ch. 5, *Hkr(Hhárf)* ch. 42; Bjarni Aðalbjarnarson 1941–1951, I, lxxv, n. 3). The author of *Ágrip* (ch. 5) likewise says that Eiríkr's reign in Norway lasted five years, but counts only two years of joint rule with Haraldr. *Hist. Norw.* (105.10) and 'Konungatal í Noregi' (*Flat.* I, 583) say that Eiríkr ruled Norway for only one year.

27. *Anno Haraldi nono vel . . . decimo*: AKSL have *regno Haraldi nono*, etc.

28. With this account of the discovery of Iceland cf. *Landnámabók* (*Sturlubók* redaction), ch. 3.

29. The term *socer* here probably renders Old West Norse *mágr* in the sense 'brother-in-law'. Hjǫrleifr was married to Ingólfr's sister Helga (cf. *Landnámabók* [*Sturlubók* redaction] ch. 6).

30. See n. 17 on the different dates given for the beginning of

Haraldr's reign. According to the *Sturlubók* redaction of *Landnámabók* (ch. 8), Ingólfr set out for Iceland in the summer of 874, when 'Haraldr hárfagri had been twelve years king of Norway'.
31. *Britannia minor*: usually 'Brittany' rather than Ireland (cf. Grässe–Benedict–Plechl 1972, I, 336, s.v.). At 7.12 Theodoricus uses the term *Britannia major* to refer to Wales/Cornwall (see below, n. 59).
32. Cf. *Íslendingabók*, ch. 1; *Landnámabók (Sturlubók* redaction), ch. 1, on the books, bells, and croziers said to have been left in Iceland by Irish anchorites.
33. Cf. *Landnámabók (Sturlubók* redaction), chs 4–5, on the voyages of Garðarr Svávarsson and Flóki Vilgerðarson. On the likelihood that Theodoricus drew his information about the discovery of Iceland from written Icelandic sources, see Sveinbjörn Rafnsson 1976, 221–229; Lange 1989, 110–111.
34. *nutricius Halstani*: cf. his vernacular sobriquet *Aðalsteinsfóstri*. On the Scandinavian tradition that Hákon was the foster-son of Æthelstan of Wessex (924–939) see Page 1981, 113–115.
35. I.e. one year together with Eiríkr, and twenty-four years as sole ruler (in peace for nineteen years, and for five years at war with his nephews). *Nóregs konunga tal* (st. 14, *Skjd.* A I, 581), *Fsk* (ch.13), and 'Konungatal i Noregi' *(Flat.* I, 583) record that Hákon's reign lasted twenty-six years. Snorri (*Hkr[Hákgóð]* ch. 28) says that Hákon ruled for twenty-six years after the flight of Eiríkr, and gives the full length of his reign as twenty-seven years in *Ólhelg(Sep)*, ch. 10. *Hist. Norw.* (106.17–18) has the same count of years. The years of Hákon's reign given in *Ágrip* add up to 24. Cf. Bjarni Aðalbjarnarson, 1941–1951, I, lxxv; Ellehøj 1965, 249 and 253.
36. *recte* Statius, *Thebaid*, i.151 (= Walther 1969, no. 22839). Sven Aggesen cites *Thebaid*, i.154–155 in *Brevis Historia Regum Dacie* xiii, 1917–1922, I, 130; Christiansen 1992, 68 and 131, n. 152.
37. Lucan, *Bell. civ.*, i.92–93 (= Walther 1969, no. 20262a), cited again below at 14.39–40. The lines are often quoted as a familiar adage; cf., for example, Sven Aggesen, *Brevis Historia Regum Dacie* xiii, 1917–1922, I, 130; Christiansen 1992, 68 and 131,

n. 151; *Magnúss saga lengri* ch. 22; Vaughan 1958, 128; Foote 1988, 199.
38. One is tempted to translate *malitia* as 'sorcery' here. Cf. Du Cange 1883–1887, s.v., 3: 'maleficium, incantatio, veneficium'. The author of *Ágrip* (ch. 6) says that a 'cook' (*matsveinn*) managed to wound Hákon with a missile 'through the witchcraft of Gunnhildr' (*með gørningum Gunnhildar*). *Hist. Norw.* (107.9–12), by contrast, treats the same episode as an act of divine vengeance for Hákon's apostasy (cf. *Ágrip* ch. 5, *Fsk* ch. 9, *Hkr[Hákgóð]* chs 17–18). The strikingly similar account of the death of Julian the Apostate in ch. 8 may make Theodoricus's discreet silence on this subject all the more surprising. No mention is made of Gunnhildr's sorcery in the accounts of Hákon's wounding in *Nóregs konunga tal* stt. 15–16 (*Skjd.* A I, 581), and *Hkr(Hákgóð)* ch. 31.
39. The same count of years is found in 'Konungatal i Noregi' (*Flat.* I, 583), although Ellehøj (1965, 250–251 and 253) suggests that the number 'xii' in that text is an error for 'xv' (the number of years which Snorri, citing Ari as his authority, says separated the death of Haraldr from that of Hákon Aðalsteinsfóstri, *Hkr[ÓlTrygg]* ch. 14). An erasure has obliterated the last part of the figure given for the length of Haraldr's reign in *Ágrip* (ch. 9: 'x..', perhaps for 'xii', perhaps 'xv'; cf. Storm 1880, n. ad 107.17; Bjarni Einarsson, 1984, 13, n. 2; Driscoll 1995, 91, n. 33). *Hist. Norw.* (107.16–17) says that Haraldr and his brothers ruled for fourteen years. *Nóregs konunga tal* st. 18 (*Skjd.* A I, 581) says that Haraldr's reign lasted only nine years, apparently assigning to Hákon jarl Sigurðarson the six years during which, according to Ari (*Hkr[ÓlTrygg]* ch. 14), Hákon and the sons of Gunnhildr struggled for power in Norway. See Ólafia Einarsdóttir 1964, 177–179.
40. Gull-Haraldr, son of Knútr Gormsson. Cf. *Nóregs konunga tal* st. 19 (*Skjd.* A I, 581), and the accounts of the battle of Háls on Limfjord in *Ágrip* ch. 10, *Jómsvíkinga saga* 1969, 81–82, *Fsk* ch. 16 and *Hkr(ÓlTrygg)* ch. 14.
41. Haraldr blátǫnn († c. 986).
42. Hákon's Machiavellian manipulation of Haraldr Gormsson and Gull-Haraldr is described in dramatic detail in *Jómsvíkinga*

saga 1969, 77–84, *Fsk* chs 15–16 and *Hkr(ÓlTrygg)* chs 9–15. It has been suggested that the story was derived from the putative **Hlaðajarla saga* (see Andersson 1985, 215 and refs).
43. See Oddr Snorrason, *ÓlTrygg* ch. 4. Bjarni Aðalbjarnarson (1941–1951, I, 227, n. 1) notes that the Hákon, 'friend of Gunnhildr', sent in pursuit of Óláfr in *Hkr(ÓlTrygg)* ch. 3, is 'a kind of double' of Hákon jarl Sigurðarson.
44. *superior provincia* is a calque on Upplǫnd (cf. ch. 15, n. 129). Cf. the use of *ad superiora* in the sense 'inland' in ch. 13 (see below, n. 98), and Fritzner s.vv. *uppi* 4: 'inde i Landet', *uppland*: 'Landskab som ligger inde i Landet, fjernt fra Søen'.
45. Cf. *Jómsvíkinga saga* 1969, 84, where it is stated that Hákon jarl sent Haraldr blátǫnn as homage sixty hawks, which he elected to pay 'in one year rather than each year'. Gjessing (1873–1876, II, 64; 1877, xiii) observes that this passage, taken together with Theodoricus's account, indicates that the stipulated payment of hawks was to be twenty a year for three years.
46. Only Theodoricus has this calculation of the length of Hákon's reign. Oddr Snorrason, *ÓlTrygg* ch. 25 (16), cites both Sæmundr inn fróði and Ari Þorgilsson as his authorities for the information that Hákon ruled Norway for thirty-three years after the death of Haraldr gráfeldr. *Nóregs konunga tal* st. 20 (*Skjd.* A I, 581) and *Hist. Norw.* 115.13 give the same figure. According to *ÓlTrygg en mesta* ch. 104, however, thirty-three years was the length, not of his rule of Norway, but of the whole period for which he was *jarl*, from the death of his father Sigurðr. 'Konungatal i Noregi' (*Flat.* I, 583) likewise records that Hákon ruled Norway for twenty years, but was *jarl* in Þrándheimr for thirteen years before that. Cf. *Hkr(ÓlTrygg)* ch. 14, where Ari is credited with the same calculation of Hákon's time as *jarl* before the death of Haraldr, and *Ágrip* ch. 12, where the length of his rule after the fall of Haraldr is given as twenty years. Cf. Bjarni Aðalbjarnarson 1941–1951, I, lxxv and n. 3; Ólafia Einarsdóttir 1964, 178–180, 195; Ellehøj 1965, 72–73, 251–253.
47. Cf. *Ágrip* ch. 11, *Hist. Norw.* 111.13–14, and the aetiological tale of Hersir's suicide in *Ágrip* ch. 15, explaining the origin of the use of the title *jarl* by the *Hlaðajarlar*.

48. Otto II of Germany (973–983) in fact invaded Denmark in 974 in reprisal for Danish raids on Holstein. (Haraldr had been converted to Christianity at least a decade before this.) Norwegian and Icelandic accounts of the battle appear to have been influenced by Adam of Bremen's erroneous claim (*Gest. Hamm.* ii.3) that Haraldr was forced to accept Christianity after an invasion by Otto I (936–973). Elsewhere Adam maintains that the work of converting Haraldr to Christianity was begun by Unni, archbishop of Hamburg-Bremen (918–936), after Henry the Fowler's victory over the Danes in 934 (*Gest. Hamm.* i.59 [61]). Widukind, *Res Gestae Saxonicae* iii.65, records that Haraldr was baptized by the German missionary Poppo (c. 965). Cf. Oddr Snorrason, *ÓlTrygg* ch. 15, *Fsk* ch. 17, *Hkr(ÓlTrygg)* chs 24–28; Weibull 1911, 37–44; Bjarni Aðalbjarnarson 1941–1951, I, 259, n.2; Abrams 1995, 225.

49. *pheodatos*: Cf. Niermeyer 1976, s.v. *feodatus* subst., 'feudatary'; *OED*, s.v. *feudatory*, B. sb. 1: 'One who holds his lands by feudal tenure; a feudal vassal.'

50. *venenum abdidisti ecclesiæ*: Hanssen (1949, 104, n. 3) regards Storm's emendation of the reading *abdidisti* found in AKS and L (Lehmann 1937, 121; rpt 1959–1962, 428 [12.3]) to *addidisti* as unnecessary. Cf. Prinz–Schneider 1967–, s.v. *abdo*, and Hanssen's own translation (1949, 105), followed here. The story recorded by Theodoricus is not to be found in any printed version of the work by Landulf Sagax identified by Lehmann (1937, 72–75; rpt 1959–1962, 384–387) as the *Romana Historia* cited in ch. 26 (see n. 252 below). The story is elsewhere told, not of Otto II, but of the emperor Constantine, who is said to have received the same angelic rebuke after making his notorious 'donation' to Pope Sylvester (cf. n. 228 below; on the fable, see Döllinger 1863, 100–101; 1871, 167–170; Laehr 1926, 172–178; Tubach 1969, no. 1217). For a full discussion of the passage, see Hanssen 1949, 104–115.

51. Cf. Oddr Snorrason, *ÓlTrygg* ch. 15: 'Otta keisari. hann er callaðr Otta hinn rauði'; cf. *ÓlTrygg en mesta* ch. 65. Hanssen (1949, 114, n. 1) notes that the epithet *pius* is applied to Otto I by Bruno of Querfurt (see Bagemihl 1913, 67; for parallels to Theodoricus's characterization of Otto II, see *ibid.*, 25–26).

52. *mittit*: literally 'sends'. We have not tried to reproduce Theodoricus's periodic vacillations between past and present tenses.
53. The manner of Gunnhildr's execution is in keeping with her reputation as a witch (cf. Ström 1942, 178–188). On N. M. Petersen's fanciful identification of the body removed from a peat bog at Haraldskjær south of Jelling in 1835 as that of Gunnhildr, and the refutation of this claim by J. J. Worsaae, see Petersen 1938, 85; Glob 1969, 55–58 and 134.
54. Cf. *Ágrip* ch. 11, *Jómsvíkinga saga* (1969, 83–84) and esp. *Flat.* I, 152–153 (cf. Ólafur Halldórsson 1958–1961, I, 170–171) where much of the phrasing of this passage is followed closely (see Bjarni Aðalbjarnarson 1937, 75–76; Lange 1989, 134–135 and refs). Nordal (1941, 141–144) emphasizes the historical unreliability of this account of Gunnhildr's death. While Old Icelandic sources consistently identify Gunnhildr's father as a certain Qzurr toti (or 'lafskegg') of Hálogaland, *Hist. Norw.* 105.5–7 records that she was the daughter of Gormr inn gamli and Þyri, and therefore the sister of Haraldr blátǫnn. Cf. Driscoll 1995, 87, n. 15; 91, n. 39.
55. Oddr Snorrason, *ÓlTrygg* ch. 18 (12), records that Hákon stopped paying tribute in the thirteenth year of his reign, after assisting Haraldr in his failed defence of Denmark against Otto II (i.e. in 974; cf. Bjarni Aðalbjarnarson 1941–1951, I, cviii–cix; Ólafia Einarsdóttir 1964, 192–198). Both Theodoricus and Oddr, therefore, calculate that Hákon ceased to pay tribute twenty years before his death (cf. above, n. 46, on different calculations of the length of Hákon's reign). According to Snorri (*Hkr[ÓlTrygg]* ch. 23), Hákon was forgiven all payment of tribute to Haraldr from the moment he came to power in Norway, in return for his help in overcoming the sons of Gunnhildr.
56. Theodoricus assumes that the rift between Hákon and Haraldr preceded rather than followed Otto's invasion of Denmark.
57. Vladimir the Great, prince of Kiev 980–1015. Cf. Oddr Snorrason, *ÓlTrygg* chs 6 (5)–8; *Hkr(ÓlTrygg)* chs 7–8, 21; *Rekstefja* st. 2 (*Skjd.* A I, 544: 'fostr i gǫrðum . . . visa'; see Bjarni Aðalbjarnarson 1941–1951, I, ci and n. 2; on the still unsolved problem of this poem's date and authorship, see Lange 1989, 202, n. 100).

58. Cf. Oddr Snorrason, *ÓlTrygg* ch. 12 (8).
59. I.e. Wales/Cornwall (cf. ch. 3, n. 31 *Britannia minor*). *Hist. Norw.* (114.6) notes that the island visited by Óláfr was 'near Wales' (*penes Britanniam*). Oddr Snorrason *(ÓlTrygg* ch. 14 [10]) notes that the Scilly Isles are situated 'a short distance from Ireland' (*scamt fra Irlandi*).
60. Oddr Snorrason, *ÓlTrygg* ch. 14 (10), has a full account of this episode, although in his version the abbot is unnamed. Most other sources (*Hist. Norw.* 114.5–115.7, *Ágrip* ch. 19, *Hkr[ÓlTrygg]* ch. 31) have instead the story of Óláfr's testing of an anchorite and subsequent baptism by him (cf. Bjarni Aðalbjarnarson 1941–1951, I, civ–cv; Strömbäck 1975, 102–104). *ÓlTrygg en mesta* chs 78–79 combines the two versions, telling first of Óláfr's encounter with the anchorite, then having him proceed to a neighbouring monastery on the islands to be baptized. According to the *Anglo-Saxon Chronicle* (C, D, E, and F versions), Óláfr was confirmed at Andover in 994, with Æthelred as his sponsor (*ASC* 1892–1899, I, 129; *EHD* I, 235). He had obviously been baptized before that.
61. For Óláfr's use of the assumed name 'Óli' or 'Áli', see Oddr Snorrason, *ÓlTrygg [A]* chs 14–15; *ÓlTrygg en mesta* chs 70, 80, 93–94; *Hkr(ÓlTrygg)* chs 32, 46–47; cf. Andersson 1979, 6, 8, 10.
62. With Theodoricus's account of Hákon's scheme, cf. Oddr Snorrason, *ÓlTrygg* ch. 19 (13).
63. The nickname is cognate with Old West Norse *klakkr* 'lump, clump'. See Lind 1920–1921, 201–202.
63a. The location of Þjálfahellir is uncertain. Schøning (1910, I, 80–81), who tramped round Agdenes in the 1770s, tentatively identified it as a small cave just east of Valset, which lies some 3 km. to the west-south-west of the tip of the Agdenes promontory. The place-name otherwise occurs only in Oddr Snorrason, *ÓlTrygg* ch. 19 (13).
64. *Sigwardum . . . episcopum*: in *Ágrip* ch. 19 the names of the clerics who accompanied Óláfr are given as Sigurðr (byskup), Þangbrandr (prestr) and Þormóðr. Oddr Snorrason, *ÓlTrygg* ch. 26 (17), says that Óláfr recruited missionaries only on a return visit to England, after he had been king for one year,

and provides a list of names which is identical to those presented in Theodoricus and *Ágrip*, except that he identifies Óláfr's bishop as 'Ión biscup' rather than Sigurðr/Sigeweard. In this, Oddr agrees with *Hist. Norw.* 115.8, which names only 'Johannem episcopum et Thangbrandem', and Adam of Bremen (*Gest. Hamm.* ii.37 [35], iv.34 [33]), who identifies 'Iohannes episcopus' as the most important of the early missionaries to Norway. Cf. Maurer 1855–1856, I, 282; Taranger 1890, 146–148.

65. The form *Theobrandus* (for **Þeodbrand*? cf. Förstemann 1900, 1425, s.v. *Theudobrand*) is found only here. He is referred to as Þorbrandr in the Þórðarbók redaction of *Landnámabók* (1968, 348, n. 4). Otherwise, his name is regularly given as Þangbrandr in both Norwegian and Icelandic sources (cf., for example, Steinunn skáldkona, *lausavísa* 1 [*Skjd.* A I, 135]; *Íslendingabók* ch. 7; *Ágrip* ch. 19; *Hist. Norw.* 115.8; Oddr Snorrason, *ÓlTrygg* ch. 26 [17]; cf. *Hauksbók* 138.5, 140: *Þanbrandr*). This form of the name is thought to be German (for OHG **Dankbrant*), although it is not attested elsewhere (see Förstemann 1900, 333, s.v. *Branda*). According to Oddr Snorrason, *ÓlTrygg [A]* ch. 41, Þangbrandr was not Flemish, but 'Saxon by race' (cf. *Hkr[ÓlTrygg]* ch. 73), and a later tradition makes him the son of a certain Count Willebald of Bremen; cf. *Kristni saga* ch. 5 (*Hauksbók* 130); *ÓlTrygg en mesta* ch. 74; *Njáls saga* ch. 100. *Kristni saga* chs 5 and 7–9 (*Hauksbók* 130–131, 132–138), *ÓlTrygg en mesta* chs 74, 81, 189 and 216–218, and *Njáls saga* chs 100–104 provide highly romanticised accounts of Þangbrandr and his mission to Iceland (see ch. 12 below). Cf. Taranger 1890, 158–160.

66. The vernacular form of his name is given as Þormóðr in ch. 12. Cf. *Ágrip* ch. 19, Oddr Snorrason, *ÓlTrygg* ch. 26 (17), *Íslendingabók* ch. 7, *Kristni saga* ch. 12 (*Hauksbók* 141).

67. *Iovinianum: Jovianum* in L (see Lehmann 1937, 121; rpt 1959–1962, 428 [15.12]). Roman emperor 363–364. Captain of the imperial bodyguard during Julian the Apostate's ill-starred Persian campaign, Jovian was hastily chosen as emperor on Julian's death (cf. Ammianus Marcellinus, *Rerum Gestarum Libri XXXI*, xxv.5). Because of his orthodoxy, he is regularly contrasted favourably with Julian by Christian historians. As Storm (1880,

n. ad 15.12) and Hanssen (1945, 167) note, the form *Iovinianus* is not uncommon in twelfth-century sources (cf., for example, *Liber exceptionum* I.viii.4; see next note).
68. Johnsen (1939, 53) argues that Theodoricus here borrows directly from Hugh of St Victor's *Exceptiones priores* (*recte* Richard of St Victor *Liber exceptionum* I.viii.4 'De Joviniano'; see n. 9 above).
69. Flavius Claudius Julianus, Roman emperor 361–363, better known as 'Julian the Apostate' for his rejection of Christianity and his promotion of traditional Roman religion. Although his polemic against Christianity, written during his Persian campaign, has not survived (Jerome, *Epist.* lxx.3, 1910–1918, I, 703–704, says it comprised not six, but seven books), much of its content can be recovered from Cyril of Alexandria's *Contra Julianum*. Johnsen (1939, 80–83) and Hanssen (1949, 96–99) see in this digression on Julian the Apostate a thinly veiled condemnation of Theodoricus's contemporary, King Sverrir the *guðníðingr*. Bagge (1989, 118 and 128–129), however, argues that Theodoricus more likely intends to draw a typological parallel with Hákon jarl, who, like Julian, rejected the Christian faith and persecuted its adherents, and who was ousted by the Christian king Óláfr just as Julian was succeeded by the devout Jovian. Cf. Lange 1989, 42–43.
70. Cf. 1 Sam. 25:39, 1 Kgs. 2:44.
71. This lurid and immensely popular account of Julian's death (see Tubach 1969, no. 2881) originates in a passage in the *Church History* of Theodore of Cyrrhus (c. 393 to c. 466), iii.25. Johnsen (1939, 54) cites 'Hugh of St Victor' (*recte* Richard, *Liber exceptionum* I.viii.3—see nn. 9 and 68 above) as Theodoricus's immediate source; but Hanssen (1945, 166–167; 1949, 97) identifies closer parallels for several details in the writings of Ado of Vienne (*Chronicon* 361, PL 123, 94), Ekkehard (*Chronicon universale* s.a. 364; 1844, 114), Matthew Paris (*Chronica majora*, I, 167), and Otto of Freising (*Chronica* iv.10; 1912, 197). Theodoricus did not know or ignored the story (repeated by many other Norse writers) that Mary sent St Mercurius to transfix Julian with a spear (cf. *Hkr[Ólhelg]* ch. 12; *Ólhelg[Sep]* ch. 23; *Knýtlinga saga* ch. 6; *Ágrip af sǫgu Danakonunga* 329; *Mariu saga* 72–73, 699–702; see, for example, Bjarni

Aðalbjarnarson, 1941–1951, II, 14, n. 1; Demidoff, 1978–1979, 30–47, esp. 44; Bjarni Guðnason, 1982, 98, n.2).
72. Cf. different accounts of the same episode in Oddr Snorrason, *ÓlTrygg* ch. 26 (17); *Orkneyinga saga* (the Danish 'Þ' text) ch. 12; *Hkr[ÓlTrygg]* ch. 47; *ÓlTrygg en mesta* ch. 98.
73. Þorfinnr was to rule Orkney from c. 1014 to c. 1065. Oddr says that the son of Sigurðr seized by Óláfr was named 'Huelpr'. *Orkneyinga saga, Hkr[ÓlTrygg], ÓlTrygg en mesta* give his name as 'Hvelpr or Hundi', and say that Óláfr took him back to Norway as surety after forcing Sigurðr to accept his terms.
74. Ps. 82:17.
75. Present-day Moster, Hordaland. Cf. n. 123.
76. Cf. Oddr Snorrason, *ÓlTrygg* ch. 64 (52); *Hkr(ÓlTrygg)* ch. 47; *ÓlTrygg en mesta* ch. 99. *Ágrip* ch. 19 merely states that Óláfr first preached Christianity in Mostr. *Hkr(Hákgóð)* ch. 18 refers to the burning of three churches built by Hákon Aðalsteinsfóstri in Møre (c. 950).
77. In another context Oddr Snorrason likewise refers to the early trading centre of Niðaróss (*ÓlTrygg* [A]) ch. 40) without stating, as all other sources do, that it was first established by Óláfr himself (cf. Oddr, *ÓlTrygg* [S] ch. 31; *Fsk* ch. 23; *Hkr[ÓlTrygg]* ch. 70; *Hkr[Ólhelg]* ch. 42). Andersson (1979, 14–16) compares *Hkr(prologus)* 6, where Snorri notes that one of Ari's ultimate source-men was Þorgeirr afráðskollr, who was 'so old that he lived on Niðarnes when Hákon jarl the Powerful was killed,' adding, 'in that same place Óláfr Tryggvason had the market town established which is there now.' Andersson argues that Ari probably mentioned a trading centre on Niðarnes in his lost *Konungaævi, that this information was used by both Theodoricus and Oddr, and that the tradition of Óláfr's founding of Niðaróss was a later development.
78. Theodoricus makes no mention of the uprising against Hákon, occasioned by his attempted abduction of either Guðrún Lundasól (according to *Ágrip* ch. 13) or the wife of a certain Brynjólfr (according to Oddr Snorrason, *ÓlTrygg* ch. 20 [14]). Both women figure in *Hkr(ÓlTrygg)* ch. 48, *ÓlTrygg en mesta* chs 101–102; cf. Andersson 1979, 3.
79. *in quendam viculum, Rimul nomine*: Here *viculus* must have

the sense 'minor estate, farmstead' (cf. Niermeyer 1976, s.v. *vicus*, 4). The farm is present-day *Romol* in Melhus, Guldalen (see Rygh 1897–1924, xiv.281; Olsen 1928, 70, 72).
80. Storm emends the form *Barke* found in AKS (and L, cf. Lehmann 1937, 121; 1959–1962, 428 [18.3]) to *Carke* (cf. *Ágrip* ch. 13, MS. *carki*; *Hist. Norw.* 115.14 *Carcus*). He is called Skopti karkr in *Jómsvíkinga saga* (1969, 185, 194) and *Fsk* ch. 22, both Karkr and Þormóðr karkr in *Hkr(ÓlTrygg)* chs 48–49 and *ÓlTrygg en mesta* ch. 102, simply Karkr in Oddr Snorrason, *ÓlTrygg* ch. 21 (15). See Lind 1920–1921, 189; Driscoll 1995, 92, n. 40.
81. Cf. *Nóregs konunga tal* st. 21 (*Skjd.* A I, 582); *Ágrip* ch. 13; Oddr Snorrason, *ÓlTrygg* ch. 21 (15); *Hist. Norw.* 115.14–18; *Hkr(ÓlTrygg)* chs 48–49; *ÓlTrygg en mesta* chs 102–104.
82. Cf. Matt. 20:1, 21:28.
83. The comma after *verba* in Storm's edition should come after *movebantur: quia minus movebantur, ad verba addidit frequenter et verbera*. For paronomasia of the type *post verba verbera*, cf. Walther 1963–1986, no. 28177 and *Register* s.v. *verba-verbera*, and *Disticha Catonis* iv.6 (1952, 200, and 202 ad loc.).
84. Cf. Luke 10:33–34. The allegorical interpretation of the Samaritan of the parable as 'dominus noster' is an exegetical commonplace. Cf., for example, Ambrose, *Exp. Lc.* vii.74; 1957, 239; Augustine, *Quaest. euang.* ii.19; 1980, 62–63; Caesarius of Arles, *Sermo* clxi.1; 1953, 661; Bede, *Exp. Lc.* iii.2245; 1960, 223.
85. Luke 14:23.
86. On the form of sorcery called *seiðr*, see Strömbäck 1935 and 1970; de Vries 1956–1957, I, 330–333; Foote and Wilson 1970, 390 and 404; Dillmann 1993; Price 2002.
87. In other sources the burning of the *seiðmenn* and the desecration of the temple at Mærin are described as separate incidents. Cf. accounts of the burning in Oddr Snorrason, *ÓlTrygg* ch. 36 (28), where Oddr cites Sæmundr as his authority; *Hkr(ÓlTrygg)* ch. 62; *ÓlTrygg en mesta* ch. 196; accounts of Óláfr's destruction of the idols at Mærin in Oddr Snorrason, *ÓlTrygg* ch. 54 (42); *Hkr(ÓlTrygg)* chs 67–69; *ÓlTrygg en mesta* chs 167–168.

88. I.e. one year after Óláfr's accession to the throne.
89. Cf. Bede, *De temporibus* vii (1980, 590), and *De temporum ratione* xxxi.58–65 (1977, 378–379); *Landnámabók* (*Sturlubók* redaction) ch. 1.
90. Ari, *Íslendingabók* ch. 7, says that Þangbrandr stayed in Iceland 'one or two winters'; cf. *Hkr(ÓlTrygg)*, ch. 73: 'two winters'; *Kristni saga* ch. 9 (*Hauksbók* 136): 'three winters'.
91. Ari, *Íslendingabók* ch. 7, records the earliest converts in Iceland as 'Hallr Þorsteinsson of Síða . . . Hjalti Skeggjason from Þjórsárdalr, Gizurr the White Teitsson . . . and many other chieftains'.
92. It was not Ísleifr (bishop of Iceland 1056–1080), but his son Gizurr (bishop of Iceland 1082–1106, of Skálaholt 1106–1118) who established the episcopal see at Skálaholt. Cf. *Íslendingabók* ch. 10; *Kristni saga* ch. 16 (*Hauksbók* 146); *Hungrvaka* (1938, 85); Jón Helgason 1925, 63–64. According to *Hungrvaka* (1938, 76), the first church at Skálaholt was built by Gizurr the White Teitsson, Ísleifr's father.
93. Storm (1880, 20, n. 9) proposed that the name Þorgils here is a mistake for Þóroddr Eyvindarson goði of Ǫlfus, the father of Skapti the Lawspeaker (1004–1030) and father-in-law of Gizurr the White; and Jón Jóhannesson (1956, 156–157; 1974, 129) suggested further that Theodoricus may have confused Þóroddr with his son-in-law Þorgils Þórðarson Ǫrrabeinsstjúpr, the hero of *Flóamanna saga*. On the other hand, it has been argued that Theodoricus's 'Thorgils de Aulfusi' could either refer to Þorgils Ǫrrabeinsstjúpr himself (see Jón Hnefill Aðalsteinsson 1978, 64–65 and refs; Lange 1989, 137–138), or represent a conflation of Þóroddr of Ǫlfus and Þorgils of Flói (see Einar Arnórsson 1950, 321; Perkins 1985, 793–795). It is not stated elsewhere that Þóroddr had become a Christian before the official acceptance of Christianity as the religion of Iceland in 999 or 1000 (unless the story told in *Kristni saga* ch. 12, *Hauksbók* 142, that opponents of Christianity during the deliberations at the Alþingi interpreted the eruption of a volcanic fire near Þóroddr's farm as a sign of divine disfavour, indicates that Þóroddr had already abandoned the old religion; see Jón Jóhannesson 1956, 156–157; 1974, 129).

According to *Flóamanna saga* (ch. 20), however, Þorgils was among the first to accept the new faith (*tók Þorgils í fyrra lagi við trú*). The saga also records (ch. 35) that Þorgils died and was buried at Hjalli in Ǫlfus. It has been noted that the author of *Flóamanna saga* might have taken his information about Þorgils's early conversion from Theodoricus's history (see Perkins 1985, 794–795; Þórhallur Vilmundarson 1991, cxlix–cl). It has also been suggested that Theodoricus's own informant here may have been Þorgils's illustrious descendant, St Þorlákr Þórhallsson, bishop of Skálaholt 1178–1193; see Jón Hnefill Aðalsteinsson 1978, 65.

94. *Íslendingabók* ch. 7, *Kristni saga* ch. 12 (*Hauksbók* 141), *Hkr(ÓlTrygg)* ch. 95, and *ÓlTrygg en mesta* ch. 228 likewise state that Þormóðr accompanied Gizurr Teitsson and Hjalti Skeggjason on their mission to Iceland. Cf. Taranger 1890, 161–164; Jón Jóhannesson 1956, 159; 1974, 132.
95. In other accounts (*Íslendingabók* ch. 7, *Kristni saga* ch. 12 [*Hauksbók* 142], *Njáls saga* chs 104–105) the confrontation between Christians and heathens is, on the contrary, presented as a stand-off, and violence is averted only when the matter is submitted to the arbitration of Þorgeirr Ljósvetningagoði.
96. Cf. Oddr Snorrason, *ÓlTrygg* [S], chs 22–23.
97. See esp. Oddr Snorrason, *ÓlTrygg* [S] ch. 58 (46); cf. *Hkr(ÓlTrygg)* ch. 87, *ÓlTrygg en mesta* ch. 222.
98. *ad superiora, scilicet Uplond*: cf. nn. 44 and 129.
99. As a by-name of Guðrøðr Bjarnarson, *sýr* 'sow' is recorded only here (cf. Lind 1920–1921, 377–378). Suhm (1783, 321 ad loc.) noted that Theodoricus was doubtless thinking of Sigurðr sýr, the stepfather of Haraldr harðráði. As Storm points out, however, Theodoricus makes no mention of this nickname in connection with Sigurðr in ch. 15.
100. This is the usual Icelandic tradition. Cf. *Hkr(ÓlTrygg)* ch. 60, *Ólhelg(Sep)* ch. 18, *Ólhelg(Leg)* ch. 8.
101. Storm (1880, ad 22.3) notes that this tradition 'kjendes ikke længer'. But Johnsen (1939, 20–21) suggests that the English connections both of St Óláfr and of Norway in the century after the saint's death could well have fostered the notion that he was baptized in England. That Óláfr accepted the Chris-

tian faith in England is stated explicitly in Eysteinn Erlendsson's *Pass. Olav.* (see next note).
102. Robert, archbishop of Rouen (989–1037), son of Duke Richard I of Normandy (942–996). Cf. William of Jumièges, *GND* v.12: 'Rex etiam Olauus . . . ortante archiepiscopo Rodberto, ad Christi fidem est conuersus, atque ab eo baptismate lotus sacroque chrismate delibutus, de precepta gratia gaudens, ad suum regnum est regressus.' This account is echoed in Eysteinn Erlendsson's *Pass. Olav.* 68.7–9: 'Hic, euangelice ueritatis sinceritate in anglia comperta, fidem toto admisit pectore, et ad baptismi gratiam in urbe rotomagi deuota animi alacritate conuolauit.' Cf. the vernacular homily 'Jn die sancti Olaui Regis et martiris' based on *Pass. Olav.* (*GNH* 1931, 109.2–4): 'á Englande toc hann á guð at trva. ok í borg þæirri er Røm hæitir. þar let hann cristna sic.'
103. As Storm notes (1880, ad 22.5), this observation appears to be a muddled reminiscence of *GND* v.10–12. The quarrels between Duke Richard II of Normandy (996–1026) and Odo II of Chartres (in the years 1013–1014) are confused with the conflicts of Richard's grandfather William Longsword (duke of Normandy c. 928–942) with Louis IV d'Outremer (king of France 936–954) and Count Arnulf I of Flanders (918–965). According to William of Jumièges, it was Richard who called upon Óláfr (and a certain 'Lacman'; cf. *GND* v.11 and van Houts 1992, II, 20, n. 1) for assistance against Odo, while King Robert the Pious (996–1031) intervened to reconcile the warring parties (*GND* v.11–12; cf. Lemarignier 1945, 87–89, and Musset 1957–1958, 23–25). Cf. the similar confusion in *Hkr(Ólhelg)* ch. 20, where 'jarlar tveir, Viljálmr ok Roðbert' are said to rule Normandy at the time of Óláfr's visit, rather than their father Ríkarðr Rúðujarl ('earl of Rouen'; cf. Bjarni Aðalbjarnarson 1941–1951, II, 27, n. 1). If the phrase *nobilissimi ducis* (at Storm 1880, 22.7) is not simply an error for *nobilissimi regis*, then Theodoricus also confuses Duke Hugh the Great of Neustria (923–956) with his son, Hugh Capet, king of France (987–996), the father of Robert the Pious.
104. Storm (1880, ad 22.11) interprets the reading *provectioris aetatis . . . quam illi dicant*, which he adopts from A and S, as

a comparative of difference with a relative adverb meaning 'than'—'it is clear that he was of *more* advanced age . . . *than* they [i.e. Icelanders] say . . .' Lange (1989, 100–101) points out, however, that the readings found in L and K—*provectioris aetatis . . . quomodo* [L] / *quemadmodum* [K] *illi dicant*—are better interpreted as a comparative of degree with a relative adverb meaning 'as': 'he was of *rather* advanced age . . . *as* they say'. Storm's suggestion that the phrase *quando martyrio coronatus est* should be omitted as an interpolation (on the grounds that the preceding passage deals with Óláfr's baptism and not his death) is also rejected by Lange (1989, 101), since Óláfr's ultimate end as 'a faithful martyr of Christ' is, in fact, mentioned earlier at 13.10.

105. *in illa terra, ubi nullus antiquitatum unquam scriptor fuerit*. Scholarly opinion has long been divided over whether Theodoricus refers here to Norway or Iceland (see bibliographical references in Lange 1989, 212 nn. 294 and 295). Lange (1989, 102–103) argues that the phrase must be interpreted in the light of what follows: if even an authority such as Jerome can (according to Theodoricus) be forced to record three conflicting views on the baptism of Constantine, it is not surprising that three different accounts of Óláfr's baptism circulate when no chronicler of these events has ever existed. Lange suggests that the phrase in question is best treated as a piece of hyperbole, and takes the words *in illa terra* in the very general sense 'auf dieser Erde'. She argues moreover that *nullus antiquitatum scriptor* is probably meant to imply 'no *eyewitness* historian' (see n. 11 above on the notion of *historia* as a record of 'things seen' by a contemporary chronicler).

106. Jerome, in fact, records only that Constantine was baptized shortly before his death by the Arian Christian Eusebius, bishop of Nicomedia (*Chronicon*, 1956, 234.3–5). The (unhistorical) legend of Constantine's baptism at Rome by Pope Sylvester figures in all versions of the *Vita* of Sylvester (cf., for example, *Liber Pontificalis*, 1886–1892, I, 170; Mombritius II, 512.15–513.13; *Silvesters saga* chs 7–8), and was confirmed as the officially sanctioned tradition in a letter from Pope Alexander III to Eysteinn Erlendsson; the letter is undated but is from

the period 1161–1172 (*Regesta Norvegica* I no. 140; see Döllinger 1863, 52–61; 1871, 89–103; Holtzmann 1938, 386 and n. 2; Hanssen 1949, 102 and 122; Vandvik 1955). We have been unable to find any other reference to a tradition that Constantine was baptized in Constantinople; but see Laehr 1926, 170, on debates over the contradictory traditions in the twelfth century.
107. Horace, *Ars poetica* 78; Walther 1969, no. 548.
108. According to *Hist. Norw.* (118.3–16), Sveinn and Óláfr Eiríksson of Sweden had thirty ships each, while Eiríkr had only eleven, a total of seventy-one ships against Óláfr's eleven (cf. *Fsk* ch. 24, and Halldórr ókristni, *Eiríksflokkr* st. 2, *Skjd.* A I, 202). *Ágrip*, ch. 20, records that Óláfr's opponents assembled a fleet of eighty-two ships. *Rekstefja* (stt. 15, 16, 18, *Skjd.* A I, 547) counts a total of seventy-five ships against Óláfr's eleven.
109. Cf. Sallust, *Catilina*, lx.4 (see Skard 1935, 120; Hanssen 1949, 84).
110. Hanssen (1949, 84) cites examples of the same formula from Orosius, *Hist. adv. pag.*, II.xv.5, and Justin, *Epitoma*, V.i.10. See *TLL* 4, s.v. *consumo*, 609.55–57; and cf. ch. 19, n. 203 below.
111. Cf. Sallust, *Catilina*, lxi.7. Hanssen (1949, 84), however, maintains that both this and all of the preceding sentence were probably borrowed *en bloc* from an intermediate source.
112. Cf. *Ágrip* ch. 20 fin.; Hallfreðr, *Erfidrápa* st. 29 (*Skjd.* A I, 166); *Rekstefja* st. 33 (*Skjd.* A I, 551–552). Rumours of Óláfr's survival began to circulate immediately after the battle, and are mentioned in Hallfreðr's *Erfidrápa* (dated 1001) stt. 20–24 (*Skjd.* A I, 163–165); cf. *Hkr(ÓlTrygg)* ch. 112. For the tradition that Óláfr escaped to end his days as a monk in Syria or Greece, see Oddr Snorrason, *ÓlTrygg*, chs 73 (61) to 75 (63), 78 (65) to 81; *ÓlTrygg en mesta* chs 267–269, 271, 283, 286; *Hemings þáttr Áslákssonar*, 1962, 57–58 (cf. Ashdown 1959).
113. All versions of the text (including L, cf. Lehmann 1937, 121; 1959–1962, 428 [24.10]) have the form *Svoln*, which Storm emends to *Svold*. *Svǫld(r)* is also identified as an island off Vindland in Oddr Snorrason, *ÓlTrygg* [A] ch. 65, [S] ch. 55

fin.; *Fsk* ch. 24; *Hkr(ÓlTrygg)* ch. 99. In *Knýtlinga saga*, ch. 122, however, *Svǫldr* is given as the name of a river in Vindland (*í ánni Svǫldr*). And Storm notes (1880, ad 24.10) that the phrase *fyrir Svaldrar mynni* in Skúli Þorsteinsson's poem on the battle (st. 2, *Skjd.* A I, 306; cf. *Rekstefja* st. 15, *Skjd.* A I, 547) suggests a river rather than an island (as do, though perhaps less certainly, *Svǫldrar vágr* in *Nóregs konunga tal* st. 25 [*Skjd.* A I, 579] and Saxo's *portus Swaldensis* at *Gesta Danorum* XIV.xliv.9). Bjarni Aðalbjarnarson (1941–1951, I, cxxxv) suggests that Icelanders unfamiliar with the place may have transferred the river-name *Svǫldr* to the island beside which Halldórr ókristni says Óláfr and Eiríkr jarl fought (see *Eiríksflokkr* st. 3, *Skjd.* A I, 203: 'iarl vaN hiálms at hólmi hriþ'; cf. Hallfreðr's *Erfidrápa* st. 17, *Skjd.* A I, 163: 'hólms . . . a uiðu sunndi'). For full discussion of the problem see Baetke 1951, Ellehøj 1958, Ólafur Halldórsson 1984, 102–105, and Lange 1989, 65–68, 108–110, 113–114 and refs. *Ágrip* ch. 20 and *Hist. Norw.* 117.14 follow Adam of Bremen (*Gest. Hamm.* ii.40 [38]) in placing the site of the battle 'beside Sjælland' in the Øresund. 'Vindland' is for Storm's emended *Vinnlandiam*; cf. B *Umlandiam*, AL *Uumlandiam*, K *Vumlandiam*, S *Wumlandiam*.

114. Cf. Oddr Snorrason, *ÓlTrygg* [A] ch. 73: 'Oc aðr en luki þessi stefnu. þa heitr Eirikr j. at taka helga skirn ef hann fengi sigraþ þenna hinn ageta konung. Oc Eirikr j. hafði aðr haft istafni a skipi sinu. Þór. en nu let hann coma istaðiN hinn helga cross. en hann brot Þor isundr ismán mola'—a passage further adapted in *ÓlTrygg en mesta* chs 252–253.

115. Lucan, *Bell. civ.* i.92–93. Cf. n. 37 above.

116. *pituita*: The usual meaning of the word is 'phlegm, catarrh'. Hanssen (1945, 174–175) suggests that its use here where one would expect *uva* 'uvula' (cf. Old West Norse *úfr*) is due to miscopying of a text in which both words appeared side by side: *(propter) pituitam (uvam) fecisset abscidi* becoming the present *pituitam fecisset abscidi*. The same account of Eiríkr's death is found in *Nóregs konunga tal* st. 27 (*Skjd.* A I, 582), *Ágrip* ch. 21, *Fsk* ch. 26, *ÓlTrygg en mesta* ch. 266, *Knýtlinga saga* ch. 16; cf. *Hkr(ÓlTrygg)* ch. 25. For discussion of the 'staphylotomy' operation in medieval Scandinavia see Grön

1908, 56–58; Finnur Jónsson 1912, 29–30; Møller-Christensen 1944, 118; 1961, 73–74; McDougall 1992, 58–59, 76–77.
117. For accounts of Óláfr's part in the restoration of Æthelred Unræd after the death of Sveinn tjúguskegg (in February 1014) cf. Óttarr svarti, *Hǫfuðlausn* st. 8 (*Skjd.* A I, 292); *Ólhelg(Leg)* ch. 10; *Hkr(Ólhelg)* chs 12–15; see Johnsen 1916, 13–14; Campbell 1949, 78–82.
118. *potens*: i.e. *inn ríki.*
119. In fact, Æthelred died in London on 23 April 1016, eight months after the beginning of Knútr's reconquest of England, but before the Danish fleet had reached the Thames. After a series of battles, culminating in the English defeat at Ashingdon on 18 October 1016, Knútr and Æthelred's successor Edmund Ironside agreed to a division of the country which lasted only until Edmund's death on 30 November 1016. Knútr then became sole ruler of England. Cf. Stenton 1971, 388–393; *Ólhelg(Leg)* ch. 10; *Hkr(Ólhelg)* ch. 26; *Hist. Norw.* 122.18–123.5. Theodoricus's account possibly bears some relation to Sigvatr Þórðarson, *Knútsdrápa* st. 2, *Skjd.* A I, 248 (cited in *Hkr[Ólhelg]* ch. 26) on Knútr's expulsion of the sons of Æthelred.
120. Cf. *Ólhelg(Leg)* ch. 18.
121. I.e. the year after Eiríkr Hákonarson's departure from Norway.
122. *cum duabus onerariis navibus*: cf. identical wording at *Hist. Norw.* 124.9. Óttarr svarti, *Hǫfuðlausn* st. 13 (*Skjd.* A I, 293), *Ólhelg(Leg)* ch. 19, *Ágrip* ch. 23, and *Fsk* ch. 28 likewise specify that Óláfr set out with two *knerrir*. On the *knǫrr* (a type of merchant-ship also used in warfare) see Falk 1912, 107–110; Shetelig–Falk 1937, 374–375; Crumlin-Pedersen and Christensen 1970.
123. Storm (1880, ad loc.) maintains that the name *Sæla* is a variant form of *Selja* (present-day Selje in Sogn og Fjordane), adopted here to allow paronomasia on Old West Norse *sæla* 'bliss'. In fact, only *Bergsbók* (Stockholm, Royal Library, perg. 1 fol.) records the name of Óláfr's landfall in the form *Selja*; all other accounts have *Sæla* in agreement with Theodoricus (*Ágrip* ch. 23, *Fsk* ch. 28, *Ólhelg[Leg]* ch. 19, *Ólhelg[Sep]* ch. 29 [cf. 57.18, v.l. from *Bergsbók: selia*], *ÓlTrygg en mesta* ch. 270 [cf. 321.15, v.l. from *Bergsbók: selia*]). Ólafur Halldórsson

(1984, 107–112) has ingeniously suggested that the otherwise unrecorded place-name *Sæla* here may, in fact, owe its existence to confusion with *Mostr*, the site of Óláfr Tryggvason's landfall on his return to Norway from England (see ch. 10 above and n. 75). Ólafur points out that the name of that island is amenable to a similar kind of word-play, since it is homophonous with Old West Norse *mostr* 'abundance, plenty'. He argues that a Latin chronicler might well have used the word *felicitas* (in the sense 'fruitfulness, fertility') to render the name *Mostr*, which might in turn have been translated back into Norse at some later stage as the otherwise non-existent place-name *Sæla* (from *felicitas* in the sense 'bliss, happiness'). For similar stories of prognostication by folk etymology (on the principle *nomen est omen*) see Pease 1920–1923 on Cicero, *De divinatione* ii.84; Whitby *Vit. Greg.* chs 10, 92–93 and 146, n. 48.

124. Present-day Sauesund beside the island Atløy in Sogn og Fjordane.

125. Cf. *Ágrip* ch. 23, *Ólhelg(Leg)* ch. 19. On the *skúta* see Falk 1912, 95–97; Shetelig–Falk 1937, 372; Crumlin-Pedersen and Christensen 1970.

126. Horace *Epodes* i.1–2. Theodoricus appears to assume that 'Liburnians' were also large ships like, rather than contrasted with, the *alta navium propugnacula* of Horace's verse. Cf., however, *OLD* s.v. *Liburna*, 'a light, fast-sailing warship, galley'. Isidore, *Etym.* XIX.i.12, defines *Liburnae* as *naves . . . negotiatorum* and quotes the same passage from Horace.

127. Cf. accounts of the stratagem in *Ágrip* ch. 23, *Fsk* ch. 28, *Ólhelg(Leg)* ch. 19, *Ólhelg(Sep)* ch. 32, *Hkr(Ólhelg)* ch. 30. See also *Nóregs konunga tal* stt. 29–30 (*Skjd.* A I, 583).

128. *noverat enim eorum facilitatem et inconstantiam*: see Introd. p. xxvi. Johnsen (1939, 78) and Hanssen (1949, 95) argue that Theodoricus's jibes against the treachery of the Þrœndir (cf. ch. 19) reflect his abhorrence of their support for Sverrir against Erlingr skakki and Magnús (and their chief adherent, Archbishop Eysteinn). Cf. *Sverris saga* ch. 43 (1920, 46–47). In the context of the battle of Stiklastaðir we have what might be taken as a verdict on the Þrœndir from the archbishop him-

self: 'indurati et pertinaces in malicia sua, ueritatis, et ideo regis, hostes erant inexorabiles' (*Pass. Olav.* 1881, 72).
129. *in superiorem provinciam*: see nn. 44 and 98.
130. Cf. *Ágrip* ch. 24, *Fsk* ch. 29, *Ólhelg(Leg)* chs 22 fin. to 24; *Ólhelg(Sep)* chs 33–35, *Hkr(Ólhelg)* chs 32–35.
131. The coastal region between Langesundsfjord in Telemark and Larviksfjord in Vestfold. Cf. *Ágrip* ch. 24, *Fsk* ch. 29, *Ólhelg(Leg)* ch. 24, *Ólhelg(Sep)* ch. 40, *Hkr(Ólhelg)* ch. 49, *Nóregs konunga tal* st. 31 (*Skjd.* A I, 583).
132. Einarr Eindriðason, married to Sveinn's sister, naturally supported him at this stage. Subsequently he became a strenuous promoter of the cult of St Óláfr and one of the principal supporters of Magnús Oláfsson (cf. chs 21, 25, 27 below). His by-name is regularly given in the form *thambaskelmir* in extant witnesses of Theodoricus's text (Storm 1880, 45.6, 50.21, 54.29; cf. Lehmann 1937, 122; rpt 1959–62, 429 [50.21]: *Thambar Kelmer*; cf. *þambaskelmir* in for example *Ágrip* ch. 24; Oddr Snorrason, *ÓlTrygg* [S] chs 16, 59, 61, 63). The alternative form, *þamba-* or *þambarskelfir*, is usually taken to mean either 'agitator of the bowstring' (with reference to Einarr's prowess as an archer) or 'gut-shaker' (with reference to a big belly); see Lind 1920–21, 405–406; Bjarni Aðalbjarnarson 1941–1951, I, 218, n. 2. Saltnessand (1968) has argued in favour of P. A. Munch's proposal that *þǫmb* may have been the name of Einarr's bow. Bjarne Fidjestol (1997a, 6–8) prefers the interpretation 'Bowstring-shaker'. Libermann (1996, 100) has argued, more deviously, that the sense 'bowstring' for *þǫmb* might have developed as a back formation from Einarr's nickname, which originally meant 'paunch-shaker'. That the nickname was later taken to mean 'farter' is suggested by a story in *Msk* 60 (see Gade 1995a–b, Sayers 1995, Libermann 1996, esp. 100–101).
133. Cf. *Hkr(ÓlTrygg)* ch. 19.
134. Cf. *Ágrip* ch. 24: 'Einarr þambaskelmir kastaði akkeri í skip Sveins ok sigldi með hann nauðgan á braut til Danmarkar', and similar accounts in *Ólhelg(Leg)* ch. 25, *Ólhelg(Sep)* ch. 40, *Hkr(Ólhelg)* ch. 49. Cf. *Fsk* ch. 29: 'Komsk jarl svá á brott með dugnaði Einars mágs síns, því at hann lét kasta streng í skip hans.'
135. *in Rusciam*: Old West Norse *Garðar/Garðaríki* (see Pritsak

1981, 217–220); cf. *Ágrip* ch. 24, *Fsk* ch. 29, *Ólhelg(Leg)* ch. 25, *Ólhelg(Sep)* ch. 42, *Hkr(Ólhelg)* ch. 55.
136. I.e. both the new churches and those which had already been established. Cf. *Ólhelg(Leg)* ch. 29: 'Ólafr Harallzson gaf fe til kirkna, þæira er Olafr Trygguason hafðe ræisa latet.'
137. Cf. *Ólhelg(Leg)* ch. 29 fin. and 38, *Hkr(Ólhelg)* ch. 58 and the verse attributed to Sigvatr there (*Skjd.* A I, 240, no. 4). There are numerous references to 'the law of the holy King Óláfr' in the older *Gulaþingslǫg*, fewer in other lawbooks; see references in *NgL* V, 417.
138. Cf. *Ágrip* ch. 25, *Fsk* ch. 30, *Ólhelg(Leg)* ch. 44, *Ólhelg(Sep)* chs 72–77, *Hkr(Ólhelg)* chs 88–93. On the confused account in *Hist. Norw.* 123.11–124.8, see Storm 1880, 123, n. ad 123.12.
139. *quam postea conjunxit Ottoni duci Saxonum*: cf. *Ágrip* ch. 25, *Fsk* ch. 30, *Ólhelg(Leg)* ch. 44, *Hkr(Mgóð)* ch. 26. In fact, the name of Úlfhildr's husband was Ordulf (duke of Saxony 1059–1072), and she was not given in marriage by Óláfr, but by her half-brother Magnús (in the autumn of 1042; cf. Adam of Bremen, *Gest. Hamm.* ii.79 [75]; *Ólhelg[Sep]* ch. 264). One is tempted to conjecture that the proper subject of *conjunxit* (**Magnus frater eius*?) has been omitted by mistake.
140. Cf. *Ólhelg(Leg)* ch. 61 fin.
141. Cf. *Nóregs konunga tal* st. 33 (*Skjd.* A I, 583), *Ólhelg(Leg)* ch. 62, *Ólhelg(Sep)* ch. 148, *Hkr(Ólhelg)* ch. 156. Knútr's bribery of Norwegian nobles is also mentioned by John of Worcester (*Chronicon* 1995–1998, II, 510, s.a. 1027).
142. Cf. *Ágrip* ch. 26.
143. Present-day Tungenes, just north of Stavanger; cf. Sigvatr, *Erlingsflokkr* st. 2 'þung var sócn fyr tungum' and st. 3 'fyr norðan tungor' (*Skjd.* A I, 244); *Ólhelg(Leg)* ch. 63: 'firir norðan Tungu'.
144. See *Ólhelg(Leg)* ch. 64: 'Aslakr Fitiaskalle var næsta brœðrongr Ærlings at frænzæmi' (cf. *Hkr[Ólhelg]* ch. 116). Cf. accounts of the slaying of Erlingr in *Ágrip* ch. 26, *Fsk* ch. 33, *Ólhelg(Sep)* ch. 172, *Hkr(Ólhelg)* ch. 176.
145. *mille ducentarum navium*: cf. *Ólhelg(Leg)* ch. 63: 'Siglir sunnan . . . með .xii.c. skipa'; *Hkr(Ólhelg)* ch. 167: 'Knútr . . . hafði eigi færa en tólf hundruð skipa.' According to the C, D,

E, and F versions of the *Anglo-Saxon Chronicle* s.a. 1028 (*ASC* 1892–1899, I, 156–157; *EHD* I, 255), Knútr left England with 50 ships.

146. *ad generum suum Olavum regem Svethiae*: Kirchmann (1684) noted: *generum (lege socerum)* (see Storm 1880, 30, textual n. 3). As Hanssen remarks, however (1945, 174), the use of *gener* in the sense 'father-in-law' is not unparalleled in medieval Latin (cf., for example, Niermeyer 1976, s.v. *gener*, 3).

147. Ruler of Kiev 1016–1054, son of Vladimir the Great (see n. 57 above). Cf. *Ólhelg(Leg)* ch. 69 fin.

148. Cf. *Ágrip* ch. 27, *Ólhelg(Leg)* ch. 70.

149. I.e. the Pentland Firth. The 'Charybdis' referred to is the infamous *Swelchie*, north-east of Stroma, Old West Norse *Svelgr(inn)* (cf. *OED* s.v. *Swelchie*; *Orkneyinga saga* ch. 74, *Hákonar saga Hákonarsonar* ch. 327; Finnbogi Guðmundsson 1965, 169, n. 2).

150. The death of Hákon Eiríksson at sea is also mentioned in *Ágrip* ch. 27, *Ólhelg(Leg)* ch. 71, and in the 'C' version of the *Anglo-Saxon Chronicle* s.a. 1030 (*ASC* 1892–1899, I, 157; *EHD* I, 255). Only Snorri (*Ólhelg[Sep]* ch. 180; *Hkr[Ólhelg]* ch. 184) shares with Theodoricus the detail that Hákon met his end in the Pentland Firth, where he was sucked into the *Swelchie* (Theodoricus: *in illam imam voraginem*; Snorri: *í svelginn*; *Ágrip* and *Ólhelg[Leg]* record only that he perished *í Englandshafi*). Bjarni Guðnason (1977, 115, n. 21) suggests that this is a case where Snorri may have borrowed directly from Theodoricus. It is interesting to note that John of Worcester (*Chronicon* 1995–1998, II, 510, s.a. 1030) appears to preserve a dim reminiscence of the same account of Hákon's death: *Predictus comes Hacun in mari periit. Quidam tamen dicunt eum fuisse occisum in Orcada insula.*

151. As Lehmann points out (1937, 72; rpt 1959–1962, 384) the passage is borrowed neither from Pliny nor from the stoic philosopher Chrysippus († c. 208–204 BC), but is taken either directly or indirectly from Isidore, *Etym.* XIII.xx.1.

152. Gen. 7:11. The same verse is cited in *Hist. Norw.* (95.8–9), in a discussion of submarine eruptions in Iceland and their origin in 'the deepest abyss' of the earth (see Storm 1880, nn.

ad 95.7–8). A reminiscence of the same scriptural verse here, however, is hardly surprising. For example, Honorius Augustodunensis, *Imago Mundi* i.41 'De voragine', likewise cites Gen. 7:11 (cf. Johnsen 1939, 47).
153. Cf. Paul the Deacon, *Hist. Lang.* i.6.
154. Paul the Deacon, *Hist. Lang.* ii.5.
155. Cf. Paul the Deacon, *Hist. Lang.* i.9; Isidore, *Etym.* IX.ii.95. For bibliography on this derivation of the name of the Lombards, see Schönfeld 1965, s.v. *Langobardi*.
156. The end of the fifty-year occupation of Pannonia by the Huns is noted by Jordanes (*Getica* xxxii.166; cf. Marcellinus Comes, *Chronicon* s.a. 427, 1894, 76.30–33) and his account is reproduced by Sigebert of Gembloux (*Chronica* s.a. 428, 1844, 307.44–45). Theodoricus's remarks here, however, sound like a confused reminiscence of Jordanes on the reception of the Vandals into Pannonia by Constantine (in 334; cf. *Getica* xxii.115). On the vexed question of the 'cession' of all or part of Pannonia to the Huns see Bury 1923, I, 166; Thompson 1948, 64; Maenchen-Helfen 1973, 87–90.
157. On Jordanes' Gothic history, the *Getica* or *De origine actibusque Getarum* (written in the 550s), see Goffart 1988, 20–111. On the name-form 'Jornandes' see Mierow 1915, 2; Goffart 1988, 44, n. 108; Giunta–Grillone 1991, xxix.
158. *de Mœotidis paludibus*: Maeotis is the ancient name of the Sea of Azov.
159. As Storm notes (1880, ad 33.2), the legend of Alexander the Great's imprisonment of various barbarous nations, identified with the biblical 'Gog and Magog', behind the 'Caspian gates' is not included in Jordanes' *Getica* (although he refers to the building of the gates at vii.50). While the earliest reference to the story would appear to be in Josephus's *Jewish War* vii.245 (AD 75–79), Anderson (1932, 18) argues that 'it was the bursting of the Caucasus barrier in 395 by tribes which the Greeks called Huns ... that provided the setting for the fusion of the building of Alexander's Gate with the Biblical legend of Gog and Magog.' The 'enclosed nations' are identified as Huns in the Syrian *Sermo de fine extremo* (probably from the end of the fourth century) and in the Syrian

Christian legend concerning Alexander (of the sixth or seventh century; see Anderson 1932, 16–24). Isidore, *Etym.* IX.ii.66 (reproduced, for example, in Rabanus Maurus, *De universo* xvi.2, PL 111, 439D) offers a close parallel for Theodoricus's account.

160. With this account of the physical appearance of the Huns cf. Jordanes, *Getica* xxiv.127 (copied verbatim in Sigebert of Gembloux, *Chronica*, 1844, 301.70–302.3).
161. Cf. Jordanes, *Getica* xxiv.123–124 (Sigebert of Gembloux, *Chronica*, 1844, 302.9–11).
162. *expanderunt se super faciem universæ terræ more locustarum*: cf. Ps. 103:30; Judg. 6:5, 7:12; Judith 2:11. Cf. n. 235 below.
163. Cf. Sigebert of Gembloux, *Chronica*, s.a. 453, 1844, 309.54; see Johnsen 1939, 49.
164. Cf. Sigebert of Gembloux, *Chronica*, s.a. 453, 1844, 310.1–13; see Johnsen 1939, 49. As Storm notes (1880, ad. 34.3), Theodoricus's use of the phrase *utriusque sexus* indicates that he has in mind the version of the Ursula legend which developed after the discovery at Cologne in 1155 of bones identified as those of Ursula and her followers. Since these included the remains of men and children as well as women, male martyrs came to be included among Ursula's 'eleven thousand' companions. See Schade 1854, 42ff.; Tout 1902, 31ff; Levison 1927, 107–120.
165. Prov. 28:1.
166. Ps. 35:13: *ibi ceciderunt qui operantur iniquitatem, expulsi sunt nec potuerunt stare.* Theodoricus has *operabantur* instead of the Vulgate reading.
167. Cf. *Ágrip* ch. 27; *Ólhelg(Leg)* ch. 71. Sveinn was Knútr's son by Ælfgifu of Northampton (see n. 216 below).
168. Cf. 1 Cor. 7:31: *praeterit enim figura huius mundi.*
169. Cf. 2 Cor. 3:5: *sufficientia nostra ex Deo est.*
170. Cf. *Pass. Olav.* 1881, 72.5: *diuino inspiratus instinctu*; *Ólhelg(Leg)* ch. 71 fin.; *Ólhelg(Sep)* ch. 184; *Hkr(Ólhelg)* ch. 188.
171. Cf. *Ólhelg(Leg)* ch. 72; *Ólhelg(Sep)* ch. 188; *Hkr(Ólhelg)* ch. 192.
172. Although other sources agree that Óláfr returned to Norway by way of Sweden, Theodoricus is alone in reporting that he spent his last winter there. And only Adam of Bremen (*Gest.*

Hamm. i.73 [71]) also speaks of Óláfr's father-in-law Óláfr sœnski Eiríksson as still living at this time. His death is usually dated c. 1020–1022 (cf. *Hkr[Ólhelg]* ch. 114).
173. Cf. *Ólhelg(Leg)* ch. 73; *Ólhelg(Sep)* ch. 200; *Hkr(Ólhelg)* ch. 204.
174. With this list of Óláfr's followers at Stiklastaðir, cf. *Ólhelg(Leg)* ch. 76; Þormóðr Bersason Kolbrúnarskáld, *lausavísa* 22 (*Skjd.* A I, 287), cited in *Ólhelg(Leg)* ch. 84. Rǫgnvaldr (later earl of Orkney 1035–1046?) is said to have rescued Óláfr's half-brother, the young Haraldr Sigurðarson, after the battle (*Orkneyinga saga* ch. 21).
175. See ch. 9.
176. Cf. Pliny, *Nat. Hist.* VII.xvi.73. On the ancient notion of the progressive deterioration of the human race see, for example, Cross 1962, 9–10. In his use of the word *exustio*, 'a burning up', Pliny alludes to the Stoic doctrine that although the post-diluvian world had survived destruction by water, it would eventually be subject to destruction by fire. Cf. Pliny, *Nat. Hist.* II.cx.236, where the fires of Mount Etna are identified as a signal of the final conflagration to come: [*In*] *illo* [sc. *Aetnae monte*] . . . *natura saevit exustionem terris denuntians.* Cf. Schilling 1977, 159.
177. Lucan, *Bell. civ.* vii.812–815.
178. Tenney Frank (1909, 83) notes that these remarks attributed to Plato are reminiscent of *Timaeus* 22C and *Laws* 677b. Theodoricus's immediate source has not been identified.
179. ϵἰ*marmenem* ALS, ϵἰμαρμένην K = Gk ϵἰμαρμένη, i.e. 'fate, destiny'; see Liddell and Scott 1925–1940, s.v. μείρομαι, III; Lampe 1961, s.v. ϵἰμαρμένη.
180. Storm (1880, n. ad 37.6) suggests that here Theodoricus may recall the description of the world (*mundus*) as encompassing the concepts of 'world' and 'time' implicit in the term *saeculum*, in Origen, *De principiis* II.iii.5: *Verumtamen multorum saeculorum finis esse dicitur hic mundus, qui et ipse saeculum dicitur.*
181. In his *Epist.* cviii.12 (1910–1918, 321) Jerome gives an account of the twelve stones of Josh. 4:1–9 preserved at Galgala, but draws no conclusions about the diminishing stature of the human

race. Theodoricus's ultimate source here is, in fact, not Jerome but the *De locis sanctis* of Adomnán of Iona (c. 624–704). See n. 183 below.
182. Ps. 113:5.
183. Cf. Adomnán, *De locis sanctis* II.xv.3–4, where not Jerome, but Adomnán's informant, the Gallic bishop and pilgrim Arnulf, gives this account of the stones and observes that 'two strong young men of our day could scarcely lift any one of them from the earth'.
184. Jerome died in 420. As Storm remarks (1880, n. ad 37.22) Theodoricus compiled his history some 760 years after that date.
185. Theodoricus apparently follows the tradition that the body of Pallas was discovered during the reign of Emperor Henry III (1046–1056). The Icelandic *Annales Regii, Flateyjarannáll,* and *Oddverja annáll* record the discovery s.a. 1053 (*Islandske Annaler* 1888, 108, 470; *Flat.* III, 508). The last two provide a full account and cite the Latin verse which identified the body. Another description, complete with an Icelandic translation of Pallas's epitaph, is included in *Breta sǫgur* ch. 4 (*Hauksbók* 237), where it is reported that the body was found during the days of Sigurðr Jórsalafari (1103–1130) and 'Emperor Henry II', evidently a mistake for Henry V, emperor from 1106 to 1125. The discovery finds frequent record in thirteenth- and fourteenth-century sources—e.g., in Helinand's *Chronicon* (s.a. 1053, PL 212, 950B), in Vincent's *Speculum historiale* XXV.xxxiv (1624, IV, 1014), in ch. 158 of *Gesta Romanorum* (1872, 538), and in Higden's *Polychronicon* I.xxiv (1865–1886, I, 222–224, where 1140 is given as the year of the discovery). The verse also circulated independently; see examples in Walther 1969, no. 6528; Baehrens 1879–1886, V, 395n. These accounts are ultimately dependent on the oldest known description of the discovery of Pallas's body, that in William of Malmesbury's *Gesta Regum* (ii.206; 1998, 384), probably compiled in the years 1119–1124. William does not associate the discovery with a specific date but assigns it to the reign of Emperor Henry III. Since Theodoricus differs from William in several details, it seems unlikely that he borrowed directly from the *Gesta Regum*. It looks, however, as though his remark that Pallas's body was

discovered 'about seventy years ago' was derived from a source of the same age as the *Gesta Regum*, written c. 1120 and referring seventy years back to c. 1050. Paasche (1934, 125–126) thought Theodoricus meant seventy years before his own time. That would envisage c. 1107–1117, firmly in the reign of Sigurðr Jórsalafari, which would also tally with the *Breta sǫgur* report, though a literary connection need hardly be assumed between this work and the *Historia* of Theodoricus. On the transmission of the Pallas story in the Middle Ages, see Graf 1923, 72, and Dittrich 1966, 573–582 (particularly on the account in the *Eneide* of Heinrich von Veldeke, completed c. 1190— here the discovery is dated 1155, in the reign of Frederick Barbarossa).

186. Augustine, *De civ. Dei* III.xi (1955, 72–73), recounts how a statue of Apollo at Cumae wept, not over the death of Pallas, but as an omen of the impending defeat (in 129 BC) of the Asian king Aristonicus at the hands of the Romans, a reflection of Apollo's grief over the loss of the Greek territory entrusted to his care. Livy, *Ab urbe condita* XLIII.xiii, has the same story, but places it during the Roman war against Perseus of Macedon in 169 BC.

187. *Filius Evandri Pallas, quem lancea Turni / Militis occidit, more suo jacet hic*: The phrase *more suo* in Pallas's epitaph has been interpreted in a variety of ways. The translator of the verse in *Breta sǫgur* reads *more suo* with *jacet*, but keeps his rendering judiciously vague: 'her liɢr Pallas *með sið sinvm* svn Avandri konvngs *ok hætti* sa sem drap spiot Tvrni Riddara' (*Hauksbók* 237). Similarly, Giles (1904, 234) provides a cautiously nebulous rendering of the same lines in William of Malmesbury's *Gesta Regum*: 'Pallas, Evander's son, lies buried here / In order due, transfix'd by Turnus's spear'. On the other hand, Sharpe (rev. Stevenson 1854, 199) interprets the verse rather differently, apparently reading *more suo* with *occidit* as a phrase describing the habitual action of Turnus's deadly spear: 'Pallas . . . whom Turnus's spear slew, *like all others whom it reached,* lies here.' Cf. John Trevisa's rendering of the epitaph in Higden's *Polychronicon* I.xxiv (1865–1886, I, 225): 'Hym Turnus þe knygt wið his spere / Slowe *in his manere*'.

In the S manuscript of Theodoricus's *Historia*, the phrase *more suo* is replaced with *morte sua* 'in his death' (see Storm 1880, 39, textual n. 3). This looks like nothing more than a rationalisation of a puzzling reading in Stephanius's exemplar, although this variant is paralleled in other versions of the epitaph. Cf., for example, the version cited in the thirteenth-century chronicle entitled *Flores temporum* (1879, 237) and in *Gesta Romanorum* (1872, 538); and 'Epitaphium Pallantis', Baehrens 1879–1886, V, 395): 'quem lanca Turni / Militis *effudit morte fera*', 'whom the spear of Turnus *despatched in savage death*'. Following a suggestion from Peter Fisher, we have taken *more suo* with *jacet* in the sense 'in accordance with his wish/will' (see *OLD*, s.v. *mos* 5.d). Michael Winterbottom (to whom we are grateful for advice on this passage) prefers to take *more suo* with *occidit*; see *Gesta Regum* 1998, 384.

188. The *Historia* reads: 'Throndenses autem audito adventu regis convenerunt in Nidrosiensem civitatem quasi vir unus adversus Dominum et adversus [*so* L] christum eius'; cf. *Pass. Olav.* (1881, 72): 'Quo comperto ueritatis hostes conuocauerunt concilium iniquitatis, et conuenerunt in unum aduersus dominum et aduersus christus eius'. This is the only very close verbal parallel to be observed between the *Passio* and the *Historia*, but each may well be independently echoing scriptural phrasing, Ps. 2:2, Acts 4:26, 27 (cf. Skard 1935, 124).

189. Hárekr ór Þjóttu is not mentioned here or in *Ágrip* ch. 30 (31), although he figures in later sources as one of Óláfr's main opponents at Stiklastaðir; cf. *Ólhelg(Leg)* ch. 80, *Fsk* ch. 34, *Hkr(Ólhelg)* chs 219–224, 229, 232. *Pass. Olav.* (1881, 72) mentions 'a certain Cnut' (i.e. Knútr the Great) as prominent among Óláfr's adversaries. *GNH* (1931, 111) identifies Kálfr Árnason as the leader of the forces assembled against Óláfr.

190. See above at 18.37.

191. *Sticlastad'er* AKL, *Sticlastader* SB, in other sources also Stiklarstaðir (modern Stiklestad in Verdal). The battle is traditionally dated 29 July 1030.

192. Cf. accounts that before the battle Óláfr dreamed of ascending a ladder to heaven: Adam of Bremen, *Gest. Hamm.* ii.61 (59), I Schol. 41 (42); Einarr Skúlason, *Geisli* (c. 1153) stt. 15–

16 (*Skjd.* A I, 461–462); *Pass. Olav.* (1881, 74); 'Lux illuxit', *Anal. Hymn.* 42, 274, no. 302.7a, *GNH* (1931, 111); *Ólhelg(Leg)* ch. 78; cf. Johnsen 1939, 27 n. 4; Tate 1978–1979. In *Hkr(Ólhelg)* ch. 214, Óláfr's dream is interpreted by Finnr Árnason as a premonition of the king's death.

193. The term used here, *dispensator*, can signify either an administrator of the royal estate, entrusted with management of the treasury, or simply 'one who dispenses alms'; see Du Cange 1883–1887, II, 139, s.v.; Niermeyer 1976, 341, s.v. Cf. *Ólhelg(Leg)* ch. 76, and the slightly more ample account in *Hkr(Ólhelg)*, ch. 207, where Óláfr is said to have appointed a local householder (*bóndi*) to see that alms were distributed for the good of the souls of those killed fighting against him at Stiklastaðir.

194. Matt. 5:44. Cf. Hoffmann 1975, 66, 79 (a comparison with St Oswald).

195. 'invective' is for *infamia*, but this word was perhaps originally *insania*, 'frenzy'.

196. Cf. Matt. 3:9, Luke 3:8: *potest Deus de lapidibus istis suscitare filios Abrahae.*

197. Cf. Acts 7:58–59. Of this parallel with St Stephen, Hoffmann 1975, 66, observes, 'Damit rückt er [St Óláfr] selbst in die Stellung des "Protomartyrs" Norwegens ein.' Cf. Introd. pp. xix–xx.

198. Here Theodoricus is evidently thinking of Óláfr's marshal, Bjǫrn digri; cf. the description of his fall at Óláfr's side in Sigvatr Þórðarson's *Erfidrápa Óláfs helga* (c. 1040) st. 18 (*Skjd.* A I, 261–262). Sigvatr, however, identifies Þórðr Fólason, not Bjǫrn, as Óláfr's standard-bearer (*Erfidrápa Óláfs* st. 7, *Skjd.* A I, 258); and this detail, supported by reference to Sigvatr, is repeated in *Hkr(Ólhelg)* ch. 212 init. and ch. 266.

199. *Ágrip* ch. 30 (31) and *Ólhelg(Leg)* ch. 81 record that Óláfr was killed by Þórir hundr Þórisson and Þorsteinn knarrarsmiðr after first being wounded by a retainer or kinsman of Kálfr Árnason. According to *Hkr(Ólhelg)* ch. 228, the king died from wounds he received from Þorsteinn, Þórir and either Kálfr Árnason or Kálfr Arnfinnsson. See Fidjestøl 1987 (trans. 1997).

200. Later Icelandic accounts are consistent in recording that several wounds were inflicted upon the king. *Ágrip* ch. 30 (31)

and *Ólhelg(Leg)* chs 81–82 record that Óláfr was first wounded in the leg and finished off by Þórir hundr and Þorsteinn knarra(r)smiðr. According to *Hkr(Ólhelg)* ch. 228, the king died of three wounds, to his left leg, abdomen and neck. See Fidjestøl 1987 (trans. 1997).

201. In other accounts Dagr Hringsson is said to enter the fray only after the battle is well under way (*Hkr[Ólhelg]* chs 227, 229; *Fsk* ch. 34), or after the king has fallen, at which point he proposes that he himself should be accepted as the king's successor (*Ólhelg[Leg]* ch. 83). Dagr is not mentioned in *Ágrip*.

202. Cf. Livy, *Ab urbe condita* XXVII.ii.8: *nox incerta victoria diremit pugnantis*. On this classical echo, see Lehmann (1937, 72; rpt 1959–1962, 384). Theodoricus makes no mention of the tradition that during Óláfr's last battle the sun was eclipsed, just as it was at the Crucifixion (see Einarr Skúlason, *Geisli* st. 19, *Skjd.* A I, 462; *Hkr[Ólhelg]* ch. 226).

203. Cf. ch. 14, n. 110 above.

204. *Pass. Olav.* (1881, 73) records the date of St Óláfr's death as: *iiiito kalendas octobris* (thus for *augusti* or perhaps for *mensis octavi*; cf. Gjerløw 1967, 562), *feria iiiita, millesimo et xxviii anno ab incarnatione domini*, i.e. Wednesday, 29 July 1028 (cf. *MHN* 131–132). In *Hkr(Ólhelg)* ch. 235, on the other hand, Snorri gives Wednesday, 29 July 1030 as the king's deathday; and Ari, *Íslendingabók* ch. 8 (1968, 19), remarks that St Óláfr fell in battle thirty years after the death of Óláfr Tryggvason, i.e. in 1030. *Ólhelg(Leg)* ch. 88 calculates the date as *fra burð Krist, drottens vars, þushundrað vætra oc ix. vætr oc xx. oc .cc. vætra*, where the last word is evidently a mistake for *nætr* or *nátta*, i.e. '1029 years and 200 [more likely than 240] nights after the birth of Christ'. This would give a date sometime in July 1030 but the number of nights would have to be manipulated to arrive at the 29th of the month. The Icelandic reckoning is usually accepted because it is the only one which can accommodate the tradition that Óláfr died on a Wednesday. 29 July fell on a Monday in 1028, on a Tuesday in 1029, on a Wednesday in 1030 (see Ólafia Einarsdóttir 1964, 75–76, 185–186, 329). We cannot tell whether Theodoricus's dating is his own compromise between conflicting sources, as suggested by Bjarni

Einarsson 1984, xxxvi, or is a date repeated from an older tradition. He is not alone in reporting 1029 as the year of Óláfr's death. The same year is given in *Ágrip* ch. 32 (33), where it was possibly derived from Theodoricus, and it has also been calculated from the addition of regnal years in *Nóregs konungatal* stt. 26, 28, 32 (*Skjd.* A I, 582–583). Theodoricus's sound observation at the beginning of the next chapter that dates and numbers in historical sources are frequently unreliable suggests that he may have been well aware of conflict over the dating of Óláfr's death. On the problem see, for example, Storm 1880, n. ad 42.6; Bjarni Aðalbjarnarson 1941–1951, II, xcii–xcviii; Lange 1989, 118–120, 125.

205. Jerome commonly uses the term *Hebraica veritas* to refer to the Hebrew text of the Bible. The phrase, however, was used ambiguously throughout the Middle Ages, and was regularly employed, as here, to refer to Jerome's Latin Vulgate. Cf. Lampe 1969, II, 188; Smalley 1983, 80, n. 2.

206. These figures are not cited directly in either the 'Chronicle' or the 'Ecclesiastical History' of Eusebius of Caesarea (c. 260 to c. 340). Jerome's Latin version of Eusebius's 'Chronicle' records that, according to the Septuagint, Abraham was born 3184 years after Adam (2242 years from Adam to the Flood, plus 942 years from the Flood to Abraham; see Jerome, *Chronicon* 1956, 15, 174), and that Christ was born 2015 years after Abraham (*Chronicon* 1956, 169). The sum of these figures provides the same *anno mundi* date of Christ's birth cited by Theodoricus, 5199. Eusebius's record of the Hebrew calculation can be deduced from the Armenian Latin version of his 'Chronicle', which records that by Hebrew reckoning Abraham was born 1948 years after the creation of Adam (Eusebius, *Chronicorum libri duo* 1866–1875, I, 95). This figure, added to the Septuagint calculation of 2015 years from Abraham to Christ, gives an *anno mundi* date of 3963, not 3971 as cited by Theodoricus. As Theodoricus points out here, however, all such calculations are subject to corruption in the course of transmission. It might be noted that another such chronological note, entered in the Icelandic miscellany manuscript AM 194 8vo in 1387, records the number of years between the Creation and

the birth of Christ as 5228 (*AÍ* I, 53–54), evidently a mistaken substitution of the Eusebian calculation of the *anno mundi* date of the Sermon on the Mount (see, for example, Tristram 1985, 180). Despite strenuous objections to the contrary by Johnsen (1939, 39–42), Storm (1880, ix, and n. ad 42.18) is probably correct in suggesting that Theodoricus knew Latin versions of the Eusebian calculations through an intermediate source (cf., for example, the Septuagint calculation in Orosius, *Hist. adv. pag.* I.i.5, and further references to various medieval calculations of the age of the world in Grotefend 1891, I, 207; Bately 1979; Tristram 1985, esp. 180–187).

207. Here Theodoricus appears to follow Isidore's calculation of the number of years from the Creation until the end of the fifth age of the world, 5154 years (*Etym.* V.xxxix.25: *VMCLIV*). According to Isidore, the sixth age began with the birth of Christ, during the reign of Octavian; but Isidore calculates that this event took place 56 years after the end of the fifth age, i.e. 5210 years after the Creation (*Etym.* V.xxxix.26; cf. Isidore, *Chronica* 1894, 453–454). Theodoricus has probably simply misinterpreted Isidore's calculation to the end of the fifth age as the time passed until the birth of Christ; or he may have worked from a corrupt source.

208. Cf. Bede, *De temporibus* (*Chronica minora*) xxii (1980, 607): *Dominus nascitur, conpletis ab Adam annis $\overline{III}DCCCCLII$, iuxta alios $\overline{V}CXCVIIII$.*

209. Remigius (c. 841–908) was master of the monastic school of St-Germain at Auxerre, and not a bishop there. He is not known to have written any chronicles or works on chronology. Remigius did write a commentary on Bede's *De arte metrica,* and is credited with another commentary on Bede's *De schematibus et tropis* (see Elder 1947; for accounts of the genuine works of Remigius, see Manitius 1911–1931, I, 504–519; II, 808–809, III, 1063, and Lutz 1962–1965, I, 11–12). Theodoricus's reference to Remigius looks like a simple mistake; it is possible that the Norwegian author had access to a manuscript of one of Remigius's commentaries which also contained chronological material by Bede. Johnsen's claim (1939, 46, 62–63) that this reference to Remigius provides clear evidence of

Theodoricus's familiarity with the French author acquired through an education abroad could hardly be farther from the truth.

210. Storm (1880, 43, textual n. 3) notes the marginal addition in AS, *septuaginta unum*, as if to record an alternative reckoning, according to the Septuagint, of 3951 years. The so-called 'Chronicle' of Hugh of St Victor (written c. 1130, really a schoolbook of history usually entitled *De tribus maximis circumstantiis gestorum*) includes several chronological tables, the second of which is a tabulation of the succession of patriarchs, judges, kings and priests from Adam to Agrippa through the six ages of the world, according to Hebrew chronology (*secundum hebraicam veritatem*). Although Hugh's 'Chronicle' evidently enjoyed a wide circulation, this section of the tables has never been published (see Green 1943, 484–493, esp. 492; Goy 1976, 36–43). The only version which we have been able to consult, in London BL MS. Egerton 3088, 102r, records Christ's birth at the end of the third age. The first event listed in the fourth age, the slaughter of the Holy Innocents, is recorded as occurring 3954 years after the beginning of the world. The testimony of Matt. 2:16, that Herod ordered the murder of children 'from two years old and under', may have given rise to a tradition that this event took place two years after the traditional Hebrew date of Christ's birth, 3952 years after the Creation (cf. Bede's calculation, above, n. 208).

211. For accounts of the miracles which occurred after Óláfr's death, see, for example, Þórarinn loftunga, *Glælognskviða* st. 8 (*Skjd.* A I, 326); Sigvatr Þórðarson, *Erfidrápa* st. 24b (*Skjd.* A I, 264); Einarr Skúlason, *Geisli* stt. 20–26, 37–41, 57–62, 67 (*Skjd.* A I, 462–472), *Pass. Olav.* 1881, 74–116; *Ólhelg(Leg)* ch. 87; *Hkr(Ólhelg)* chs 236, 238, 240, 244–245; and cf. Holtsmark 1937; Whaley 1987; Fidjestøl 1987, 42–43 (trans. 1997, 173–175); Lange 1989, 79–81.

212. The same precise count of the interval between the king's death and his translation is given in for example *Geisli* st. 25 (*Skjd.* A I, 463) and *Hkr(Ólhelg)*, ch. 244; on the foundation for it cf. Introd. p. xix. Theodoricus's note that Grímkell was a nephew of Bishop Sigurðr/Sigeweard (see n. 64 above) is

paralleled in the Flateyjarbók version of *Óláfs saga Tryggvasonar*, where the information about their kinship is attributed to Oddr Snorrason: 'Suo segir brodir Oddr . . . at Grimkell byskup sa er uar med hinum heilaga Olafi Haralldzsyni ok efldi kristinndom j Noregi væri systurson Sigurdar byskups' (*Flat.* I, 516). On Grímkell see also Adam of Bremen, *Gest. Hamm.* ii.57 (55), iv.34 (33); Taranger 1890, 167–173; Abrams 1995, 223.

213. It is usually assumed that Theodoricus refers here to a lost written account (or to more than one) of St Óláfr's translation and miracles, sometimes referred to as *Translatio Sancti Olavi*; see Storm 1880, xxxiv and n. ad 44.3; Nordal 1914, 10–12; Skard 1935, 125; Bjarni Aðalbjarnarson 1937, 6; Turville-Petre 1967, 171; Bjarni Guðnason 1977, 108. Lange (1989, 52–53) has argued that Theodoricus's words, *memoriae tradita sunt*, are not unambiguous and might refer to oral accounts or scaldic verse rather than to a particular written source. This seems less likely, however, in view of the fact that the Latin idiom, *memoriae tradere*, normally means 'to record in writing'; cf. Lewis and Short, s.v. *trado* II.B.2.b; *OLD*, s.v. *memoria* 8.b.

214. The unidentified text which Theodoricus calls *catalogus regum Norwagiensium* has been the subject of much speculation. It is commonly assumed that Theodoricus here refers to a Norwegian source, perhaps in Latin; see, for example, Storm 1873, 20; Bjarni Aðalbjarnarson 1937, 5–6, 51; Johnsen 1939, 18; Beyschlag 1950, 124, 127; Ellehøj 1965, 297; Andersson 1985, 202; Introd. p. xiv above. It has also been suggested, however, that the **Catalogus* might be a vernacular work, perhaps a version of Ari's **Konungaævi* (Lange 1989, 53–54, and 200, n. 70; cf. Sverrir Tómasson 1988, 37 on Icelandic works which circulated under Latin titles); or the title might refer to a lost Latin work on the kings of Norway by Sæmundr inn fróði (see, for example, Gjessing 1873–1876, II, 36; Finnur Jónsson 1929, xii; Lange 1989, 54). It has been argued that the **Catalogus* must be Norwegian, since the chronological details which Theodoricus draws from this hypothetical source differ from Icelandic texts supposedly based on lost works by Sæmundr and Ari. Theodoricus, following the **Catalogus*, notes that Knútr and Sveinn ruled Norway for five years (i.e. one year together

with Óláfr and then for four years after his death). In *Nóregs konunga tal*, however, which cites Sæmundr as one of its sources (see st. 40, *Skjd*. A I, 584), it is calculated that Sveinn Álfífuson ruled Norway for six years (st. 36, *Skjd*. A I, 583–584; cf. n. 216 below). Snorri, on the other hand, records that Knútr ruled Norway for seven years (*Hkr[Mgóð]* ch. 5). However, such differences between accounts of a single chronological detail recorded in Theodoricus and later Icelandic texts offer only the most indirect evidence of differences between the putative sources used—the hypothetical *Catalogus* and lost works by Sæmundr and Ari. There are drastically divergent opinions regarding the form and content of the *Catalogus*. Storm (1880, n. ad 44.11) and Johnsen (1939, 18) assume that the work began with the reign of Óláfr Haraldsson; Finnur Jónsson (1920–1924 II, 593; 1928, 264) and Ellehøj (1965, 184) conjecture that the work may have begun with Haraldr hárfagri. Bjarni Aðalbjarnarson (1937, 6) postulates that this text was nothing more than a list of king's names together with calculations of the length of their reigns; whereas Ellehøj (1965, 182–196, 278) speculates that the *Catalogus* contained narrative passages as well, and goes so far as to suggest that this lost work provided the basis for Theodoricus's history. For a succinct account of the difficulties which surround this hypothetical text, see Lange 1989, 53–55 and 200–201, nn. ad loc.

215. I.e. three years after St Óláfr's translation. As Storm notes (1880, n. ad 44.13), Magnús was five years old when Óláfr left Russia, and therefore six when his father died. Magnús returned to Norway four years after Óláfr's death (*Ágrip* ch. 34 [35], *Ólhelg[Leg]* ch. 89) when, as Theodoricus states at 21.6, the young king was ten years of age.

216. Ælfgifu 'of Northampton', daughter of Earl Ælfhelm of Northumbria, and Knútr's concubine before his marriage to Ælfgifu/Emma of Normandy. In 1030 Knútr appointed her regent of Norway on behalf of their son Sveinn, but the severity of her rule and of the new forms of taxation she imposed made her so unpopular that by 1035 she and Sveinn were forced to flee to Denmark (cf. *ASC* 1892–1899, II, 211; Stenton 1971, 397–398, 405–406). On the miseries of the *Álfífuǫld* see *Ágrip* chs

27–29, 32 (33); *Ólhelg(Leg)* chs 71, 88; *Hkr(Ólhelg)* ch. 239; Sigvatr Þórðarson, *lausavísa* 28, *Skjd.* A I, 274 (cited in *Ágrip* ch. 32 [33], *Ólhelg[Leg]* ch. 88).
217. *Tham Baskelme* AKSL (Storm 1880, 45, textual n. 3; Lehmann 1937, 122; rpt 1959–1962, 429); see n. 132 above.
218. *bryggyofot*: *Bryggytfot* ABKL, *Bryggyfot* S (Storm 1880, 45, textual n. 4; Lehmann 1937, 122; rpt 1959–1962, 429). On this nickname see Lind 1920–1921, 46.
219. On this diplomatic mission, see also *Ágrip* ch. 33 (34). In *Ólhelg(Leg)* ch. 89, Rǫgnvaldr Brúsason does not figure among the emissaries sent to Russia, since he is said to have fled Norway after the battle of Stiklastaðir (*Ólhelg[Leg]* ch. 83). In *Orkneyinga saga* ch. 21 and *MgóðHharðr* (*Msk* 17–19, *Flat.* III, 261–262) Rǫgnvaldr is said to have been a leading member of Jaroslav's court at the time of the Norwegian delegation. *Fsk* chs 44–45 and *Hkr(Ólhelg)* ch. 251 mention neither Rǫgnvaldr nor Sveinn bryggjufótr among the men sent to persuade Magnús to take up the Norwegian crown. Magnús's triumphant return from the east is described by Arnórr Þórðarson jarlaskáld, *Magnúsdrápa* stt. 1–2 (*Skjd.* A I, 338) and by Þjóðólfr Arnórsson, *Magnúsflokkr* (c. 1045) stt. 1–2 (*Skjd.* A I, 361); cf. Johnsen 1939, 28, nn. 4–5.
220. The flight of Sveinn Álfífuson to Denmark is described in Arnórr jarlaskáld, *Magnúsdrápa* stt. 3–4 (*Skjd.* A I, 339); Þjóðólfr Arnórsson, *Magnúsflokkr* stt. 3–5 (*Skjd.* A I, 361–362); Bjarni Hallbjarnarson gullbrárskáld, *Kalfsflokkr* st. 6 (*Skjd.* A I, 395); cf. Johnsen (1939, 28, nn. 4–5). On Sveinn's departure, his subsequent death and the death of Knútr the Great, cf. *Ágrip* chs 34–35 (35–36), *Fsk* chs 46–47, *MgóðHharðr* (*Msk* 20–22, *Flat.* III, 263–264), *Hkr(Mgóð)* chs 4–5.
221. *Brennojar*: sic S, *Brennorar* AB, *Brennoiar* KL; off the mouth of the Göta älv in present-day west Sweden.
222. *Hartha Knut* ABK, *Harha Knut* S; the only son of Knútr and Emma of Normandy. He was king of Denmark 1035–1042, of England 1040–1042.
223. On the events leading up to an eventual treaty between Magnús and Hǫrðaknútr, cf. *Ágrip* 35 (36) and *Hkr(Mgóð)* ch. 6. *Fsk* ch. 47 and *MgóðHharðr* (*Msk* 22, *Flat.* III, 264) refer to open warfare between Denmark and Norway before the conflict was

settled by a truce. The terms of the treaty are expressed somewhat differently in *Ágrip*, where it is stated that whichever king outlived the other should take control of both kingdoms (*sá þeira, er lengr lifði, skyldi taka við báðum lǫndum*). Other sources agree with Theodoricus, that the treaty stipulated that only if one king were to die without an heir (*barnlauss*) would the surviving king be entitled to take over the other's kingdom. The oldest reference to this treaty appears in the anonymous *Chronicon Roskildense* (*SmhDmæ.* I, 22), written c. 1140. See Driscoll 1995, 101, n. 104.

224. Theodoricus has confused Liutprand, king of the Langobards from 712 to 744, with the last Langobard king, Desiderius (reigned 757–774), to whom Carloman's widow fled with her children in 771 (see, for example, Einhard, *Vit. Karol.* iii.3).

225. Here Theodoricus has confused various separate occasions on which different popes appealed for Frankish aid. His reference to Liutprand suggests that Theodoricus is actually recalling the appeals for help against Liutprand sent by Pope Gregory III to Charlemagne's grandfather, Charles Martel, in 739 and 740. Hanssen (1949, 90–91) suggests that Theodoricus's erroneous account of a pope besieged in Pavia may depend on confusion of *Papia* ('Pavia') and *papa* ('Pope') in a source such as Ado of Vienne's account of Charlemagne's capture of Pavia in 774 (PL 123, 126A).

226. *Iam rapido cursu Cæsar superaverat Alpes*: a partial misquotation of Lucan, *Bell. civ.* i.183: *Iam gelidas Caesar cursu superaverat Alpes* ('Now in haste Caesar had crossed the frozen Alps'). On this quotation see Frank 1909, 82; Hanssen 1949, 88.

227. *Ego non corporalem sed spiritualem fero gladium.* For discussion of this statement in connection with parallel passages in St Bernard and Hugh of St Victor, see Hanssen 1949, 117–120.

228. Theodoricus refers here to the so-called 'Donation of Constantine', a document fabricated probably in the Frankish empire during the late eighth or early ninth century, to strengthen the power of the Church in Rome (see, for example, Buchberger 1957–1968, VI, 483–484: 'Konstantinische Schenkung'; Cross and Livingstone 1983, 419). Cf. Hanssen 1949, 105–120; Vandvik 1955.

229. Kirchmann (1684) objected that here Theodoricus ought to have written 'roughly two hundred years' (*annos plus minus ducentos*, instead of *trecentos*; see Storm 1880, n. ad 48.6). Since the Langobards established a kingdom in Italy under Alboin in 568, and their last king, Desiderius, was defeated by Charlemagne in 774, the period of Langobard rule lasted only slightly longer than two centuries.

230. *cum Wandalis*: Theodoricus's use of *Wandali* to refer not to 'Vandals', but to the Wends (cf. 24.12: 'Wandali, quos nos materna lingua vocamus *Windir*'; Storm 1880, 48.17), is paralleled in Adam of Bremen, *Gest. Hamm.* ii.21 (18) 'Sclavania igitur, amplissima Germaniae provintia, a *Winulis* incolitur, qui olim dicti sunt *Wandali.*' Here Adam confuses both the Langobards (*Winili*, see Zeuss 1837, 57, 472; Paff 1959, 119; Latham 1965, 522, s.v. *Winilus*) and the Vandals with the Wends. In the same way, the *Continuatio Valcellensis* appended to the Chronicle of Sigebert of Gembloux, in recording the death of St Vicelin in 1154, refers to the so-called 'apostle of the Wends' as *Vicelinus Wandalorum apostolus* (1844, 460). Saxo similarly refers to the inhabitants of Vendsyssel as *Wandali* (*Gesta Danorum* XI.xiv.6; cf. Blatt 1957, 603, s.v. *Wandali*). On confusion of terms for Vandals and Wends, see generally Hoops 1911–1919, IV, 478–479; Storm 1880, n. ad 48.17; Paff 1959, 221. Magnús's battles against the Wends are described by Arnórr jarlaskáld, *Magnúsdrápa (Hrynhenda)* stt. 11–13 (*Skjd.* A I, 335–336), *Magnúsdrápa* st. 8 (*Skjd.* A I, 340), Þjóðólfr Arnórsson, *Magnúsflokkr* stt. 6–7 (*Skjd.* A I, 362–363), and in Oddr kikinaskáld's poem on Magnús (c. 1046) st. 1 (*Skjd.* A I, 354–355); cf. Johnsen 1939, 28, nn. 4–6.

231. Hǫrðaknútr died in 1042 at a wedding-feast 'as he stood at his drink'. See *ASC* (C and D versions), 1892–1899, I, 162 (*EHD* I, 260); Stenton 1971, 423.

232. Ástríðr was the daughter of Sveinn Haraldsson tjúguskegg and half-sister of Knútr the Great. Her husband Úlfr was the son of Þorgils sprakaleggr. Sveinn Úlfsson (usually called Estridsson, using the Danish form of his mother's name) ruled Denmark after the death of Magnús, from 1047 to 1076.

233. The battle of Helganes? Cf. *Ágrip* ch. 36 (37) and n. 239 below.

234. *Ágrip* ch. 36 (37) is alone in claiming that after his defeat at Helganes Sveinn Úlfsson returned to Denmark with an army he had recruited among the Wends. On the plural *Vindir*, older *Vinðr*, *Vindr*, see Noreen 1923, § 414.
235. *operientes faciem terræ more locustarum*: cf. n. 162.
236. With this account of Magnús's vision of St Óláfr before the battle of Hlýrskógsheiðr, cf. Einarr Skúlason, *Geisli* st. 28 (*Skjd.* A I, 464) and discussion in Johnsen (1939, 27–28); cf. also accounts in *Ágrip* ch. 37 (38), *Fsk* ch. 50, *MgóðHharðr* (*Msk* 42–43, *Flat.* III, 278–279), *Hkr(Mgóð)* ch. 27.
237. On this reference to the preservation of Óláfr's battle-axe at Niðaróss and similar stories of the survival of ancient objects of historical significance, see Perkins 1989, 248.
238. *Luirscogs-heithr*. The battle was fought on 28 September 1043, north-west of Hedeby, supposedly on the site of present-day Lürschau in Schleswig (see Finnur Jónsson 1929, 37, n. 8). Arnórr jarlaskáld (*Magnúsdrápa [Hrynhenda]* st. 13, *Skjd.* A I, 336) and Þjóðólfr Arnórsson (*Magnúsflokkr* st. 6, *Skjd.* A I, 362) describe Magnús's victory over an overwhelming army of Wends near the river *Skotborgará* (according to Þjóðólfr, at a place 'south of Skotborgará' and 'near Hedeby'). *Ágrip* ch. 37 (38) and *Hkr(Mgóð)* ch. 26 describe Hlýrskógsheiðr as situated beside Skotborgará (cf. *MgóðHharðr*, *Msk* 38, 42–43; *Flat.* III, 275, 278–279); but this detail is erroneous, for the river in question (present-day Kongeå) lies far north of Hedeby. On the battle, cf. Adam of Bremen, *Gest. Hamm.* ii.79 (75), and *Fsk* ch. 50. The author of *Ágrip* draws his own very detailed account of the course of the battle from an unknown source.
239. Magnús's victory at Helganes is described by Arnórr jarlaskáld, *Magnúsdrápa (Hrynhenda)* st. 15 (*Skjd.* A I, 336–337), *Magnúsdrápa* st. 12 (*Skjd.* A I, 341), and by Þjóðólfr Arnórsson, *Magnúsflokkr* st. 21 (*Skjd.* A I, 366). According to *Ágrip* ch. 36 (37), Magnús and Sveinn Úlfsson fought a naval battle at Helganes before the battle of Hlýrskógsheiðr. According to other sources, this encounter took place after the defeat of the Wends at Hlýrskógsheiðr; cf. *Fsk* ch. 50, *MgóðHharðr* (*Msk* 49–50; *Flat.* III, 283–284); *Hkr(Mgóð)* ch. 33.

240. Áróss, Latin *Aros*: present-day Århus. Magnús's victory over an army of Wends south of Århus is described in Oddr kikinaskáld's poem on Magnús, st. 1 (*Skjd.* A I, 354–355). Cf. the description of Sveinn's defeat in Jutland in Arnórr jarlaskáld's *Magnúsdrápa* st. 15 (*Skjd.* A I, 342), and accounts in *Fsk* ch. 50, *MgóðHharðr* (*Msk* 50–51; *Flat.* III, 284); *Hkr(Mgóð)* chs 30, 35. Cf. also the reference to three battles (interpreted by Snorri, *Hkr(Mgóð)* ch. 35, as those fought between Magnús and Sveinn) in Þjóðólfr Arnórsson's *Magnúsflokkr* st. 25 (*Skjd.* A I, 368).

241. The A text reads *non multa* 'not many', over which is written *nulla*, to mark alteration to *non nulla* 'not none, a good many' (see Storm 1880, 50, textual n. 1). Cf. *non nulla* KL (Lehmann 1937, 122; rpt 1959–1962, 429), *nonnulla multa* S.

242. Haraldr's nickname (*Hardrad'r* S, *Hardradr* AK, *Hardraðr* L, see Lehmann 1937, 122; rpt 1959–1962, 429) appears in the title to this chapter, but not in the text. On this nickname, see Lind 1920–1921, 136.

243. *Ourarsund* S, *Ourarsunt* ABK (Storm 1880, 50, textual n. 3) = *Eyrarsund*, the Øresund.

244. *purpuram renitebat*: i.e. 'shone with iridescent shot silk' (see e.g. Dodwell 1982, 145–50). Cf. the descriptions of Haraldr's ship returning from the east in *Fsk* ch. 50, *MgóðHharðr* (*Msk* 55; *Flat.* III, 287).

245. All texts read *Thambar Kelmer* (Storm 1880, 50, textual n. 4; Lehmann 1937, 122; rpt 1959–1962, 429). See n. 132 above.

246. In *Ágrip* ch. 38 (39) Einarr þambaskelmir is not present at the meeting between Haraldr and Magnús, and uncle and nephew divide the kingdom amicably between them. The statement in ch. 27 below, that after this meeting Haraldr left Denmark for Norway and there agreed to join forces with Sveinn Úlfsson, is at variance with other sources. They say that Haraldr made a pact with Sveinn in Sweden either after or before his interview with Magnús (*Fsk* ch. 52, *MgóðHharðr* [*Msk* 89; *Flat.* III, 307]; *Hkr[HSig]* chs 17–20). *Ágrip* subsequently has no account of hostility between Haraldr and Einarr and does not tell of the death of Einarr and Eindriði, his son. The hostility is plain in the *Fsk* account, but the deaths of Einarr and Eindriði are reported there only in bare fashion in ch. 47. A more de-

tailed and graphic description is in *MgóðHharðr* (*Msk* 178–180; *Flat.* II, 344–345, 349–350) and *Hkr(HSig)* chs 43–44.
247. See 2 Sam. 15:1–18:33.
248. Mithridates VI, Eupator Dionysus ('the Great'), was king of Pontus from 120 to 63 BC, when his son Pharnaces II led the revolt which drove his father to his death, for which Pharnaces was remembered as an emblem of filial treachery. See, for example, Lucan, *Bell. civ.* x.475–478.
249. Here the reading in AL, *spiculatori* 'to the executioner', is to be preferred over S, *speculatori* 'to the watchman'(?), adopted in Storm's edition. *Speculator* is, in any case, a common variant spelling of *spiculator* (see, for example, Niermeyer 1976, 983, s.v. *speculator* 2; 984, s.v. *spiculator*). Cf. Mark 6:27, where *speculator* (v.l. *spiculator*) is the term used to refer to John the Baptist's executioner (cf. Hanssen 1945, 173; Christiansen 1992, 108, n. 21).
250. *Barbarico vix consummato* [sic] *veneno*: a partial citation of Lucan, *Bell. civ.* i.336–337: *lassi Pontica regis / Proelia barbarico vix consummata veneno* 'the lingering warfare of the king of Pontus, scarcely ended by barbarous poison'. Lucan describes how, after years of protracted war against Rome, Mithridates took poison in a fit of despair; but it failed to kill him. Theodoricus may have drawn the line from accounts of Mithridates' war against Rome in Orosius, *Hist. adv. pag.* VI.i.29, or Otto of Freising, *Chronicon* ii.45 (1912, 121), where the same isolated phrase is cited (see Hanssen 1949, 86–87). A close parallel to this account of Pharnaces' murder of his father is contained in Orosius, *Hist. adv. pag.* VI.v.4–7.
251. Only the final remark, about Mithridates' polyglot judicial decisions, appears in Pliny, *Nat. Hist.* VII.xxiv.88: *Mithridates duarum et viginti gentium rex totidem linguis jura dixit, pro contione singulas sine interprete affatus.* All of the remarks attributed to Pliny here are found in Landulf Sagax, *Historia Romana* vi.13 (see next note). Cf. discussion in Hanssen 1945, 169.
252. On Theodoricus's references to *Romana Historia*, see nn. 50, 251, and 257–259. Lehmann (1937, 75; rpt 1959–1962, 386–387) suggests that here Theodoricus refers to the expanded versions of Eutropius's Roman history by Paul the Deacon and

Landulf Sagax, both of which circulated under the title *Historia Romana* (see Reynolds 1983, 159–162). Lehmann points out (1937, 72–73; rpt 1959–1962, 384–385) that a close parallel to the beginning of ch. 26 of Theodoricus's history is provided by Landulf's text, which incorporates Orosius's account of Pharnaces' overthrow of his father Mithridates (see n. 248 above); cf. Storm 1880, 51.14–25 and Landulf Sagax, *Historia Romana* vi.13 (1912–1913, I, 147–148); cf. Paul the Deacon, *Historia Romana* vi.12 (1914, 86–87).

253. *scripturam quæ fertur de exaltatione sanctæ crucis*: See *BHL* 4178; Mombritius 1910, I, 379–381; cf., for example, *GNH* 1931, 135–36, Salvesen–Gunnes 1971, 179; Vincent of Beauvais, *Speculum Historiale* XXIII.xii (1624, IV, 903).

254. On the *Decretum Gelasianum*, traditionally ascribed to Pope Gelasius I (d. 496), but probably a private work compiled in the sixth century, see Hanssen 1949, 92–93; Buchberger 1957–1968, IV, 630; Cross and Livingstone 1983, 385. It makes no mention of a *scriptura de exaltatione crucis*, although it does mention a *scriptura de inventione crucis*. See *Decretum Gelasianum* 1912, 10.226. Theodoricus may have worked from a commonplace version of the decree or may have muddled the name of the text to which he here refers.

255. *Cui beatus Augustinus plurimis in locis attestatur eodem sensu et pæne iisdem verbis*: Hanssen (1949, 92) doubts that a specific source is referred to here. He argues that the verb *attestatur* need only mean 'corresponds with', and that Theodoricus may simply be saying that Gelasius and Augustine are in agreement on this point.

256. On this list of apocryphal works, see *Decretum Gelasianum* 1912, 11.263, 265–268, 273, 275, 279, 280; cf. Storm 1880, n. ad 52.10.

257. On the title *Romana Historia*, cf. nn. 50 and 252 above. The accounts which follow (Storm 1880, 53.5–20), of the defeat of a Persian giant by the Byzantine emperor Heraclius (575–641), and of the dealings of Chosroes II Parvēz (king of Persia 590–628; see Kazhdan 1991, 432) with his sons, Mardasa and Syrois (Kavād-Shīrūya, king of Persia, Feb.–Sept./Oct. 628; see Kazhdan 1991, 1117), are paralleled in Landulf Sagax, *Historia*

Romana xx.26 and xx.47–50 (1912–1913, II, 116, 126–128; cf. Lehmann 1937, 73–74; rpt 1959–1962, 385–386).

258. *comedat aurum et argentum, pro quo multos impie peremit et orbem terrarum delevit*: cf. Landulf Sagax, *Historia Romana* xx.49 (1912–1913, II, 127): *Comedat aurum quod incassum collegit et propter quod etiam multos fame necauit mundumque deleuit.* Cf. traditional accounts of misers, usurers and exortionists force-fed gold and silver as one of the torments of Hell, Dunn 1934, 54; Tubach 1969, nos 454, 5039.

259. The story of Chosroes' ultimatum to Heraclius's ambassadors is found in Landulf Sagax, *Historia Romana* xx.6 (1912–1913, II, 105).

260. Very similar accounts of Titus's famous *dictum* are given in Jerome, *Chronicon* (1956, 189.4–8); *idem, Comm. in Epistolam ad Galatos* (PL 26, 433); Isidore, *Chronica* (1894, 456–457). But the story circulated widely. Cf., for example, Ps. Aurelius Victor, *Epitome* x.9; Sedulius Scottus, *Collectaneum Miscellaneum* LXXX.x.3; John of Salisbury, *Policraticus* III.xiv.185–194; *Alphabetum narrationum* (1904–1905, I, 303, no. 443); Tubach 1969, no. 1459. Bately (1979, 190–191) discusses examples of the anecdote in the Old English *Orosius* (1980, 138.23–139.2, see n. ad loc.) and *ASC* s.a. 81.

261. The author's rather morbid pun on *persecutio . . . persequamur* is lost in our translation.

262. I.e. Lake Mjøsa in Oppland. Cf. the accounts of this compact in *Fsk* ch. 52, *MgóðHharðr* (*Msk* 93–95, *Flat.* III, 309), *Hkr(HSig)* ch. 23. According to *MgóðHharðr* the settlement was made at a place called Skjaldarakr, referred to in *Fsk* as 'Akr'. This place has been identified as Aker in Vang in Hedmark, just east of Hamar (see Bjarni Aðalbjarnarson 1941–1951, III, 97, n. 2).

263. *thambaskelmis* K, *Thambas Kelmis* AS (Storm 1880, 54, textual n. 8); see n. 132 above.

264. Cf. Matt. 12:25.

265. Proba, *Cento Virgilianus de Christo*, 1–2 and 8 (in Schenkl, 1888, 569); cf. Walther 1969, no. 9696. On Theodoricus's mistaken attribution of these lines to Virgil, see Johnsen 1939, 36.

266. Lucan, *Bell. civ.*, i.666–669.

267. *Ágrip* ch. 39 (40), *Fsk* ch. 54, and *Hkr(HSig)* ch. 28 likewise record that Magnús died the year after he had divided Norway with Haraldr and expelled Sveinn from Denmark. According to *MgóðHharðr* (*Msk* 137; *Flat.* III, 326), Magnús and Haraldr reigned jointly for two years after Sveinn's expulsion from Denmark.

268. Cf. *Ágrip* ch. 39 (40), *MgóðHharðr* (*Msk* 144; *Flat.* III, 331), *Hkr(HSig)* ch. 28.

269. Theodoricus's pithy characterisation of Haraldr harðráði, 'sui tenax, alieni cupidus', neatly compresses Gregory the Great's questioning characterisation of unregenerate man: 'Quid enim vetus, quid carnalis homo noverat, nisi sua retinere, aliena rapere, si posset; concupiscere, si non posset?' (*Hom. 32 in Evang.*, PL 76, 1232D). *Ágrip* ch. 40 (41) is the only source to say that Sveinn and his ally, the Norwegian chieftain Finnr Árnason, initiated hostilities and sent an army to Norway against Haraldr. On Haraldr's forays into Denmark cf. *Hkr(HSig)* chs 32, 34–35, 58–65.

270. Tostig (ON *Tósti*), the brother of Harold, son of Earl Godwine of Wessex, had been made earl of Northumbria in 1055, but was deposed and driven out of England after a popular revolt against him in 1065. See *ASC* (C, D, and E versions), 1892–1899, I, 185–86, 190–93 (*EHD* II, 133, 141–42); Stenton 1971, 570, 578–79.

271. Cf. *Ágrip* ch. 41 (42), *Fsk* chs 58–60, *MgóðHharðr* (*Msk* 263–264; *Flat.* III, 387–389), *Hkr(HSig)* chs 77–79.

272. Storm (1880, n. ad 56.13) remarks that this explanation of the late arrival of the English king in Yorkshire suggests that Theodoricus falsely assumed that Harold, like William the Conqueror and his successors, ruled over Normandy as well as England. On the other hand, Theodoricus may have had in mind the tradition that around the year 1064 Harold was held hostage by Guy de Ponthieu and swore allegiance to William of Normandy in Bayeux (see Stenton 1971, 577–578; cf. the account of Harold's sojourn in Normandy in *Hkr[HSig]* ch. 76). The same detail, that Harold was away in Normandy when Haraldr landed, is included in *Ágrip* ch. 41 (42).

273. *quid faciant pauci contra tot milia fortes*: Ovid, *Fasti* ii.229.

Hanssen (1945, 170; 1949, 83) is inclined to believe that Theodoricus quotes this verse from a florilegium, rather than directly from Ovid.
274. Cf. the phrase uttered by Haraldr in *Ágrip* ch. 41 (42), *Sjaldan fór svá, þá er vel vildi*, reminiscent of Erlingr skakki's remark, in different circumstances: *Eigi for þa sva er vel villdi* (*Sverris saga* 1920, 35). By contrast, in *Fsk* ch. 68, *MgóðHharðr* (*Msk* 274, *Flat.* III, 393), and *Hkr(HSig)* ch. 90, Haraldr interprets his fall from horseback as an auspicious sign, remarking: *Fall er farar heill.* Harold Godwineson, looking on, interprets this ominous fall as a clear indication that the Norwegian king's luck has deserted him. The same proverb, *Fall er farar heill*, is uttered by Erlingr skakki after he slips when jumping ashore, not long before his death in the battle of Niðaróss, 19 June 1179 (*Sverris saga* 1920, 36). Analogous stories of a military commander who falls when first setting foot on the land he wishes to conquer are told of Scipio Africanus, Julius Caesar and William the Conqueror, among others (see Moberg 1940).
275. A convenient summary of medieval chronicles and histories which associate the appearance of this comet with political events in England in 1066 is provided by Freeman 1867–1879, III, 645–650; cf. Storm 1880, n. ad 57.9. Almost all European accounts agree that the comet appeared not just before the battle of Hastings (14 October) as Theodoricus suggests, but rather on the eve of the Major Rogation (25 April). A date in April accords with other reports of the appearance of Halley's comet recorded by writers for whom events in England in 1066 had no significance. See Ho Peng Yoke 1962, 184–185, no. 380; Stephenson and Walker 1985, 57; Keynes 1992, 162.
276. *Blaland* ABK, *Blaaland* S: *Bláland* usually refers to 'Ethiopia', but here designates either 'North Africa', or perhaps 'Palestine'; see Fritzner 1886–1896, s.v. (On the vague geographic limits of 'Ethiopia' for medieval European writers, see Friedman 1981, 8.) Haraldr's military adventures in the east are described or alluded to in Haraldr's own *gamanvísur* (c. 1040), stt. 3–4, 6–7 (*Skjd.* A I, 357–358; cf. *lausavísa* 15, *Skjd.* A I, 359); in Þjóðólfr Arnórsson's *Sexstefja* (c. 1065), stt. 1–8 (*Skjd.* A I, 369–371); in Arnórr Þórðarson's *erfidrápa* on Haraldr (c.

1067), st. 19 (*Skjd.* A I, 353); in Stúfr Þórðarson's *Stúfsdrápa* (c. 1067), stt. 2–4 (*Skjd.* A I, 404–405); in Bǫlverkr Arnórsson's *drápa* on Haraldr harðráði, stt. 1–5 (*Skjd.* A I, 385–386); in verses by Illugi Bryndœlaskáld (*Skjd.* A I, 384, st. 4) and Valgarðr á Velli (*Skjd.* A I, 390–391, stt. 1, 4–5); and in Einarr Skúlason's *Geisli* (1153), stt. 51–53 (*Skjd.* A I, 468–469). Cf. *Fsk* ch. 51, *MgóðHharðr* (*Msk* 58–87; *Flat.* III, 289–306), *Hkr(HSig)*, chs 2–12; and discussion in Blöndal 1978, 54–102.

277. *id locorum* KL (see Storm 1880, 57, textual n. 10; Lange 1989, 184, n. 21); *ab id locorum* AS. On the expressions *id locorum / id loci* 'there, in that region', see *TLL* 7.2, s.v. *is*, 482.72–74.

278. Theodoricus refers to the story of Haraldr's escape from a prison in Constantinople, and of how he took revenge by putting out the eyes of the Greek emperor who had detained him, apparently Michael V Kalaphates, who was blinded in April 1042 (Kazhdan 1991, 1336), in Norse sources incorrectly identified as his successor, Constantine IX Monomachos, emperor from 1042 to 1055 (Kazhdan 1991, 504). The story is referred to in Þjóðólfr Arnórsson's *Sexstefja* st. 6 (*Skjd.* A I, 370), Þórarinn Skeggjason's *drápa* on Haraldr harðráði (c. 1050–60, *Skjd.* A I, 400), and Stúfr Þórðarson's *Stúfsdrápa* st. 4 (*Skjd.* A I, 405). Cf. the accounts in *Fsk* ch. 51, *MgóðHharðr* (*Msk* 80–84; *Flat.* III, 304–305), *Hkr(HSig)* chs 13–15, and discussion of Þjóðólfr's stanza by Bjarni Aðalbjarnarson 1951, 87 n.; Turville-Petre 1976, 98; and Frank 1978, 134; cf. Blöndal 1978, 70, 88–100.

279. Þórir of Steig (in Gudbrandsdal, central Norway) was the son of Þórðr Guttormsson and his wife, Ísríðr Guðbrandsdóttir. Ísríðr was sister of Ásta, the mother of St Óláfr Haraldsson. The description of Þórir as 'born to high station among his own people' presumably refers to his local prominence in Gudbrandsdal; cf. *Hkr(Ólhelg)* ch. 128 on the marriage and prestige of his father Þórðr.

280. 'After this'—i.e. after Haraldr's death at Stamford Bridge, evidently referring to the first words of the chapter, 'After Haraldr was killed . . .'—Óláfr shared two years of rule with his brother Magnús (cf. *Ágrip* ch. 42 [43]) and was sole ruler for only twenty-four years after Magnús's death. Theodoricus must mean

here that after the death of his father, Haraldr harðráði, Óláfr was the legitimate ruler of Norway for twenty-seven years; cf. *Ágrip* ch. 44 (45), *Fsk* ch. 79. The author of *Msk* clearly counted the year in which Óláfr was absent from Norway after Stamford Bridge as the first year of his reign, for he too says that Óláfr had been king of Norway for twenty-seven years when he died (*Msk* 296). Snorri, on the other hand, counts the reign as starting only when Óláfr was accepted as king on his return to Norway a year after the death of his father. He allots him a reign of twenty-six years in all (*Hkr[Ólkyrr]* ch. 8). The 'peace and concord' of his rule are of course reflected in his nickname, *kyrri*, 'the quiet' or 'the peaceful' (see Lind 1920–1921, 36, 231).

281. In *Hkr(Ólkyrr)* ch. 6 the church containing the sacred relics of St Óláfr is mistakenly referred to as Kristskirkja, the name usually applied to Niðaróss cathedral. The mistake is made good in *Hulda–Hrokkinskinna*, where the dedication to the Trinity stands in agreement with Theodoricus (see Louis-Jensen 1977, 148). In the 1170s the St Mary's church built in stone by Haraldr harðráði was taken down and rebuilt by Archbishop Eysteinn as the church of his Augustinian foundation at Elgeseter, but an author could say that 'it may be seen to this day' both before and after its change of site. Cf. *Ágrip* ch. 42 (43); *Hkr(HSig)* ch. 38.

282. The same comparison with the peace and prosperity of Haraldr hárfagri's reign is made in *Ágrip* ch. 42 (43) and *Msk* 291.

283. Cf. *Ágrip* ch. 44 (45), *Fsk* ch. 79, *Msk* 296, *Hkr(Ólkyrr)* ch. 8.

284. In the title of this chapter all witnesses to Theodoricus's text give Magnús's nickname as *berfort*, evidently a corruption of *berfótr* or, better, *berfœttr*. Here Theodoricus uses the calque *nudipes* 'barefoot', although the vernacular nickname really means 'bareleg'. In *Ágrip* chs 45 (46), 50 (51), Magnús's cognomen is given as *berleggr*. Snorri, *Hkr(Mberf)* ch. 16, explains that Magnús was called *berfœttr* or *berbeinn* because after his sojourn in the west he and his men adopted the dress fashionable in Scotland and Ireland, and 'went barelegged about the streets and wore short tunics and cloaks' (*hann hafði mjǫk þá siðu ok klæðabúnað, sem títt var í Vestrlǫndum, ok margir hans menn. Gengu þeir berleggjaðir um stræti ok hǫfðu kyrtla*

stutta ok svá yfirhafnir). It is generally accepted by historians of costume that this describes the brat-and-léine, or mantle-and-tunic, garb common in early Ireland and Scotland. There is no clear evidence that anything quite like the kilt was worn in those parts before the Renaissance (see McClintock 1949, 3; 1950, 5–6, 8; Dunbar 1962, 23; 1981, 21–22) and indeed the garment now adopted as the national dress of Scotland appears to have been invented by an English Quaker from Lancashire some time in the 1730s (see Trevor-Roper 1983). Cf. Lind 1920–1921, 19–21, s.vv. *Berbeinn, Berfœttr, Berleggr.* Saxo, *Gesta Danorum* XIII.i.1 (1931, 342), records that Magnús earned his nickname from his shameful barefoot flight from an army of Hallanders. Cf. Christiansen 1980–1981, I, 292, n. 3; Driscoll 1995, 103–104, n. 127.
285. Cf. *Ágrip* ch. 45 (46), on the taxes rescinded by Hákon (perhaps some of those first imposed by Sveinn and Álfífa, see *Ágrip* chs 28–29, and Bjarni Einarsson, 1984, xii); see also *Fsk* ch. 80, *Msk* 297, *Hkr(Mberf)* ch. 1. *Ágrip* presents a rather more detailed account of the friction between Magnús and Hákon.
286. Hákon died suddenly of a mysterious illness after chasing a ptarmigan on Dovrefjell (see *Ágrip* ch. 46 [47], *Fsk* ch. 80, *Msk* 298, *Hkr[Mberf]* ch. 2).
287. Cf. *Ágrip* ch. 47 (48) fin., and *Hkr(Mberf)* ch. 7.
288. The portents foreshadowing Charlemagne's death mentioned here are catalogued in Einhard, *Vit. Karol.* ch. 32; see Hanssen 1949, 85–86.
289. The number eight (*octo*) is included as a superscript addition in K, and added in the margin in A (see Storm 1880, 59, textual n. 4). This detail differs from Einhard, *Vit. Karol.* ch. 32.2, where it is stated that the bridge was built over a period of ten years. According to Einhard, it was destroyed by fire in May 813, one year before the death of Charlemagne (*Vit. Karol.* ch. 17.2; cf. Sigebert of Gembloux, *Chron.*, s.a. 811 [1844, 337]).
290. In fact, the wooden arcade of the church at Aachen did not collapse until 817, three years after the emperor's death (see *Annales regni Francorum* 1895, 146; trans. Scholz 1970, 102).
291. According to Einhard, *Vit. Karol.* ch. 32.3, this event took place during Charlemagne's last expedition against the Dan-

ish king Godfred. Einhard (*Vit. Karol.* ch. 14.3) and the Royal Frankish Annals (*Annales regni Francorum* 1895, 131; Scholz 1970, 92) record that Godfred was murdered by one of his retainers in 810. Theodoricus, or his immediate source, has confused the warlike Godfred with his successor Hemming who, during his short reign (810–812), made peace with Charlemagne. According to the Royal Frankish Annals, Hemming was Godfred's nephew (*filius fratris eius, Annales regni Francorum* 1895, 133; Scholz 1970, 93), although Adam of Bremen calls Hemming Godfred's cousin (*patruelis, Gest. Hamm.* i.14 [16]), and Saxo represents Hemming as the son of a certain Olaf and grandson of Godfred (*Gøtricus*, see Saxo, *Gesta Danorum* viii.249–ix.250; cf. Fisher–Davidson 1979–1980, II, 147 n. 175, 150 n. 1).
292. Cf. Notker Balbulus, *Gest. Karol.* ii.12. The same story is told of the Merovingian king Chlothar II (584–629) in the *Liber Hist. Franc.* ch. 41 (1888, 314), the Life of Bishop Faro of Meaux (*Vita Faronis* ch. 77; 1910, 192–193), and the *Gesta Dagoberti*, ch. 14 (1888, 405).
293. *quo semel imbuta recens fuit, servavit* [*servabit* S] *odorem testa diu*: Horace, *Epistulae* I.ii.69–70: *Quo semel est imbuta recens, servabit odorem testa diu.* See Walther 1963–1986, no. 25711.
294. Cf. the very similar account of events in *Ágrip* ch. 47 (48) init.: 'En eptir fráfall Hákonar þá mátti Þórir eigi víkva skapi sínu til Magnúss, er þá tók við ríki, ok reisti upp mann þann, er Sveinn var kallaðr, sonr Haralds flettis, fyr ofmetnaðar sakar.' Cf. *Fsk* ch. 80, *Msk* 298–299. Snorri (*Hkr[Mberf]* ch. 4) says that Sveinn was of Danish descent.
295. According to *Ágrip* ch. 47 (48) and *Hkr(Mberf)* ch. 6, Þórir and Egill were captured on the island on which Hesjutún (modern Hestun) is situated, i.e. Hamnøya, a bit to the north of the mouth of Velfjorden (Nordland fylke), and were later taken to be hanged on Vambarhólmr (modern Vomma, off Hamnøya). Storm (n. ad 61.5) thought Theodoricus was wrong in reporting that Þórir was captured on Vambarhólmr. His account agrees, however, with that of *Msk* (302–304); and *Fsk* ch. 80 records that, while the followers of Þórir and Egill were captured at Hesjutún, 'Þórir varð ok handtekinn í hólmi þeim, er heitir Vambarhólmr,' and they were hanged there. The defeat of Þórir and Egill is

referred to in Þorkell hamarskáld's *Magnúsdrápa* (c. 1104), st. 1 (*Skjd.* A I, 438).
296. *cum quodam alio principe, nomine Eigil, viro probo et valde eloquente*: cf. *Ágrip* ch. 47 (48): *Egill Áskelssonr á Forlandi enn vaskasti maðr*, and *Msk* 303–304: *Egill af Forlandi enn cvrteisasti mapr, oc allra manna vascastr*. Snorri (*Hkr[Mberf]* ch. 4) is alone in giving the name of Egill's father as 'Áslákr'. For biographical details see *NBL* 3, 447–448; Lind 1931, 203. With the reference here to Egill's 'eloquence', cf. the biting insult which he is said to have directed at Magnús's servants just before being hanged, commemorated in a verse attributed to Þorkell hamarskáld (*Skjd.* A I, 439, st. 2; cf. *Fsk* ch. 80, *Msk* 304–305, *Hkr[Mberf]* ch. 6).
297. *Dalr, Hofuth, Wear*: cf. *Ágrip* ch. 48 (49): 'Magnús fór margar herfarar ok fekk þat fyrst til ákalls á Gautland austr, at hann kvað Dal ok Véar ok Varðynjar með réttu eiga at liggja til Nóregs, kvað sína forellra haft hafa forðum . . .'; cf. *Msk* 323. Magnús's military exploits are described in Þorkell hamarskáld's *Magnúsdrápa* stt. 2–5 (*Skjd.* A I, 438–439). On the Gautish campaign, cf. *Fsk* ch. 82, *Msk* 323–329, *Hkr(Mberf)* chs 12–14. *Ágrip* is alone in representing Magnús as victorious in each of his expeditions against Gautland.
298. *arma tenenti omnia dat*: An extract from Caesar's address to his troops at *Bell. civ.* i.348–349: *Viribus utendum est, quas fecimus. Arma tenenti / Omnia dat, qui iusta negat*. 'The strength we have created must be used. He who denies his due to the man bearing weapons grants him everything.' The words quoted by Theodoricus circulated independently as an aphorism (see Walther 1963–1986, no. 1353a).
299. Snorri (*Hkr[Mberf]* ch. 14) recounts how Ǫgmundr Skoptason disguised himself in the king's doublet, thereby duping the enemy into pursuing him and affording Magnús a chance to escape. *Ágrip*, ch. 49 (50), merely mentions Ǫgmundr among the men who accompanied Magnús on the Gautish campaign. The author of *Msk* (332), apparently working from a source similar to the list in *Ágrip* of Magnús's followers in Gautland, represents Ǫgmundr as one of the men who accompanied Magnús on his last expedition to Ireland.

300. King of Sweden c. 1080–1110.
301. On this settlement and Magnús's marriage to Margrét Ingadóttir, cf. *Ágrip* ch. 48 (49) fin., *Fsk* ch. 83, *Msk* 329, *Hkr(Mberf)* ch. 15.
302. *ulstrengr* AK, *Ulstrenger* SB (Storm 1880, 62, textual n. 1). On the nickname of Sigurðr ullstrengr Loðinsson see Lind 1920–1921, 391.
303. Theodoricus's statement that Sigurðr ullstrengr established the monastery on Niðarhólmr is confirmed by *Ólhelg(Leg)* ch. 75 (cf. Taranger 1890, 177; Blom 1956, 127 and 512, n. 11). In the Icelandic *Gísls þáttr Illugasonar* in *Jóns saga helga* (*Bps*. I, 226) it is likewise reported that during the reign of Magnús berfœttr a Benedictine house (*svartmunkaklaustr*) was established on Niðarhólmr, the island which Sigurðr had received from King Magnús and which he bequeathed to the monastery, together with his patrimony at Viggjar (now Viggja, on Orkdalsfjord in Sør-Trøndelag). Matthew Paris, however, (*Chronica majora*, V, 42) apparently refers to Niðarhólmr when he remarks that Knútr the Great had founded a Benedictine monastery in Norway (*coenobium in Norwegia . . . quod dicitur coenobium sancti Benedicti de Holm*), together with a kindred house in England with the same name, that is, the monastery of St Benet's of Holme in Norfolk. A similar report is included in the fifteenth-century chronicle attributed to John Brompton (*Chron.*, 1652, 912–913; cf. Langebek 1772–1878, IV, 415, n. b.; Lange 1856, 199–200; Taranger 1890, 177). There is, on the other hand, ample evidence from later Norse sources that at least the estates at Viggjar had once belonged to Sigurðr's family, and that by the fourteenth century this land had passed into the possession of the monastery on Niðarhólmr (see Louis-Jensen 1977, 118–119, n. 33). For discussion of the possibility that Theodoricus was himself a monk at Niðarhólmr, see Introd. pp. ix–x; Lange 1856, 200; Storm 1880, vii; Daae 1895, 400; Nordal 1914, 7–8; Bjarni Aðalbjarnarson 1937, 5; Johnsen 1939, 86–89; Ellehøj 1965, 176; Lange 1989, 19.
304. Magnús's killing of a certain 'Earl Hugh' in Anglesey is commemorated in Bjǫrn krepphendi's *Magnúsdrápa* (c. 1100), st. 9 (*Skjd*. A I, 436–437), and Gísl Illugason's *erfikvæði* on Magnús berfœttr (c. 1104), stt. 11–13 (*Skjd*. A I, 442); cf. Þorkell

hamarskáld, *Magnúsdrápa* (c. 1104), st. 3 (*Skjd.* A I, 438). *Ágrip* ch. 49 (50) agrees with Theodoricus in reporting that Magnús defeated and killed 'jarl þann, er Hugi hét enn digri'. Later Icelandic sources (*Fsk* ch. 81, *Msk* 318–319, *Hkr[Mberf]* ch. 10, *Orkneyinga saga* ch. 39, *Magnúss saga skemmri* ch. 3, *Magnúss saga lengri* ch. 9) record that Magnús fought against two earls named Hugh at Anglesey, 'Hugi prúði' and 'Hugi digri', and that the former was killed and the latter put to flight. These later accounts accord with information in British sources, which confirm that Hugh of Montgomery, earl of Shrewsbury, died at the battle of Anglesey in July 1098; see, for example, the *Peterborough Chronicle* (1970, 27), John of Worcester, *Chronicon* (1995–1998, I, 86–88, s.a. 1098), William of Malmesbury, *Gesta Regum* iv.329 (1998, 570), Orderic Vitalis, *Hist. eccl.* X, 5 (1969–1980, V, 222–224)—while Hugh of Avranches ('the stout'), earl of Chester, died on 27 July, 1101 (Orderic Vitalis, *Hist. eccl.* X, 19; 1969–1980, V, 314; *Brut y Twysogyon* 1955, 41). See Bugge 1914, 38–40; Charles 1934, 116–122.

305. Cf. *Ágrip* ch. 49 (50): 'Tekr hann í Orkneyjum síðan jarlinn Erlend með sér ok Magnús, son hans, áttján vetra gamlan, er nú er heilagr.' On the part of Magnús Erlendsson, later St Magnús of Orkney (d. 1117), in this expedition, cf. also *Fsk* ch. 81, *Msk* 316, *Hkr(Mberf)* ch. 23, and the detailed accounts in *Orkneyinga saga* chs 39–40, *Magnúss saga skemmri* chs 3–4, *Magnúss saga lengri* chs 9–10. On his miracles, see *Orkneyinga saga* ch. 57, *Magnúss saga skemmri* chs 19–20, *Magnúss saga lengri* chs 30, 33–35.

306. *Witheuthr* ASKL (for *Withcuthr*, see Storm 1880, 63, textual n. 1; cf. Lehmann 1937, 122; 1959–1962, 429). Cf. similar lists of the names of those who accompanied Magnús on his expedition to Orkney in *Ágrip* ch. 49 (50), *Fsk* ch. 84, *Msk* 332, *Hkr(Mberf)* ch. 23, *Orkneyinga saga* ch. 39, *Magnúss saga lengri* ch. 9.

307. On the death of Nikulás Sigurðarson at the hands of Eysteinn meyla Eysteinsson's army of Birkibeinar, see *Fsk* ch. 126, *Hkr(MErl)* ch. 40; on Eysteinn, see *Fsk* chs 122, 127–129; *Hkr(MErl)* chs 36–37, 41–42. It is difficult to say what Theodoricus means to imply in his reference to Eysteinn as *infelix tyrannus*; cf. Introd. pp. xi, xiii. As Hanssen (1949, 94–95) points out, there

was originally no great difference in meaning between the Latin terms *rex* and *tyrannus,* which had a general sense 'monarch, sovereign' (see *OLD* s.v. *tyrannus,* 1), and *tyrannus* only secondarily came to be associated with evil rulers or despots. Cf., for example, Isidore, *Etym.* IX.iii.19–20: 'Tyranni Graece dicuntur. Idem Latine et reges. Nam apud veteres inter regem et tyrannum nulla discretio erat . . . Fortes enim reges tyranni vocabantur. Nam tiro fortis . . . Iam postea in usum accidit tyrannos vocari pessimos atque inprobos reges' (cf. *Etym.* I.xxxi). Depending on how Theodoricus intended to represent Eysteinn's career here, the phrase used to describe him, *infelix tyrannus,* might be interpreted as 'a baleful tyrant', or simply 'an unfortunate king' (cf. the description of Óláfr Haraldsson at *Hist. Norw.* 121.3 as *beatissimus tyrannus Olavus* 'blessed king Óláfr'). For conflicting views on the implied sense of *tyrannus* here, see Skard 1930, 23 and Bjarni Aðalbjarnarson 1937, 29. It is perhaps significant in this regard that Theodoricus does not Latinise Eysteinn's name as *Augustinus* as he does when referring to both Eysteinn Erlendsson and Eysteinn Magnússon (cf. n. 316).
308. The title reads thus: 'De morte ejusdem Magni et filii ejus'; in the chapter headings, p. 4 above, it appears as 'De morte ejusdem Magni et de filiis ejus'.
309. Cf. *Ágrip* ch. 49 (50) fin. and ch. 50 (51) init.: 'Vendi heim ór þessi herfǫr með hlǫðnum skipum gulls ok silfrs ok gersima. En fám vetrum síðarr gørðisk hann vestr til Írlands með skipastóli ok ferr með miklu liði ok ætlar at vinna landit ok vann nekkvern hlut í fyrstunni. Dirfðisk hann af því ok gerðisk síðan óvarari, með því at í fyrstu gekk hónum með vildum sem Haraldi fǫðurfeðr hans, er hann fell á Englandi, drógu hann til lífláts ok in sǫmu svik, því at Írir sǫmnuðu á mót Magnúsi konungi óvígjum her með leynd.' On Magnús's ill-starred final expedition to Ireland, cf. *Fsk* chs 84–85, *Msk* 331–337, *Hkr(Mberf)* chs 23–25. See Driscoll 1995, 105, n. 143 and refs.
310. On the accession of Magnús's sons, cf. *Ágrip* ch. 51 (52), *Fsk* ch. 85 fin., *Msk* 337, *Hkr(Msona)* ch. 1.
311. Instead of Storm's text (1880, 64.1): *Siwardum suum duxerat,* we follow the reading in L: *Siwardum secum duxerat* (overlooked by Lehmann 1937, 122; 1959–1962, 429; but noted by

Lange 1989, 184 n. 21). Skånland (1957, 147–148), unaware of this variant in L, suggested that *Siwardum suum* should be read as a haplography for *Siwardum filium suum* 'his son Sigurðr'.
312. *tertio anno post patris obitum.* For *tertio* 'third', probably read *tertio decimo* 'thirteenth'. Óláfr died twelve years after his father's death (*Ágrip* ch. 51 [52], *Msk* 337), i.e. in the thirteenth year of the reign of the sons of Magnús (*Fsk* ch. 93), on 22 December 1115 (*Hkr[MSona]* ch. 18).
313. *rebus humanis decessit*: i.e. 'he died'; cf. *TLL* 6.3 s.v. *humanus* 3090.4–6, 18. Snorri likewise notes that Eysteinn ruled Norway for twenty years (*Hkr[MSona]* ch. 23; cf. *Fsk* ch. 93). The section of *Ágrip* which covered the reign of Eysteinn is now lost (see Bjarni Einarsson 1984, 49 n. 3 ad ch. 54; Driscoll 1995, 106, n. 151).
314. In *Msk* 352 and *Hkr(Msona)* ch. 14 Eysteinn is likewise credited with establishing a monastery at Nordnes in Bergen and ordering the construction of St Michael's church there.
315. On the improvements made during Eysteinn's reign, cf. *Msk* 352–353, 384; *Hkr(Msona)* chs 14, 23; and the fragmentary text of *Fsk* ch. 92. On the haven at Agðanes, see Jasinski 1995.
316. Theodoricus's use of a Latinised form of Eysteinn's name, *Augustinus*, permits a ready association with his near namesake Augustus Caesar, which is obscured in our translation.
317. Geoffrey of Monmouth records that the legendary Cornish king Dunwallo Molmutius granted similar immunities on roads leading to cities and temples, and that these laws were confirmed by his son Belinus (*Historia Regum Britanniae* 1984–1991, I, 24, 26; II, 30, 34; cf. the anonymous thirteenth-century poem *Gesta Regum Britannie, ibid.*, V, 52; the Welsh version of *Historia Regum Britanniae* 1929, 275, 282; Higden, *Polychronicon* II, 42–44). Comparable accounts of safety and prosperity associated with the reign of any powerful king are a commonplace of medieval history (cf., for example, the description of the reign of Edwin of Northumbria in Bede, *Hist. eccl.* II.xvi), although the detail of the king's highway as a sanctuary for criminals is less common. On the popular notion of the king's highway as a place of peculiar legal sanctuary, see Pollock 1890, 80–83; Pollock and Maitland 1898, I, 44–45; II, 464.

318. The date implied here is 1106, seven years after the liberation of Jerusalem, 15 July 1099 (see Storm 1880, n. ad 65.9). This account of Sigurðr's departure from Norway accords with *Msk* 338, where it is stated that Sigurðr travelled abroad three years after the death of his father (in 1103), or as calculated in *Fsk* ch. 86 init., after the sons of Magnús had governed the country for three years. *Ágrip* ch. 52 (53) and *Hkr(Msona)* ch. 3 report that Sigurðr went abroad four years after his father's death, i.e. in 1107, the date recorded in the *Annales regii* (ed. Storm 1888, 111). Neither of these calculations is corroborated by foreign sources. The English *Annales Radingenses* (Liebermann 1879, 10) record that Sigurðr arrived in England, his first stop on his journey south, in 1108. This accords with the statement by Albert of Aachen that Sigurðr (incorrectly referred to as 'Magnus') spent two years travelling to Jerusalem (i.e. from 1108 to 1110); see Albert of Aachen, *Hist. Hier.* XI.xxvi (1879, 675).

319. Sigurðr's trip to Jerusalem and the conquest of Sidon are recalled in Einarr Skúlason's *Sigurðardrápa* stt. 3–5 (*Skjd.* A I, 455–456). Cf. the references to Sigurðr's exploits on this expedition in Halldórr skvaldri's *Útfarardrápa* (c. 1120?) st. 11 (*Skjd.* A I, 488), and accounts in *Ágrip* chs 52–54 (53–55), *Fsk* chs 88–89, *Msk* 341–351, 383, and *Hkr(Msona)* chs 10–11. See also the account in Fulcher of Chartres, *Hist. Hier.* II.xliv (1913, 543–548); cf. Riant 1865, 194–203. On Arabic sources see *KLNM* 1, 196–197.

320. The episode of the robber's cave is alluded to in Halldórr skvaldri's *Útfararkviða* (*Skjd.* A I, 485) and *Útfarardrápa* stt. 7–8 (*Skjd.* A I, 487), and in Þórarinn stuttfeldr's *Stuttfeldardrápa* st. 4 (*Skjd.* A I, 490). Cf. versions of the story based on some or all of these verses in *Fsk* ch. 86, *Msk* 345–347 and *Hkr(Msona)* ch. 6.

321. On Sigurðr's sojourn at the court of Baldwin I (king of Jerusalem 1100–1118), cf. *Fsk* ch. 88, *Hkr(Msona)* chs 10–11.

322. *Fsk* ch. 88 and *Hkr(Msona)* ch. 11 likewise record that Baldwin gave Sigurðr this sacred relic. According to *Ágrip* ch. 53 (54), Sigurðr persuaded the king of Jerusalem (who is not named) to give him a splinter of the cross. Sigurðr had it kept as a dedicatory relic in the Holy Cross church he built in the border-

fortress at Konungahella; see for example *Hkr(Msona)* ch. 32. For accounts of the proliferation of pieces of the True Cross distributed as relics, see Brewer 1884, 269–270; Buchberger 1957–1968, VI, 615, 'Kreuzpartikel'.
323. Sigurðr's madness is described in *Hkr(Msona)* ch. 22, but Snorri makes no mention of poison as the cause of the king's malady. The author of *Ágrip* (ch. 55 [56]) refers euphemistically to the onset of Sigurðr's bouts of madness as his *óhœgyndi* 'discomfort'. Cf. Driscoll 1995, note 154.
324. *de Scotia*: *Scotia*, 'Scotland', is generally distinguished from *Hibernia*, 'Ireland', and in all other instances (see above, 3.21, 7.10, 32.15) Theodoricus refers to Ireland as *Hibernia*. On the other hand, although it is not common, *Scotia* can be used as a synonym of *Scotia Maior*, i.e. 'Ireland' (see Grässe–Benedict–Plechl 1972, II, 237, s.v. *Hibernia*), and it is possible that this is the sense which Theodoricus means to attach to the word here. The heading to this chapter refers to Haraldr Magnússon as 'Irish' (*Hyberniensis*). The accounts in *Flat.* II, 440 and *Msk* 391 suggest that Haraldr came from the Hebrides. *Ágrip* ch. 57 (58) and *Fsk* ch. 93 state that Haraldr came from Ireland. Snorri (*Hkr[Msona]* ch. 26) tries to accommodate these conflicting reports by describing Haraldr as a man from Ireland whom Hallkell húkr Jóansson had taken aboard his ship in the Hebrides. Haraldr's nickname was *gilli* (cf. *Ágrip* ch. 57 [58]: *gillikrist*, from Irish *gille-Críst* 'servant of Christ'; cf. Lind 1920–1921, 110).
325. Ordeal was allowed or prescribed as a means of proof in the 'laws of the land' and not finally abolished till the middle of the thirteenth century; cf. references in *NgL* V 325, s.vv. *járn, járnburðr*. Cf. the account in *Sverris saga* ch. 59 (1920, 64–65) of Eiríkr who proved himself a son of King Sigurðr munnr by carrying hot iron. As most relevant to the situation of Haraldr gilli and this Eiríkr may be cited article VIII 16 in the Frostathing laws (for Trøndelag and other parts of northern Norway); see *NgL* I, 207. On the prohibition of this kind of ordeal by church law see Hanssen 1945, 168; 1949, 95–96; cf. Hamre 1960, 551–553. Accounts of Haraldr gilli's ordeal are also in *Ágrip* ch. 57 (58), *Fsk* ch. 93, *Hkr(Msona)* ch. 26.
326. *hominem exuit*: i.e. 'he died'. For this euphemism see, for

example, *DMLBS*, s.v. *exuere* 2.b.; cf. *TLL* 5.2, s.v. *exuo*, 2114.51–55, 81.
327. Ovid, *Metamorphoses* i.128–131.
328. Lucan, *Bell. civ.* vii.552–554.
329. Lucan, *Bell. civ.* vii.556. Theodoricus's reference to this line as appearing *alio loco* suggests that he is unaware that it is part of the same passage as the preceding citation from Lucan, separated from the earlier quotation by only a single line. Hanssen (1949, 88) points to this together with earlier misquotation of Lucan (see above, n. 226) as evidence that Theodoricus did not know the *Bell. civ.* at first hand.
330. *non visa sed audita*: see n. 11.
331. For classical antecedents of this humility formula see Skard 1930, 75.

BIBLIOGRAPHY AND ABBREVIATIONS

I. PRIMARY SOURCES: EDITIONS AND TRANSLATIONS

Adam of Bremen, *Gest. Hamm.* = *Magistri Adam Bremensis Gesta Hammaburgensis ecclesiae Pontificum.* 1978. Ed. W. Trillmich and R. Buchner. *Quellen des 9. und 11. Jahrhunderts zur Geschichte der hamburgischen Kirche und des Reiches*, 135–499.

Adomnán, *De locis sanctis.* 1965. Ed. L. Bieler. CCSL 175, 175–234.

Ágrip 1984: in *Ágrip af Nóregskonunga sǫgum. Fagrskinna— Nóregs konunga tal.* Ed. Bjarni Einarsson. ÍF 29.

Ágrip 1995: in *Ágrip af Nóregskonungasǫgum. A twelfth-century synoptic history of the kings of Norway.* Ed. and trans. M. J. Driscoll. Viking Society for Northern Research. Text series 10. (Where chapter references in this edition differ from *Ágrip* 1984, they are added in parentheses.)

Ágrip af sǫgu Danakonunga: see *Danakonunga sǫgur*, 323–336.

AÍ = *Alfrœði Íslenzk. Islands encyclopædisk litteratur* I–III. 1908–1918. Ed. Kr. Kålund and N. Beckman. STUAGNL 37, 41, 45.

Albert of Aachen, *Hist. Hier.* = *Alberti Aquensis Historia Hierosolymitana.* 1879. Ed P. Meyer. *Recueil des historiens des croisades. Historiens occidentaux* 4, 265–713.

Alphabetum narrationum = *An Alphabet of Tales.* 1904–1905. Ed. Mary M. Banks. EETS, O.S. 126, 127.

Ambrose, *Exp. Lc.* = *Sancti Ambrosii Mediolanensis . . . Expositio Evangelii secundum Lucam.* 1957. Ed. M. Adriaen. CCSL 14.

Ammianus Marcellinus, *Rerum Gestarum Libri XXXI.* 1935–1940. Ed. and trans. J. C. Rolfe. 3 vols.

Anal. Hymn. = *Analecta Hymnica medii aevi.* 1886–1922. Ed. C. Blume and G. M. Dreves. 55 vols.

Annales regni Francorum. 1895. Ed. F. Kurze. MGH. SS. rer. Germ. in usum scholarum.

ASC = *Anglo-Saxon Chronicle.* 1892–1899. Ed. C. Plummer and J. Earle. *Two of the Saxon chronicles parallel.* Rpt 1952 with bibl. by D. Whitelock. 2 vols.

Augustine, *De civ. Dei* = *Sancti Aurelii Augustini De civitate Dei libri I–XXII.* 1955. Ed. B. Dombart and A. Kalb. CCSL 47–48.

Augustine, *Quaest. euang.* = *Sancti Aurelii Augustini Quaestiones Evangeliorum.* 1980. Ed. A. Mutzenbecher. CCSL 44B.

Baehrens, E. 1879–1886. *Poetae Latini Minores.* 6 vols.

Bede, *De temporibus.* 1980. Ed. C. W. Jones. CCSL 123C, 579–611.

Bede, *De temporum ratione.* 1977. Ed. C. W. Jones. CCSL 123B.

Bede, *Exp. Lc.* = *Bedae Venerabilis . . . In Lucae Evangelium expositio.* 1960. Ed. D. Hurst. CCSL 120, 1–425.

Bede, *Hist. Eccl.* = *Bede's Ecclesiastical History of the English People.* 1969. Ed. B. Colgrave and R. A. B. Mynors.

Biblia sacra iuxta Vulgata versionem. 1975. Ed. R. Weber et al. 2 Aufl.

Boethius, *Cons. phil.* = *Anicii Manlii Severini Boethii Philosophiae Consolatio.* 1984. Ed. L. Bieler. CCSL 94.

Bps. = *Biskupa sögur.* 1858–1878. Ed. Guðbrandur Vigfússon and Jón Sigurðsson. 2 vols.

Brennu-Njáls saga. 1954. Ed. Einar Ól. Sveinsson. ÍF 12.

Brut y Twysogyon = *Brut y Twysogyon or the Chronicle of the princes. Red Book of Hergest version.* 1955. Ed. T. Jones.

Caesarius of Arles, *Sermones.* 1953. Ed. G. Morin. 2nd ed. CCSL 103–104.

Catalogus regum Danie: in *SmhDmæ.* I, 159–160.

CCCM = Corpus Christianorum. Continuatio Mediaevalis.

CCSL = Corpus Christianorum. Series Latina (1953–).

Chronicon Roskildense. 1917–1922. Ed. M. Cl. Gertz. *SmhDmæ.* I, 14–33.

Cicero, *De Divinatione.* 1920–1923. Ed. A. S. Pease. University of Illinois Studies in Language and Literature 6 (1920), 161–500 and 8 (1923), 153–474; rpt 1963.

Continuatio Valcellensis: see Sigebert of Gembloux.

CSEL = Corpus scriptorum ecclesiasticorum latinorum.

Danakonunga sǫgur: Skjǫldunga saga. Knýtlinga saga. Ágrip af sǫgu Danakonunga. 1982. Ed. Bjarni Guðnason. ÍF 35.

Decretum Gelasianum = *Das Decretum Gelasianum. De libris recipiendis et non recipiendis.* 1912. Ed. E. von Dobschutz. Texte und Untersuchungen zur Geschichte des altchristlichen Literatur 38 (3R. 8).

Disticha Catonis. 1952. Ed. M. Boas.

E.A. = Editiones Arnamagnæanæ.

EETS. OS. = Early English Text Society, Original Series.
EETS. SS. = Early English Text Society, Supplementary Series.
EHD I = *English Historical Documents*. I. *c. 500–1042*. 1979. Ed. D. Whitelock. 2nd ed.
EHD II = *English Historical Documents*. II. *1042–1189*. 1981. Ed. D. C. Douglas and G. W. Greenaway. 2nd ed.
Einhard, *Vit. Karol.* = *Vita Karoli imperatoris*, in *Einhard's Life of Charlemagne*. 1915. Ed. H. W. Garrod and R. B. Mowat.
Ekkehard, *Chronicon universale*. 1844. Ed. G. Waitz. MGH. SS. 6, 33–231.
Eusebius, *Chronicorum libri duo*. 1866–1875. Ed. A. Schoene. 2nd ed. 2 vols.
Flat. = *Flateyjarbók* I–III. 1860–1868. Ed. Guðbrandur Vigfússon and C. R. Unger.
Flóamanna saga. 1991. In *Harðar saga*. Ed. Þórhallur Vilmundarson and Bjarni Vilhjálmsson. ÍF 13, 229–327.
Flores temporum. 1879. Ed. O. Holder-Egger. MGH. SS. 24, 228–250.
Fsk = *Fagrskinna*, in *Ágrip af Nóregskonunga sǫgum. Fagrskinna— Nóregs konunga tal*. 1984. Ed. Bjarni Einarsson. ÍF 29.
Fulcher of Chartres, *Hist. Hier.* = *Fulcheri Carnotensis Historia Hierosolymitana*. 1913. Ed H. Hagenmeyer.
Geoffrey of Monmouth, *Historia Regum Britanniae* = *The Historia Regum Britannie of Geoffrey of Monmouth* I–V. 1984–1991. Ed. N. Wright and J. Crick; *The Historia Regum Britanniae of Geoffrey of Monmouth . . . together with a literal translation of the Welsh Manuscript No. LXI of Jesus College Oxford*. 1929. Ed. A. Griscom and R. E. Jones.
Gesta Dagoberti = *Gesta Dagoberti I. Regis Francorum*. 1888. Ed. B. Krusch. MGH. SS. rer. Merov. 2. 326–425.
Gesta Romanorum. 1872. Ed. H. Oesterley.
Giles 1904: see William of Malmesbury.
GND: see William of Jumièges.
GNH = *Gamal Norsk Homiliebok. Cod. AM 619 4°*. 1931. Ed. G. Indrebø; *Gammelnorsk Homiliebog*. 1971. Trans. A. Salvesen, introduction and notes by E. Gunnes.
Hákonar saga Hákonarsonar. 1887. Ed. Guðbrandur Vigfússon. R.S. 88, vol. 2, 1–360.

Hauksbók. 1892–1896. Ed. Finnur Jónsson and Eiríkur Jónsson.
Hemings þáttr Áslákssonar. 1962. Ed. G. Fellows Jensen. E.A., B. 3.
Higden, Ranulph, *Polychronicon* I–IX. 1865–1886. Ed. C. Babington. R.S. 41.
Hist. Norw. = *Historia Norwegiæ.* In *MHN,* 69–124.
Hkr = Snorri Sturluson, *Heimskringla* I–III. 1941–1951. Ed. Bjarni Aðalbjarnarson. ÍF 26–28.
Hkr(Hákgóð) = *Hákonar saga góða.*
Hkr(Hhárf) = *Haralds saga ins hárfagra.*
Hkr(HSig) = *Haralds saga Sigurðarsonar.*
Hkr(Mberf) = *Magnúss saga berfœtts.*
Hkr(Mgóð) = *Magnúss saga góða.*
Hkr(Msona) = *Magnússona saga.*
Hkr(Ólhelg) = *Óláfs saga helga (Haraldssonar).*
Hkr(Ólkyrr) = *Óláfs saga kyrra.*
Hkr(ÓlTrygg) = *Óláfs saga Tryggvasonar.*
Honorius Augustodunensis, *Imago Mundi.* 1983. Ed. V. Flint. Archives d'histoire doctrinale et littéraire du moyen âge 49.
Horace, *Epistulae. Ars poetica.* 1929. Ed. and trans. H. R. Fairclough in *Horace: Satires, Epistles, and Ars Poetica,* 250–440, 450–488.
Horace, *Epodes.* 1927. Ed. and trans. C. E. Bennett in *Horace: The Odes and Epodes,* 359–417.
Hungrvaka. 1938. Ed. Jón Helgason in *Byskupa sǫgur* I, 25–115.
ÍF = Íslenzk fornrit.
Isidore of Seville, *Etym.* = *Isidori Hispalensis episcopi etymologiarum siue originum libri xx.* 1911. Ed. W. M. Lindsay.
Isidore of Seville, *Chronica.* 1894. Ed. Th. Mommsen. MGH, AA. 11.2, 424–488.
Islandske Annaler indtil 1578. 1888. Ed. G. Storm.
Íslendingabók. Landnámabók. 1968. Ed. Jakob Benediktsson. ÍF 1.
Jerome, *Chronicon.* 1956. Ed. R. Helm in *Die Chronik des Hieronymus. Hieronymi Chronicon. Die griechischen christlichen Schriftsteller der ersten drei Jahrhunderte. Eusebius Werke* 7.
Jerome, *Epist.* = *Sancti Eusebii Hieronymi epistulae* I–III. 1910–1918. Ed. I. Hilberg. CSEL 54–56.
John Brompton, *Chron.* = *Chronicon Johannis Bromton Abbatis Jornalensis.* 1652. Ed. R. Twysden. *Historiæ anglicanæ scriptores* X, 725–1284.

John of Salisbury, *Policraticus* = *Ioannis Saresberiensis Policraticus* I–IV. 1993. Ed. K. S. B. Keats-Rohan. CCCM 118.

John of Worcester, *Chronicon* = *The Chronicle of John of Worcester.* 1995–1998. Ed. R. R. Darlington and P. McGurk. 2 vols.

Jómsvíkinga saga. 1969. Ed. Ólafur Halldórsson.

Jordanes, *Getica* = *De origine actibusque Getarum, alias Getica.* 1882. Ed. Th. Mommsen. MGH, AA. 5.1, 53–138; *Iordanis De origine actibusque Getarum.* 1991. Ed. F. Giunta and A. Grillone. Fonti per la storia d'Italia 117; *The Gothic History of Jordanes.* 1915. Trans. C. C. Mierow.

Josephus, *The Jewish war.* 1956–1957. Ed. and trans. H. St J. Thackeray in *Josephus* II–III.

Justin, *Epitoma* = *M. Iuniani Iustini epitoma historiarum philippicarum Pompeii Trogi.* 1972. Ed. O. Seel.

Knýtlinga saga: in *Danakonunga sǫgur*, 91–321.

Kristni saga: in *Hauksbók* 126–149.

Kristnisaga. 1905. Ed. B. Kahle. Altnordische Saga-Bibliothek 11, 1–57.

Landnámabók: see *Íslendingabók. Landnámabók.*

Landulf Sagax, *Historia Romana.* 1912–1913. Ed. A. Crivellucci in *Landolfi Sagacis Historia Romana* I–II. Fonti per la storia d'Italia 49–50.

Langebek J., ed., 1772–1878. *Scriptores rerum Danicarum medii ævi.* 9 vols.

Liber Hist. Franc. = *Liber Historiae Francorum.* 1888. Ed. B. Krusch. MGH. SS. rer. Merov. 2, 215–328.

Liber Pontificalis. 1886–1892. Ed. L. Duchesne. 2 vols; additions and corrections vol. 3. 1957. Ed. C. Vogel.

Liebermann, F., ed., 1879. *Ungedruckte anglo-normannische Geschichtsquellen.*

Livy, *Ab urbe condita.* 1919–1959. Ed. and trans. B. O. Foster et al. in *Livy.* 14 vols.

Lucan, *Bell. civ.* = *De Bello civili.* 1928. Ed. and trans. J. D. Duff in *Lucan.*

Magnúss saga lengri. Magnúss saga skemmri: in *Orkneyinga saga* 1965.

Marcellinus Comes, *Chronicon.* 1894. Ed. T. Mommsen. MGH. AA. 11, 37–108.

Mariu saga. 1871. Ed. C. R. Unger.
Matthew Paris, *Chronica majora.* 1872–1883. Ed. H. R. Luard. 7 vols. R.S. 57.
MGH = Monumenta Germaniae Historica. AA. = Auctores Antiquissimi. SS. = Scriptores. SS. rer. Germ. = Scriptores rerum Germanicarum. SS. rer. Lang. Ital. = Scriptores rerum Langobardicarum et Italicarum. SS. rer. Merov. = Scriptores rerum Merovingicarum.
MgóðHharðr = *Magnúss saga góða ok Haralds harðráða* (in *Msk* 1–286, and *Flat.* III, 249–400).
MHN = *Monumenta Historica Norvegiæ: Latinske kildeskrifter til Norges historie i middelalderen.* 1880. Ed. G. Storm. Rpt 1973.
Mombritius, B., ed., 1910. *Sanctuarium, seu Vitae Sanctorum.* 2 vols.
Msk = *Morkinskinna.* 1932. Ed. Finnur Jónsson. STUAGNL 53.
NgL = *Norges gamle Love indtil 1387.* 1846–1895. Ed. R. Keyser et al.
Njáls saga: see *Brennu-Njáls saga.*
Notker Balbulus, *Gest. Karol.* = *Gesta Karoli Magni imperatoris.* 1959. Ed. Hans F. Haefele in *Notker der Stammler: Taten Kaiser Karls des Grossen.* MGH SS. rer. Germ., N.S. 12.
Oddr Snorrason, *ÓlTrygg* = *Saga Óláfs Tryggvasonar af Oddr Snorrason munk.* 1932. Ed. Finnur Jónsson. (Numbers in brackets refer to the S text, Stock. perg. 4:o nr 18.)
Old English Orosius. 1980. Ed. J. Bately. EETS. SS. 6.
Ólhelg(Leg) = *Olafs saga hins helga. Die 'Legendarische Saga' über Olaf den Heiligen (Hs. Delagard. saml. nr. 8^{11}).* 1982. Ed. A. Heinrichs, D. Jahnsen, E. Radicke, H. Röhn.
Ólhelg(Sep) = [*Separate saga of Óláfr helgi*] *Saga Óláfs konungs hins helga. Den Store Saga om Olav den Hellige* I–II. 1941. Ed. O. A. Johnsen and Jón Helgason.
ÓlTrygg en mesta = *Óláfs saga Tryggvasonar en mesta.* 1958–1961. Ed. Ólafur Halldórsson. E.A., A 1–2.
Orderic Vitalis, *Hist. eccl.* = *The ecclesiastical history of Orderic Vitalis.* 1969–1980. Ed. M. Chibnall. 6 vols.
Origen, *De principiis* = *Origène. Traité des Principes . . . La Version de Rufin.* 1978–1984. Ed. H. Crouzel and M. Simonetti. 5 vols.
Orkneyinga saga. 1965. Ed. Finnbogi Guðmundsson. ÍF 34.

Orosius, *Hist. adv. pag.* = *Pauli Orosii Historiarum adversum paganos libri VII.* 1882. Ed. K. Zangemeister. CSEL 5.

Otto of Freising, *Chronica* = *Ottonis Episcopi Frisingensis Chronica sive Historia de duabus civitatibus.* 1912. Ed. A. Hofmeister. MGH. SS. rer. Germ. in usum scholarum.

Ovid, *Metamorphoses.* 1966–1968. Ed. and trans. F. J. Miller. 2 vols.

Pass. Olav. = *Passio et miracula beati Olavi.* 1881. Ed. F. Metcalfe.

Paul the Deacon, *Hist. Lang.* = *Historia Langobardorum.* 1878. Ed. L. Bethmann and G. Waitz. MGH. SS. rer. Lang. Ital. saec. vi–ix, 12–187.

Paul the Deacon, *Historia Romana.* 1914. Ed. A. Crivellucci. Fonti per la storia d'Italia 51.

Peterborough Chronicle. 1970. Ed. C. Clark in *The Peterborough Chronicle 1070–1154.*

PL = Patrologia Latina (Patrologiæ cursus completus series secunda). 1844–1905. Ed. J.-P. Migne.

Pliny, *Nat. hist.* = *Naturalis historia.* 1940–1962. Ed. and trans. H. Rackham et al. in *Pliny: Natural History.* 10 vols.

Ps. Aurelius Victor, *Epitome* = *Sexti Aurelii Victoris Liber de Caesaribus . . . subsequitur Epitome de Caesaribus.* 1911. Ed. F. Pichlmayr.

Regesta Norvegica. I, *822–1263.* 1989. Ed. E. Gunnes.

Richard of St Victor, *Liber exceptionum.* 1958. Ed. J. Chatillon. Textes philosophiques du Moyen Âge 5.

Roger of Wendover, *Flores Historiarum.* 1841–1844. Ed. H. O. Coxe. 4 vols and appendix.

R.S. = Rolls Series.

Sabatier, P., ed., 1743–1749. *Bibliorum sacrorum latinae versiones antiquae, seu Vetus Italica.* 3 vols.

Sallust, *Catilina.* 1931. Ed. and trans. J. C. Rolfe in *Sallust*, 1–129.

Salvesen, A., trans., 1969. *Norges historie. Theodoricus Munk: Historien om de gamle norske kongene. Historien om Danenes ferd til Jerusalem.*

Salvesen–Gunnes 1971: see *GNH.*

Saxo Grammaticus, *Gesta Danorum.* 1931. Ed. J. Olrik and H. Ræder in *Saxonis Gesta Danorum* I.

Saxo Grammaticus, *History of the Danes.* 1979–1980. Trans. P. Fisher and H. R. Ellis Davidson. 2 vols.

Saxo Grammaticus, *Danorum Regum Heroumque Historia. Books X–XVI. The text of the first edition with translation and commentary in three volumes.* 1980–1981. Ed. E. Christiansen. BAR [British Archaeological Reports] International Series 84, 118 (i–ii).

Schenkl, K. et al., eds., 1888. *Poetae christiani minores* I. CSEL 16.

Scholz, B. W., with B. Rogers, eds, 1970. *Carolingian Chronicles.*

Sedulius Scottus, *Collectaneum Miscellaneum.* 1988. Ed. D. Simpson. CCCM 67.

Series regum Danie: in *SmhDmæ.* I, 157–158.

Sigebert of Gembloux, *Chronica.* 1844. Ed. D. L. C. Bethmann. MGH. SS. 6, 300–374; *Chronica Sigeberti. Continuatio Valcellensis.* Ed. D. L. C. Bethmann. MGH. SS. 6, 458–460.

Silvesters saga. 1877. Ed. C. R. Unger in *Heilagra manna søgur* II, 245–280.

Skard, E., trans., 1932. *Soga um dei gamle norske kongane av Tjodrek munk.*

Skjd. = *Den norsk-islandske Skjaldedigtning.* 1912–1915. Ed. Finnur Jónsson. A I–II, Tekst efter Håndskrifterne; B I–II, Rettet Tekst.

SmhDmæ. = *Scriptores minores historiæ Danicæ medii ævi.* 1917–1922. Ed. M. Cl. Gertz. 2 vols.

Statius, *Thebaid.* 1928. Ed. and trans. J. H. Mozley in *Statius* I, 339 to II, 505.

Stevenson 1854: see William of Malmesbury.

Storm, G., ed., 1880. *Monumenta Historica Norvegiæ.*

Storm, G., ed., 1888: see *Islandske Annaler indtil 1578.*

STUAGNL = Samfund til Udgivelse af Gammel Nordisk Litteratur.

Sven Aggesen, *Brevis Historia Regum Dacie.* 1917–1922. Ed. M. Cl. Gertz. *SmhDmæ.* I, 94–141. Trans. E. Christiansen 1992. *The works of Sven Aggesen.* Viking Society for Northern Research. Text series 9.

Sverris saga = *Sverris saga etter Cod. AM 327 4°.* 1920; rpt 1981. Ed. G. Indrebø.

Theodoricus monachus. *Historia de antiquitate regum Norwagiensium.* In *MHN*, 1–68. A = AM 98 fol. B = Det kongelige bibliotek, Copenhagen, Kalls samling, no. 600. K = ed. princeps, Bernhard Caspar Kirchmann, Amsterdam 1684. L = Staatsbibliothek Preußischer Kulturbesitz, Berlin, Ms. lat. fol.

356. M = Det kongelige bibliotek, Copenhagen, Thotts samling, no. 1541 4to. S = Universitetsbiblioteket, Uppsala, Ms. De la Gardie no. 32.

vet. lat.: see Sabatier 1743–1749.

Vincent of Beauvais, *Speculum Historiale*. In *Speculum Maius sive Quadruplex* I–IV 1624, rpt 1964–1965. Vol. IV.

Vita Faronis = *Vita Faronis episcopi Meldensis*. 1910. Ed. B. Krusch and W. Levison. MGH. SS. rer. Merov. 5, 171–203.

Västgötalagens litterära bilagor. 1941. Ed. I. Lindquist.

Whitby *Vit. Greg.* = *De vita atque virtutibus beati Gregorii papae urbis Romae*. 1968, rpt 1985. Ed and trans. B. Colgrave in *The earliest Life of Gregory the Great. By an anonymous monk of Whitby*.

Widukind, *Res gestae Saxonicae*. 1935. Ed. G. Waitz and K. A. Kehr in *Die Sachsengeschichte des Widukind von Korvei*. 5th ed. by H.-E. Lohmann and P. Hirsch. MGH. SS. rer. Ger. in usum scholarum.

William of Jumièges, *Gesta Normannorum Ducum*. 1992. Ed. E. M. C. van Houts in *The Gesta Normannorum Ducum of William of Jumièges, Orderic Vitalis, and Robert of Torigni*. 2 vols.

William of Malmesbury, *Gesta Regum Anglorum*, vol. I. 1998. Ed. and trans. R. A. B. Mynors, R. M. Thomson and M. Winterbottom. Trans. J. Stevenson 1854 in *The church historians of England* III.1: *The history of the kings of England . . . by William of Malmesbury*. Revision of a translation by John Sharpe 1815. Trans. J. A. Giles 1904 in *William of Malmesbury's Chronicle of the kings of England*.

II. SECONDARY LITERATURE

(Includes editions to which reference is made for commentary rather than text)

Abrams, L. 1995. 'The Anglo-Saxons and the Christianization of Scandinavia', *Anglo-Saxon England* 24 (1995), 213–249.

Anderson, A. R. 1932. *Alexander's Gate, Gog and Magog and the inclosed nations*.

Andersson, T. M. 1979. 'Ari's *Konunga Ævi* and the earliest accounts of Hákon Jarl's death', in *Opuscula* 6. Bibliotheca Arnamagnæana 33, 1–17.

Andersson, T. M. 1985. 'Kings' sagas (Konungasögur)', in Carol Clover and John Lindow, eds, *Old Norse-Icelandic literature. A critical guide.* Islandica 45, 197–238.
Ashdown, M. 1959. 'An Icelandic account of the survival of Harold Godwinson', in P. Clemoes, ed., *The Anglo-Saxons*, 122–136.
Baetke, W. 1951. 'Das Svoldr-Problem', *Berichte über die Verhandlungen der sächsischen Akademie der Wissenschaften zu Leipzig.* Philol.-hist. Klasse, Bd. 98, Heft 6, 59–135.
Bagemihl, G. 1913. *Otto II und seine Zeit im Lichte mittelalterlicher Geschichtsauffassung.*
Bagge, S. 1989. 'Theodoricus Monachus—clerical historiography in twelfth-century Norway', *Scandinavian Journal of History* 14, 113–133.
Bately, J. 1979. 'World history in the Anglo-Saxon Chronicle: its sources and its separateness from the Old English Orosius', *Anglo-Saxon England* 8, 177–194.
Beyschlag, S. 1950. *Konungasögur.* Bibliotheca Arnamagnæana 8.
BHL = *Bibliotheca Hagiographia Latina Antiquae et Mediae Aetatis.* 1898–1901. Ed. Socii Bollandiani (*Subsidia Hagiographica* 6), 2 vols; *Supplementum* 1911 (*Subsidia Hagiographica* 12); *Novum Supplementum* 1986 (*Subsidia Hagiographica* 70).
Bjarni Aðalbjarnarson 1937. *Om de norske kongers sagaer.* Skrifter utg. av Det Norske Videnskaps-Akademi i Oslo. II. Hist.-Filos. Klasse. 1936, no. 4.
Bjarni Aðalbjarnarson 1941–1951: see *Hkr.*
Bjarni Einarsson 1984: see *Ágrip.*
Bjarni Guðnason 1977. 'Theodoricus og íslenskir sagnaritarar', in Einar G. Pétursson and Jónas Kristjánsson, eds, *Sjötíu ritgerðir helgaðar Jakobi Benediktssyni*, 107–120.
Bjarni Guðnason 1982: see *Danakonunga sǫgur.*
Blatt, F. 1957. *Saxonis Gesta Danorum* II: *Index verborum.*
Blom, G. A. 1956. *Trondheim bys historie* I: *St. Olavs by, ca. 1000–1537.*
Blöndal, Sigfús 1978. *The Varangians of Byzantium.* Trans. and rev. B. S. Benedikz.
Brewer, E. C. 1884. *A dictionary of miracles.*
Buchberger, M. et al. 1957–1968. *Lexikon für Theologie und Kirche.* 2. Aufl.

Bugge, A. 1914. *Smaa bidrag til Norges historie paa 1000-tallet.*
Bury, J. B. 1923. *History of the later Roman empire from the death of Theodosius I to the death of Justinian.* 2 vols. Rpt 1958.
Campbell, A., ed., 1949. *Encomium Emmae Reginae.*
Charles, B. G. 1934. *Old Norse Relations with Wales.*
Chatillon, J. 1948. 'Le contenu, l'authenticité et la doute du "Liber Exceptionum" et des "Sermones centum" de Richard de Saint Victor', *Revue de moyen âge latin* 4, 23–52, 343–366.
Christiansen 1980–1981: see Saxo Grammaticus.
Christiansen 1992: see Sven Aggesen.
Coens, M. 1920. 'Les Vierges martyres de Cologne', *Analecta Bollandiana* 48, 89–110.
Cross, F. L., and E. A. Livingstone 1983. *The Oxford Dictionary of the Christian Church.* 2nd ed., 4th impression.
Cross, J. E. 1962. 'Aspects of microcosm and macrocosm in Old English literature', *Comparative Literature* 14, 1–22.
Crumlin-Pedersen, O. and E. Christensen 1970. 'Skibstyper', *KLNM* 15, 482–493.
Daae, L. 1895. 'Om Historieskriveren "Theodoricus monachus" og om Biskop Thore af Hamar', *[Norsk] Historisk Tidsskrift.* 3. rk. III, 397–411.
Demidoff, L. 1978–1979. 'The death of Sven Forkbeard—in reality and later tradition', *Mediaeval Scandinavia* 11, 30–47.
Dillmann, F.-X. 1993. 'Seiður og shamanismi í Íslendingasögum,' *Skáldskaparmál* 2, 20–33.
Dittrich, Marie-Luise 1966. *Die 'Eneide' Heinrichs von Veldeke.*
DMLBS = *Dictionary of medieval Latin from British sources.* I–V (A–L) 1975–1997. Ed. R. E. Latham, D. R. Howlett et al.
Dodwell, C. R. 1982. *Anglo-Saxon Art. A new perspective.*
Döllinger, Johann J. Ign. von 1863. *Die Papst-Fabeln des Mittelalters. Ein Beitrag zur Kirchengeschichte.* Trans. A. Plummer 1871 in *Fables respecting the Popes of the Middle Ages.*
Driscoll 1995: see *Ágrip.*
Du Cange, C. Du Fresne 1883–1887. *Glossarium Mediae et Infimae Latinitatis.* Rev. G. A. L. Henschel and L. Favre. 10 vols.
Dunbar, J. T. 1962. *History of Highland Dress.*
Dunbar, J. T. 1981. *The Costume of Scotland.*
Dunn, T. F. 1934. *The Facetiae of the Mensa Philosophica.* Washington University Studies. New series. Language and Literature 5.

Einar Arnórsson 1950. *Árnesþing á landnáms- og söguöld.*
Elder, J. P. 1947. 'Did Remigius of Auxerre comment on Bede's *De schematibus et tropis?*', *Mediaeval Studies* 9, 141–150.
Ellehøj, S. 1958. 'The location of the fall of Olaf Tryggvason', *Árbok hins íslenzka fornleifafélags*, Fylgirit, 68–73.
Ellehøj, S. 1965. *Studier over den ældste norrøne historieskrivning.* Bibliotheca Arnamagnæana 26.
Falk, H. 1912. 'Altnordisches Seewesen', *Wörter und Sachen* 4, 1–122.
Fidjestøl, B. 1987. 'Legenda om Tore Hund', in J. R. Hagland, J. T. Faarlund and J. Rønhovd, eds, *Festskrift til Alfred Jakobsen*, 38–51. Rpt 1997, 'The legend of Þórir hundr', in B. Fidjestøl, *Selected Papers*. Ed. O. E. Haugen and E. Mundal. Trans. P. Foote, 168–183.
Fidjestøl, B. 1997a. 'Tre norrøne tilnamn. Þambaskelmir, hárfagri og hornklofi', *Nordica Bergensia* 14, 6–14.
Finnbogi Guðmundsson 1965: see *Orkneyinga saga.*
Finnur Jónsson 1912. *Lægekunsten i den Oldnordiske Oldtid.*
Finnur Jónsson 1920–1924. *Den Oldnorske og Oldislandske Litteraturs Historie.* I–III. 2nd ed.
Finnur Jónsson 1928. 'Ágrip', *Aarbøger for Nordisk Oldkyndighed og Historie.* 3. R. 18, 261–317.
Finnur Jónsson, ed., 1929. *Ágrip af Nóregs konunga sǫgum.* Altnordische Saga-Bibliothek 18.
Fisher-Davidson 1979–1980: see *Saxo Grammaticus.*
Foote, P. G. and D. M. Wilson 1970. *The Viking Achievement.*
Foote, P. G. 1988. 'Observations on Orkneyinga saga', in B. Crawford, ed., *St Magnus Cathedral and Orkney's twelfth-century renaissance*, 192–207.
Frank, R. 1978. *Old Norse court poetry: the* dróttkvætt *stanza.* Islandica 42.
Frank, T. 1909. 'Some classical quotations from the Middle Ages', *Classical Philology* 4, 82–83.
Freeman, E. A. 1867–1879. *The History of the Norman Conquest of England.* 6 vols.
Friedman, J. B. 1981. *The Monstrous Races in Medieval Art and Thought.*
Fritzner, J. 1886–1896. *Ordbog over det gamle norske Sprog.* I–III. 1972. IV. *Rettelser og Tilleg.* Ed. F. Hødnebø.
Förstemann, E. 1900. *Altdeutsches Namenbuch. Erster Band: Personennamen.* 2nd ed.

Gade, K. E. 1995a. 'Einarr Þambarskelfir's last shot', *Scandinavian Studies* 67, 153–161.
Gade, K. E. 1995b. 'Einarr Þambarskelfir, Again'. *Scandinavian Studies* 67, 547–550.
Giunta–Grillone 1991: see Jordanes, *Getica*.
Gjerløw, L. 1967. 'Olav den hellige. Liturgi', *KLNM* 12, 561–567.
Gjessing, A. 1873–1876. *Undersøgelse af Kongesagaens Fremvæxt*. I–II.
Gjessing, A. 1877. *Jómsvíkinga saga i Latinsk oversættelse af Arngrim Jonsson*.
Glob, P. V. 1969. *The Bog People*. Trans. R. Bruce-Mitford.
Goffart, W. 1988. *The Narrators of Barbarian History (A.D. 550–800)*.
Goy, Rudolf. 1976. *Die Überlieferung der Werke Hugos von St. Viktor*. Monographien zur Geschichte des Mittelalters Bd. 14.
Grässe–Benedict–Plechl 1972 = J. G. T. Grässe, F. Benedict, H. Plechl, S.-C. Plechl. *Orbis Latinus: Lexikon lateinischer geographischer Namen des Mittelalters und der Neuzeit*. 3 vols.
Graf, A. 1923. *Roma nella memoria e nelle immaginazioni del medio evo*.
Green, W. M. 1943. 'Hugo of St Victor: *De tribus maximis circumstantiis gestorum*', *Speculum* 18, 484–493.
Grön, F. 1908. *Altnordische Heilkunde*, extract of *Janus* 13.
Grotefend, H. 1891. *Zeitrechnung des deutschen Mittelalters und der Neuzeit*. I–II.
Guenée, B. 1980. *Histoire et culture historique dans l'Occident médiéval*.
Gunnes, E. 1973. 'Om hvordan Passio Olavi ble til', *Maal og Minne*, 1–11.
Hamre, L. 1960. 'Gudsdom: Norge', *KLNM* 5, 551–553.
Hanssen, J. S. Th. 1945. 'Observations on Theodoricus Monachus and his History of the Old Norwegian Kings, from the end of the xii. sec.', *Symbolae Osloenses* 24, 164–180.
Hanssen, J. S. Th. 1949. 'Theodoricus monachus and European literature', *Symbolae Osloenses* 27, 70–127.
Ho Peng Yoke. 1962. 'Ancient and mediaeval observations of comets and novae in Chinese sources', *Vistas in astronomy* 5, 127–225.

Hoffmann, E. 1975. *Die heiligen Könige bei den Angelsachsen und skandinavischen Völkern.*
Holtsmark, A. 1937. 'Sankt Olavs liv og mirakler', in *Festskrift til Francis Bull.* Rpt in A. Holtsmark 1956. *Studier i norrøn diktning*, 15–24.
Holtsmark, A. 1961. 'Historia de antiquitate regum Norvagiensium', *KLNM* 6, 583–585.
Holtzmann, W. 1938. 'Krone und Kirche in Norwegen im 12. Jahrhundert (Englische Analekten III)', *Deutsches Archiv für Geschichte des Mittelalters* 2, 341–400.
Hoops, J. 1911–1919. *Reallexikon der germanischen Altertumskunde.* I–IV.
van Houts 1992: see William of Jumièges.
Jasinski, M. 1995. 'Kong Øysteins havn på Agdenes', *Viking* 58, 73–105.
Johnsen, O. A. 1916. *Olav Haraldssons ungdom indtil slaget ved Nesjar.* Skrifter utgitt av Videnskapsselskapet i Kristiania. Hist.-Filos. Klasse, no. 2.
Johnsen, A. O. 1939. *Om Theodoricus og hans Historia de antiquitate regum Norwagiensium.* Avhandlinger utg. av Det Norske Videnskaps-Akademi i Oslo. II. Hist.-Filos. Klasse, no. 3.
Jón Helgason 1925. *Islands kirke fra dens grundlæggelse til reformationen. En historisk fremstilling.*
Jón Hnefill Aðalsteinsson 1978. *Under the cloak.* Acta universitatis Upsaliensis. Studia ethnologica Upsaliensia 4.
Jón Jóhannesson 1956. *Íslendinga saga* I.
Jón Jóhannesson 1974. *A History of the Old Icelandic Commonwealth.* Trans. Haraldur Bessason.
Kazhdan, A. P. et al. 1991. *The Oxford dictionary of Byzantium.* 3 vols.
Keynes, Simon. 1992. 'The comet in the Eadwine Psalter', in M. Gibson, T. A. Heslop, R. W. Pfaff, eds, *The Eadwine Psalter: Text, image, and monastic culture in twelfth-century Canterbury*, 157–164.
Kirchmann 1684 = Theodoricus monachus K.
KLNM = *Kulturhistorisk Leksikon for Nordisk Middelalder.* 1956–1978. 22 vols.

Laehr, G. 1926. *Die konstantinische Schenkung in der abendländischen Literatur des Mittelalters bis zur Mitte des 14. Jahrhunderts.* Historische Studien. Heft 116.
Lampe, G. W. H. 1961. *A patristic Greek lexicon.*
Lampe, G. W. H. 1969. *The Cambridge history of the Bible.*
Lange, Chr. C. A. 1856. *De Norske Klostres Historie.* 2nd ed.
Lange, G. 1989. *Die Anfänge der isländisch-norwegischen Geschichtsschreibung.* Studia Islandica/Íslensk fræði 47.
Latham 1965. *Revised medieval Latin word-list from British and Irish sources.*
Lehmann, P. 1937. *Skandinaviens Anteil an der lateinischen Literatur und Wissenschaft des Mittelalters.* Sitzungsberichte der Bayerischen Akademie der Wissenschaften, Philos.-hist. Abteilung, Jahrg. 1936, Heft 2 and Jahrg. 1937, Heft 7. Rpt in P. Lehmann 1959–1962. *Erforschung des Mittelalters*, V, 275–300, 331–429.
Lemarignier, J. F. 1945. *Recherches sur l'hommage en marche et les frontiers féodales.*
Levison, W. 1927. 'Das Werden der Ursula-Legende', *Bonner Jahrbücher* 132, 1–164.
Lewis, C. T., and C. Short. 1879. *A Latin Dictionary.*
Libermann, A. 1996. 'Gone with the wind. More thoughts on medieval farting', *Scandinavian Studies* 68, 98–104.
Liddell, H. G., and R. Scott 1925–1940. *A Greek-English Lexicon.* 9th ed., rev. H. S. Jones, with supplement 1968.
Lind, E. H. 1920–1921. *Norsk-isländska personbinamn från medeltiden.*
Lind, E. H. 1931. *Norsk-isländska dopnamn ock fingerade namn från medeltiden. Supplementband.*
Lutz, Cora E. 1962–1965. *Remigii Autissiodorensis commentum in Martianum Capellam.* 2 vols.
Louis-Jensen, J. 1977. *Kongesagastudier: Kompilationen Hulda–Hrokkinskinna.* Bibliotheca Arnamagnæana 32.
Maenchen-Helfen, O. J. 1973. *The world of the Huns.* Ed. M. Knight.
Manitius, M. 1911–1931. *Geschichte der lateinischen Literatur des Mittelalters.* 3 vols.
Maurer, K. 1855–1856. *Die Bekehrung des norwegischen Stammes zum Christenthume.* 2 vols.
McClintock, H. F. 1949. *Old Highland Dress and Tartans.*

McClintock, H. F. 1950. *Old Irish and Highland Dress and that of the Isle of Man.* 2nd ed.

McDougall, I. 1992. 'The third instrument of medicine: Some accounts of surgery in medieval Iceland', in S. Campbell, B. Hall and D. Klausner, eds, *Health, disease and healing in medieval culture,* 57–83.

Mierow 1915: see Jordanes.

Moberg, O. 1940. 'Olav Haraldssons hemkomst: En historiografisk undersökning', *[Norsk] Historisk Tidsskrift* 32, 545–575.

Momigliano, A. 1961–1962. 'Historiography on written tradition and historiography on oral tradition', *Atti della Accademia delle Scienze di Torino* 96, 1–12. Rpt in A. Momigliano, *Studies in historiography* 1966, 211–220.

Musset, L. 1957–1958. 'Actes inédits du XIe siècle, iii: les plus anciennes chartes normandes de l'abbaye de Bourgueil', *Bulletin de la société des antiquaires de Normandie* 54, 15–54.

Møller-Christensen, V. 1944. *Middelalderens lægekunst i Danmark.*

Møller-Christensen, V. 1961. 'Halssygdomme', *KLNM* 6, 72–74.

NBL = Norsk Biografisk Leksikon. 1923–1983. Ed. E. Bull et al. 19 vols.

Niermeyer, J. F. 1976. *Mediae Latinitatis lexicon minus.*

Nordal, Sigurður 1914. *Om Olaf den helliges saga.*

Nordal, Sigurður 1941. 'Gunnhildur konungamóðir', *Samtíð og saga* 1, 135–155.

Noreen, A. 1923. *Altisländische und altnorwegische Grammatik.* 4th ed.

OED = The Oxford English Dictionary 1884–1928. Ed. J. A. H. Murray et al. 2nd ed. 1989. Ed. J. A. Simpson and E. S. C. Weiner.

Ólafia Einarsdóttir 1964. *Studier i kronologisk metode i tidlig islandsk historieskrivning.*

Ólafur Halldórsson 1958–1961: see *ÓlTrygg en mesta.*

Ólafur Halldórsson 1984. 'Mostur og Sæla', *Gripla* 6, 101–112.

OLD = Oxford Latin Dictionary 1968–1982. Ed. P. G. W. Glare et al.

Olsen, Magnus 1928. *Farms and fanes of ancient Norway.* Instituttet for sammenlignende kulturforskning. Serie A: Forelesninger 9.

Paasche, F. 1934. 'Über Rom und das Nachleben der Antike im norwegischen und isländischen Schrifttum des Hochmittelalters', *Symbolae Osloenses* 13, 114–145.
Paff, W. J. 1959. *The geographical and ethnic names in the Þiðriks saga: A study in Germanic heroic legend.*
Page, R. I. 1981. 'The audience of Beowulf and the Vikings', in C. Chase, ed., *The dating of Beowulf*, 113–122.
Paris, Gaston 1865. *Histoire poétique de Charlemagne.*
Pease 1920–1923: see Cicero, *De Divinatione.*
Perkins, R. 1985. 'Christian elements in Flóamanna saga', *The Sixth International Saga Conference 28.7–2.8, 1985. Workshop papers.* II, 793–811.
Perkins, R. 1989. 'Objects and oral tradition in medieval Iceland', in R. McTurk and A. Wawn, eds, *Úr dölum til dala: Guðbrandur Vigfússon centenary essays*, 239–266.
Petersen, C. S. 1938. *Stenalder, Bronzealder, Jernalder. Bidrag til nordisk arkæologis literærhistorie 1776–1865.*
Pollock, F. 1890. 'The King's Peace', in *Oxford lectures and other discourses*, 65–90.
Pollock, F. and F. W. Maitland 1898. *The History of English Law before the time of Edward I.* I–II. 2nd ed. rev. 1968.
Price, Neil. 2002. *The Viking Way: religion and war in late Iron Age Scandinavia.*
Prinz–Schneider 1967– = O. Prinz and J. Schneider. *Mittellateinisches Wörterbuch bis zum ausgehenden 13. Jahrhundert.*
Pritsak, O. 1981. *The Origin of Rus'.* I. *Old Scandinavian Sources other than the Sagas.*
Reynolds, L. D. 1983. 'Eutropius', in L. D. Reynolds et al. *Texts and Transmission. A survey of the Latin classics*, 159–162.
Riant, P. 1865. *Expéditions et pèlerinages des Scandinaves en Terre Sainte au temps des croisades.*
Richter, H. 1938. *Englische Geschichtschreiber des 12. Jahrhunderts.*
Rygh, Oluf. 1897–1924. *Norske Gaardnavne.*
Saltnessand, E. 1968. 'Hva betyr tilnavnet Tambarskjelve?' *[Norsk] Historisk Tidskrift* 47, 143–148.
Salvesen 1969: see Primary Sources.
Sayers, W. 1995. 'The honor of Guðlaugr Snorrason and Einarr Þambarskelfir. A reply', *Scandinavian Studies* 67, 536–547.

Schade, O. 1854. *Die Sage von der heiligen Ursula und den elftausend Jungfrauen.*

Schilling, R. 1977. *Pline l'ancien: Histoire Naturelle Livre VII.*

Schulz, M. 1909. *Die Lehre von der historischen Methode bei den Geschichtschreibern des Mittelalters (vi.–xiii. Jahrhundert).* Abhandl. z. Mittl. u. Neueren Geschichte 13.

Schönfeld, M. 1965. *Wörterbuch der altgermanischen Personen- und Völkernamen.* 2nd ed.

Schøning, G. 1910. *Reise . . . gennem en deel af Norge i de aar 1773, 1774, 1775.* 2 vols.

Seeberg, A. 1978–1981. 'Five kings', *Saga-Book* 20, 106–113.

Shetelig–Falk 1937 = H. Shetelig and H. Falk. *Scandinavian Archaeology.* Trans. E. V. Gordon.

Skard, E. 1930. *Målet i Historia Norwegiae.* Skrifter utgitt av Det Norske Videnskaps-Akademi i Oslo. II. Hist.-Filos. Klasse, no. 5.

Skard, E. 1935. 'Kirchliche Olavus tradition bei Theodoricus monachus', *Symbolae Osloenses* 14, 119–125.

Skard, E. 1941. Review of Lehmann 1937 and Johnsen 1939, *[Norsk] historisk tidsskrift* 32, 267–277.

Skånland, V. 1957. 'Einige Bemerkungen zu der *Historia de profectione Danorum in Hierosolymam*', *Symbolae Osloenses* 33, 37–155.

Skånland, V. 1966. 'The Year of King Harald Fairhair's Access to the Throne according to Theodoricus Monachus', *Symbolae Osloenses* 41, 125–128.

Smalley, B. 1983. *The study of the Bible in the Middle Ages.* 3rd ed.

Steenstrup, J. C. H. R. 1876–1882. *Normannerne.* I–IV.

Stefán Karlsson 1977. 'Ættbogi Noregskonunga', in Einar G. Pétursson and Jónas Kristjánsson, eds, *Sjötíu ritgerðir helgaðar Jakobi Benediktssyni*, 677–704.

Stenton, F. M. 1971. *Anglo-Saxon England.* 3rd ed.

Stephenson, F. R. and C. B. F. Walker 1985. *Halley's comet in history.*

Storm, G. 1873. *Snorre Sturlassöns Historieskrivning, en kritisk Undersögelse.*

Storm, G. 1880 = *MHN*; 1888 = *Islandske Annaler indtil 1578.*

Ström, F. 1942. *On the Sacral Origin of the Germanic Death Penalties.* Kungliga Vitterhets Historie och Antikvitets Akademiens Handlingar 52.

Strömbäck, D. 1935. *Sejd*. Nordiske texter och undersökningar 5.
Strömbäck, D. 1970. 'Sejd', *KLNM* 15, 76–79.
Strömbäck, D. 1975. *The Conversion of Iceland: A Survey*. Trans. P. Foote.
Suhm, P. F. 1783 = Langebek 1772–1878, vol. V.
Sveinbjörn Rafnsson 1976. 'Aðferðir og viðhorf í Landnámurannsóknum', *Skírnir* 150, 213–238.
Sverrir Tómasson 1988. *Formálar íslenskra sagnaritara á miðöldum*. Stofnun Árna Magnússonar á Íslandi. Rit 33.
Taranger, A. 1890. *Den angelsaksiske Kirkes Indflydelse paa den norske*.
Tate, G. S. 1978–1979. 'The Cross as Ladder: *Geisli* 15–16 and *Líknarbraut* 34', *Mediaeval Scandinavia* 11, 258–264.
Thompson, E. A. 1948. *A history of Attila and the Huns*.
TLL = *Thesaurus Linguae Latinae*. 1900– . 10 vols: A–pro.1.
Tout, Mrs Thomas F. 1902. 'The legend of St Ursula and the eleven thousand virgins', in T. F. Tout and J. Tait, eds, *Historical essays*, 17–56.
Trevor-Roper, Hugh. 1983. 'The Invention of Tradition: The Highland Tradition of Scotland', in Eric Hobsbawn and Terence Ranger, eds, *The Invention of Tradition*, 15–41.
Tristram, H. L. C. 1985. *Sex aetates mundi. Die Weltzeitalter bei den Angelsachsen und den Iren. Untersuchungen und Texte*.
Tubach, Frederic C. 1969. *Index Exemplorum. A handbook of medieval religious tales*. Folklore Fellows Communications no. 204.
Turville-Petre, E. O. G. 1967. *Origins of Icelandic Literature*.
Turville-Petre, E. O. G. 1976. *Scaldic Poetry*.
Ulset, T. 1983. *Det genetiske forholdet mellom Ágrip, Historia Norwegiæ og Historia de antiquitate regum Norwagiensium*.
Vandvik, E. 1955. 'Donatio Constantini and early Norwegian church policy', *Symbolae Osloenses* 33, 131–137.
Vaughan, R. 1958. *Matthew Paris*. Rpt 1979.
de Vries, J. 1956–1957. *Altgermanische Religionsgeschichte*. 2nd ed. 2 vols.
Walther, H. 1963–1986. *Proverbia sententiaeque latinitatis medii aevi. Lateinische Sprichwörter und Sentenzen des Mittelalters in alphabetischer Anordnung*. 9 vols.

Walther, H. 1969. *Initia carminum ac versuum medii aevi posterioris latinorum. Alphabetisches Verzeichnis der Versanfänge mittellateinischer Dichtungen.* 2. Aufl.

Weibull, L. 1911. *Kritiska undersökningar i Nordens historia omkring år 1000.*

Whaley, D. 1987. 'The Miracles of St Olaf in Snorri Sturluson's Heimskringla', in J. Knirk, ed., *Proceedings of the Tenth Viking Congress. Larkollen, Norway, 1985*, 325–342.

Zeuss, K. 1837. *Die Deutschen und die Nachbarstämme.*

Þórhallur Vilmundarson 1991: see *Flóamanna saga*.

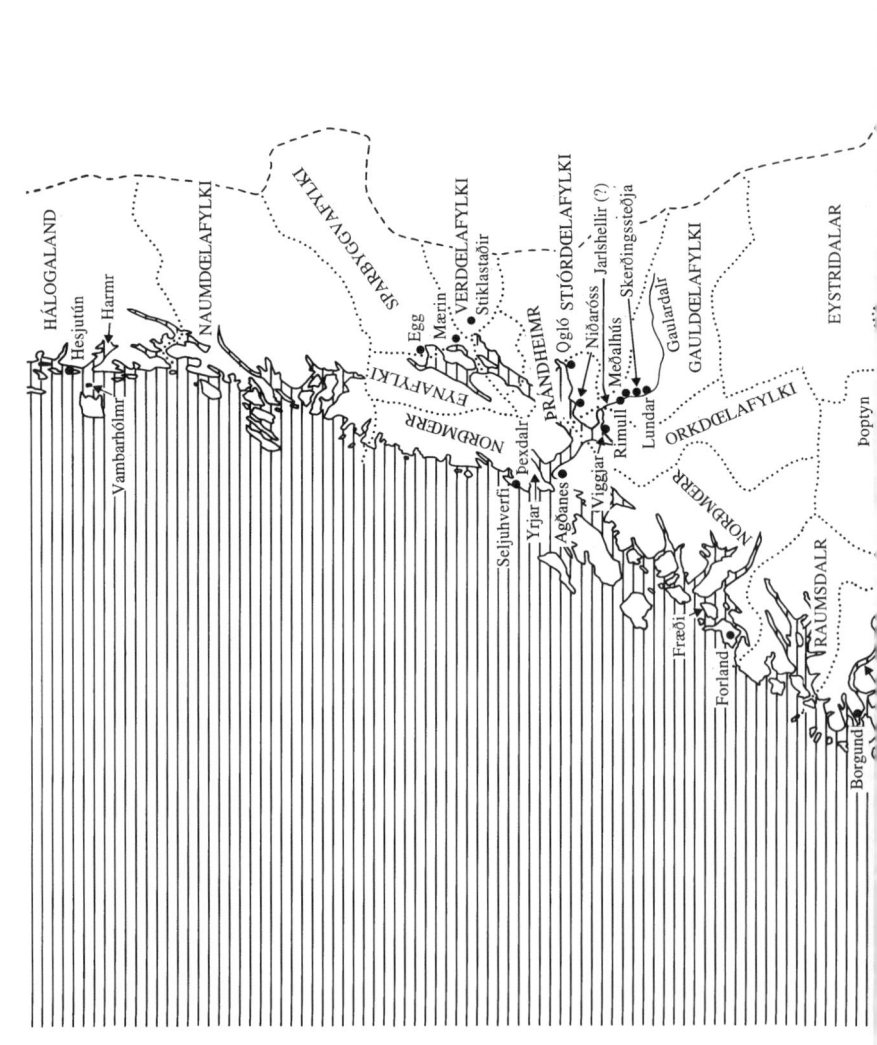

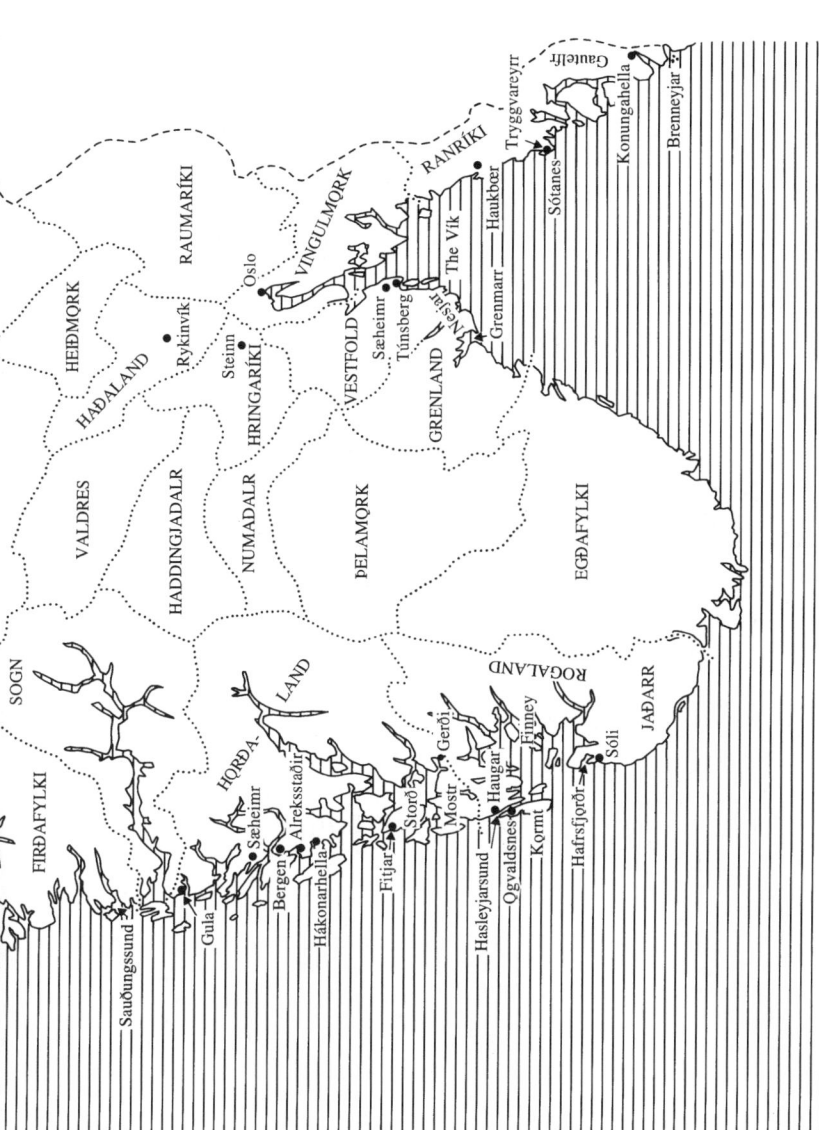

Central and South Norway

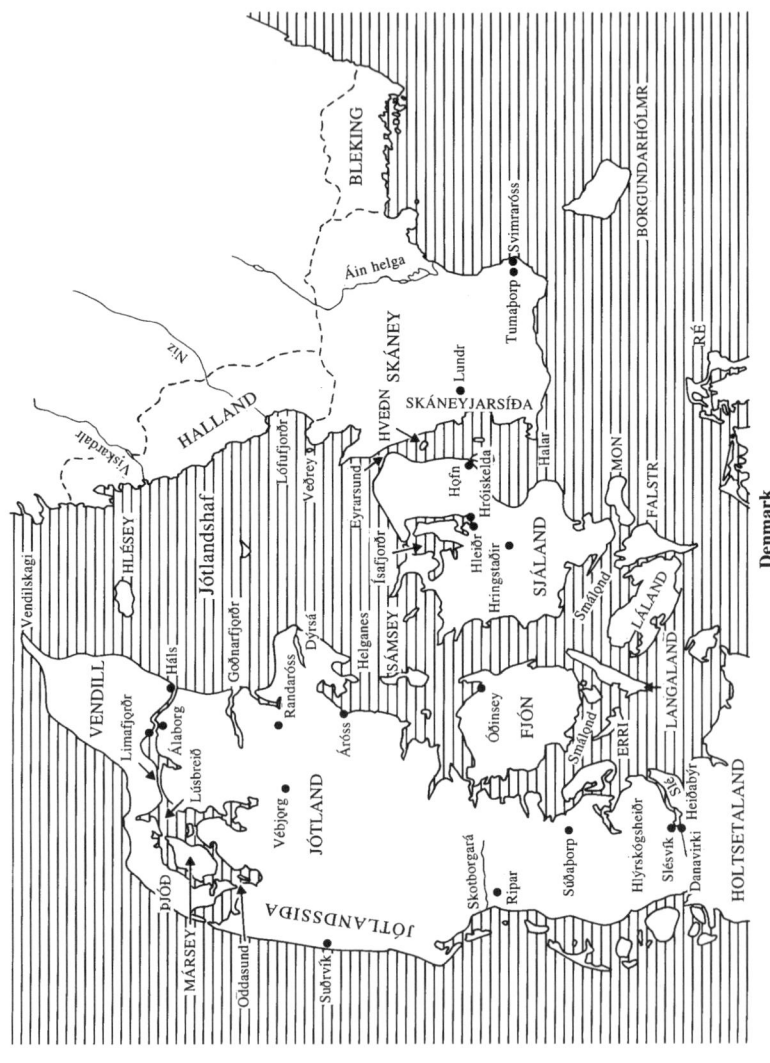

Denmark

INDEXES

Authors mentioned or quoted in the *Historia* are listed in Index 3. Abbreviations used are: abp = archbishop; b. = brother; bp = bishop; d. = daughter; D = Danish; E = English; Emp. = emperor; f. = father; J = jarl, earl; K = king; m. = mother; N = Norwegian; O = Orkney; Q = queen; R = Russian; s. = son; S = Swedish; w. = wife. References are to chapter and line; t. = chapter title.

1. PERSONS

(Appellations of the Almighty and Christ are not recorded)

Abraham 19.54
Absalom 26.6
Adam 20.32
Æthelred, EK 15.2, 5
Æthelstan, EK 2.5, 10; 4.1
Alexander the Great 17.28
Álfífa, m. of Sveinn, s. of Knútr Sveinsson 'the mighty' 21.5
Áslákr fitjaskalli 16.42
Ásta, m. of St Óláfr 13.12; 15.51
Ástríðr, d. of SK Óláfr and w. of St Óláfr 16.22, 26
Ástríðr, d. of DK Sveinn, m. of Sveinn, s. of Úlfr 24.8
Ástríðr, m. of Óláfr Tryggvason 7.24
Ástríðr, sister of Óláfr Tryggvason 13.4
Attila, Hun K, 17.38
Augustus Caesar 32.39–48
Baldwin, K (of Jerusalem) 33.14
Benedict, St 31.32
Bergljót, d. of Hákon Sigurðarson 15.61
Bernard, E abbot 7.13
Bjǫrn, s. of Haraldr Fair-hair 13.14–15
Bjǫrn, standard-bearer of St Óláfr 19.69
Brúsi Sigurðarson, OJ 18.41
Carloman, b. of Charles the Great 23.t., 3–5; his sons and widow 23.5–7
Charles the Great, Emp. 23.t., 1–7, 11–44, 50, 54–60; 30.t., 16–65
Chosroes, Persian K 26.t., 35–36, 64–96; his sons 26.84–85
Constantine the Great, Emp. 13.36–39; 23.51
Constantius, Emp. 13.36
Dagr (Eilífsson), f. of Gregorius 31.47
Dagr Hringsson 18.36; 19.77–80
Domitian, Emp. 26.97–98, 106, 112–114
Egill (Áskelsson) 31.11
Einarr þambaskelmir 15.59–62; 21.10; 25.24–29, 34–39; 27.14; his son (Eindriði) 25.38
Eiríkr, NJ, s. of Hákon Sigurðarson 14.3, 20–48; 16.1
Eiríkr, NK, called 'brothers' bane', s. of Haraldr Fair-hair, 2.t., 1–3, 7, 9–12; 4.15
Erlendr (Þorfinnsson), OJ 31.43
Erlingr Skjálgsson 13.4; 16.36–42
Eutropia, St 17.42
Evander, f. of Pallas 18.109, 121
Eysteinn (Erlendsson), abp Prol. 4, 49–54
Eysteinn (meyla, s. of Eysteinn, s. of Magnús berfœttr) 31.49
Eysteinn, NK, s. of Magnús berfœttr 32.14, 22–25, 27–38; 33.18
Finnr Árnason, NJ 18.37; 19.13, 25
Flóki, voyager to Iceland 3.27
Garðarr, voyager to Iceland 3.26
Gizurr of Skálaholt 12.13, 19, 24–26
Gormr Haraldsson, DK 4.22
Gregorius Dagsson 31.47
Grímkell, bp 20.38; 27.13
Guðrøðr sýr, s. of Bjǫrn, s. of Haraldr Fair-hair 13.12

Guðrøðr, s. of Eiríkr and Gunnhildr 5.7; 13.5
Gundabunda, Persian commander 26.70
Gunnhildr, NQ, w. of Eiríkr, s. of Haraldr Fair-hair 2.7; 4.14, 18, 29, 32; 5.8; 6.t., 1–4, 10–19
Hákon, NJ, s. of Eiríkr, s. of Hákon Sigurðarson 14.42, 49; 15.23, 34–42; 16.32, 57, 60–65; 18.2; 20.55
Hákon, NK, s. of Haraldr Fair-hair and foster-son of Æthelstan 2.4, 8, 12; 4.t., 1–16
Hákon, NK, s. of Magnús, s. of Haraldr Sigurðarson 29.7; 30.3–8; 31.1–2
Hákon Sigurðarson, NJ, called 'the evil' 4.26–30; 5.t., 1–9; 6.t., 1–5, 7–9, 20–24; 7.t., 1, 17–37; 10.t., 7–10, 25–34; 11.18; 14.3; 20.49
Halfdan the Black, f. of Haraldr Fair-hair 1.2
Hallr of Síða 12.12
Haraldr Fair-hair, NK Prol. 19, 39; 1.t., 1–4; 2.1, 3; 3.1, 17; 4.1, 35; 13.15; 29.21
Haraldr gráfeldr, NK, s. of Eiríkr, s. of Haraldr Fair-hair 4.16, 24–28; his brothers 4.17, 28–29
Haraldr Gormsson, DK 4.21–25; 5.2–6, 9–12; 6.8–14, 17–18, 23–24, 26
Haraldr (Knútsson), nephew of Haraldr Gormsson 4.20
Haraldr, s. of Guðrøðr sýr and f. of St Óláfr 13.13
Haraldr, NK, s. of Magnús berfœttr 34.t., 1–9
Haraldr Sigurðarson, NK, half-b. of St Óláfr 18.35; 25.t., 9–43; 27.t., 1–17, 33; 28.t., 1–15, 23–32, 38–47; 29.1, 17; 30.11, 12–14
Harold, EK 28.10, 15–19, 31
Helena, Empress 13.37; 23.51
Hemming, DK 30.39–41, 53–55
Heraclius, governor of Africa 26.57
Heraclius, Emp. 26.57–64, 88
Hjalti of Þjórsárdalr 12.17, 19, 24–26
Hjǫrleifr, b.-in-law of Ingólfr 3.15
Hringr Dagsson 18.36
Hugh Capet, Duke 13.24
Hugh, Earl of Cornwall 31.41
Hyrningr, b.-in-law of Óláfr Tryggvason 13.7
Hǫrðaknútr, DK, s. of Knútr Sveinsson 'the mighty' 22.10, 12–22; 24.2–3 (Knútr)
Ingi Steinkelsson, SK 31.25–28
Ingigerðr, d. of SK Óláfr and w. of RK Jaroslav 16.24, 49; 18.18; 21.15, 17–21
Ingólfr, first settler of Iceland 3.13–18, 24
Ísleifr, bp in Iceland, s. of Gizurr 12.14
Jaroslav, RK 16.49, 52; 18.18; 21.14, 16
Jósteinn, uncle of Óláfr Tryggvason 7.22–37; 8.2; 10.8–11
Jovian, Emp. 8.12–16, 38, 41–46
Julian, Emp. 8.16–36, 40
Julius Caesar 18.58–60; 23.29
Kálfr Árnason 16.36; 18.38; 19.11, 13; 21.11
Karkr, slave of Hákon Sigurðarson 10.28–34
Karlshǫfuð, uncle of Óláfr Tryggvason 7.22–37; 8.2; 10.8–11
Knútr = Hǫrðaknútr 24.2–3
Knútr Sveinsson, EK and DK, 'the mighty' (the Great) 15.4; 16.29–35, 43, 55–60; 18.1–3, 12; 20.51, 54; 22.4, 11; 24.9
Laurence, St 31.33–34
Liutprand, Langobard K 23.7–10, 32–34, 40–45, 54–57
Magnús, St, OJ, s. of Erlendr 31.44–46
Magnús, NK, s. of Haraldr Sigurðarson 29.3–6; 30.3 (uncle of Magnús berfœttr); 31.1

Magnús, NK, s. of St Óláfr 16.53; 18.18; 21.t., 5–6, 13, 15, 18, 21, 25; 22.t., 2, 6–22; 24.t., 2–11, 20–38, 41; 25.1–34, 40–44; 27.t., 1–17, 34–49; 28.3
Magnús, NK, called 'berfœttr', s. of Óláfr, s. of Haraldr Sigurðarson 30.t., 1–3, 8–11; 31.t., 4–29, 36–42; 32.t., 1–16; 34.3
Mardasa, s. of Chosroes 26.66
Margareta, d. of SK Ingi Steinkelsson 31.27
Mithridates, K of Pontus 26.9–33

Narses, the patrician 17.17
Nero, Emp. 26.98, 114
Nicasius, abp, St 17.41
Nikulás Sigurðarson 31.49

Óláfr (Eiríksson), SK 14.2, 23, 30; 16.22, 47; 18.20
Óláfr, s. of Haraldr Fair-hair 4.35
Óláfr, St, NK, s. of Haraldr, s. of Guðrøðr sýr 10.23; 13.t., 10–12, 15–22, 29–33; 15.t., 1–3, 7–55; 16.t., 2–28, 39, 41, 43–54; 18.t., 4, 13–39; 19.t., 1–82, 87; 20.36–42, 47–51; 21.t., 3, 5, 7, 10, 12, 20; 24.25–30, 33–34; 25.10, 13; 27.t.; 28.1; 29.16–17
Óláfr, NK, s. of Haraldr Sigurðarson 29.t., 1–2, 10–24; 30.1, 10; 31.1
Óláfr, NK, s. of Magnús berfœttr 32.14, 18–22
Óláfr Tryggvason, NK 4.28, 30–34; 7.t., 2–20, 22–23, 27, 30, 33, 35, 37–40; 8.t., 1–11; 9.t., 1–15; 10.t., 1–15, 18, 24–25, 33; 11.t., 1–11, 19–24; 12.t., 1, 20–25; 13.2–10, 17–18; 14.t., 1–18; 16.7; 20.39–40
Ole, pseudonym of Óláfr Tryggvason 7.16
Otto, Duke of Saxony 16.27–28
Otto, Emp., 'the pious' 5.25–26
Otto, Emp. 'Rufus' 5.11–20, 25–26; 6.25–28

Pallas, s. of Evander 18.109–126
Peter, St 12.16; 23.48, 53
Pharnaces, s. of Mithridates 26.8–17
Philip, K (of Macedon) 17.28
Pope (unnamed; see n. 225) 23.9, 11–18, 41, 44–54

Robert, abp of Rouen 13.20
Robert Capet, K of France 13.23–28
Rǫgnvaldr Brúsason, OJ 18.40; 21.8

Sigeweard, bp 8.t., 4–5; 20.39
Sigurðr Hranason 31.48
Sigurðr, NK, s. of Magnús berfœttr 32.14–17, 22–26; 33.t., 1–24; 34.1–8, 10, 18
Sigurðr, step-f. of St Óláfr 15.51
Sigurðr (Hlǫðvisson), OJ 9.t., 3–19; 18.41–43
Sigurðr ullstrengr 31.30–35
Steigar-Þórir, fosterer of NK Hákon, s. of Magnús 29.7–8; 31.2–10
Stephen, St 19.62–63
Sveinn bryggjufótr 21.10
Sveinn, NJ, s. of Hákon Sigurðarson 14.31–32, 36, 43, 49; 15.42–44, 53–63; 20.48
Sveinn, DK, s. of Haraldr Gormsson and f. of Knútr 'the mighty' 14.2, 23, 28–29; 16.31
Sveinn Haraldsson, 'pseudo-king' 31.4–5, 12
Sveinn, s. of Knútr Sveinsson 'the mighty' 18.2; 19.3; 20.51, 55; 21.4; 22.1–4, 11
Sveinn, DK, s. of Úlfr and Ástríðr 24.8–11, 40–41; 25.2, 42; 27.1–5, 35–41; 28.6
Sylvester, St, pope 13.39
Syrois, s. of Chosroes 26.34, 67–83, 96

Theobrand, priest 8.6; 12.1, 7–9, 19–22
Theodoricus, monk Prol. 1, 5; incipit p. 5; explicit p. 54
Thermo, priest (= Þormóðr) 8.7; 12.23–29

Titus, Emp. 26.99–111
Tostig, b. of EK Harold 28.9–15, 31–32
Tryggvi, s. of Óláfr and f. of Óláfr Tryggvason 4.28, 31, 34–37
Turnus 18.110, 121
Úlfhildr, d. of St Óláfr 16.27
Úlfr Hranason 31.48
Úlfr, f. of DK Sveinn by Ástríðr, d. of Sveinn and half-sister of Knútr 'the mighty' 24.8
Ursula, St 17.45
Valdemar, RK 7.4
Viðkunnr Jóansson 31.47–48
William, Duke of Normandy 13.21, 26, 27
Þóra, concubine of Hákon Sigurðarson 10.28
Þorfinnr Sigurðarson, OJ 9.10
Þorgeirr, b.-in-law of Óláfr Tryggvason 13.4, 8
Þorgils of Ǫlfus 12.18
Þórir, half-b. of Magnús, s. of St Óláfr 27.39
Þórir hundr 16.37; 19.11, 70
Þórir klakka 7.26; 10.16
Þormóðr, priest = Thermo
Ǫgmundr Skoptason 31.24

2. PLACES AND PEOPLES

Aachen 30.24
Africa 26.57
Agðanes, N 7.30; 10.4; (port at) 32.38
Agrippina (= Cologne) 17.44
Alps 23.27, 29
Áróss, D 24.43
Auxerre 20.23
Bergen, N 32.32, 35, (palace at) 35–37
Bithynia 13.38
Bláland, see Ethiopia
Brenneyjar 22.10
Bretland, see Cornwall
Britain, Greater 7.12
Britain, Lesser (= Ireland) 3.21
Britons 17.45
Brundisium 32.40
Caesarea 20.13
Charybdis 16.62–64; 17.t., 1–13
Cologne 17.44
Constantinople (and emperors of) 13.38; 17.22–26; 28.44–46
Cornwall (= *Bretland*) 31.39–41 (see n. 304)
Dalr (part of Gautland) 31.15, 27–28
Denmark (Danes, Danish kings) 4.20, 21, 23; 5.2; 6.8, 11, 17, 26; 7.5; 14.2, 28; 15.4; 16.29; 20.52; 22.t., 3, 7, 9; 24.t., 4, 13, 17; 25.13, 18, 43; 27.5, 6, 10, 11, 34, 40; 28.7; 30.40
England (the English) 2.5, 9; 7.2, 14, 25; 9.1; 10.16; 13.19, 29; 14.41; 15.t., 2, 7, 41; 16.29, 59, 60; 18.1; 20.40, 51; 22.4; 24.9; 28.t., 9, 10, 13, 15, 17, 32, 36; 29.1, 5
Ethiopia (*Bláland*) 28.40
Eyrarsund 25.3
Faroe Islands 3.3
Fitjar, N 4.11
Flanders (and count of) 8.7; 13.25
France (and king of) 13.23, 28
Francia (kingdom of Charles the Great) 23.12
Garðarshólmr (early name for Iceland) 3.27
Gaul, Gaulish provinces Prol. 31, 36; 17.38
Gautland (and kings of the Gautar) 31.13, 17, 25
Greece 25.t., 10, 29
Hálogaland, N 31.9
Helganes, D 24.42
Hlýrskógsheiðr, D 24.49
Hungary (= Pannonia) 17.21
Huns 17.t., 21, 26–49

Indexes

Hǫfuð (part of Gautland) 31.15–18, 27–28
Hǫrðaland, N 3.14
Iceland (Icelanders) Prol. 12; 1.7; 3.t., 19; 12.t., 2, 3, 30
Ireland, also called Lesser Britain (and the Irish) 3.21; 7.10; 32.4–7, 9–12, 15; 34.t.
Israel (sons of) 18.93
Italy 17.16; 23.7, 51, 62
Jerusalem 28.41; 33.3–5
Jordan, river 18.94, 97
Langobards 17.t., 17–19; 23.8, 32, 39, 59, 61
Loire, river Prol. 36
Longobarbs = Langobards
Maeotic swamps 17.27
Mainz 30.17
Mostr, N 10.2–4
Mærin, N 11.16
Nesjar, N 15.55
(Niðarhólmr, N 31.32–35; see n. 303)
Niðaróss (city, cathedral, diocese), N Prol. 5; 10.19; 11.16; 19.7; 20.42; 24.35; 29.16, 23; 31.35, 50
Normandy 13.22, 27; 28.16
Northmen Prol. 29, 35
Northumbria 28.14
Norway (Norwegians, Norwegian kings) Prol. 2–3, 9; 1.3; 2.11; 3.10; 4.19, 36; 5.7, 8; 6.1; 8.t.; 9.3; 10.1, 3; 14.33; 15.t., 13, 40; 16.31, 35, 56; 18.3, 17; 20.53–54; 21.1–2, 17, 23; 22.8; 23.62; 25.10, 13, 21, 28, 41; 27.t., 2, 6, 8, 10; 29.2, 20; 31.3, 6, 16; 32.2, 16; explicit p. 54
Orkney Islands 9.t., 2–4; 16.63–64; 18.42; 31.36, 43; 32.16
Pannonia (= Hungary) 17.11, 15, 20
Paris Prol. 27; 20.26
Parthians (= Persians) 8.19
Pavia 23.10

Pentland Firth = Petlandsfjǫrðr
Persia (Persians) 8.12, 44; 26.60, 62; 33.5. See Parthians, Saracens
Petlandsfjǫrðr 16.63
Phoenicia 33.9
Pontus 26.9, 28
Red Sea 18.95
Rheims 17.42, 43
Rhine, river 30.17
Rimull, N 10.27
Rome 13.39; 18.110; 34.31
Rouen 13.21, 29
Russia 7.3; 15.62; 16.t., 48; 21.15; 28.40
(Saracens, see Persians, 33.5)
Sauðungssund, N 15.22
Saxony (Saxons) 23.21; 30.41–53
Scilly Isles 7.11
Scotland 31.39; 34.2
Scythia, Nether Prol. 29–30
Scythia, Upper (= Sweden) Prol. 30–31
Seine, river Prol. 32
Seville 20.21
Sicily 28.43
Sidon 33.8–9
Síða, in Iceland 12.13
Skálaholt, in Iceland 12.13
Slavia (= Vindland) 14.19
Sóli, N 16.36
Stiklastaðir, N 19.25
Storð, N 4.11
Svǫldr 14.19
Sweden Prol. 32; 14.2, 30; 16.48; 18.20
Sæla, N 15.17
Thule 3.6; 12.3
Tours Prol. 37
Tunga, N 16.41
Upplǫnd, N 4.37; 13.9; 15.50; 19.2; 27.13
Vambarhólmr, N 31.9
Véar (part of Gautland) 31.15, 27–28
Vienne 23.55

The Vík, N 13.5; 15.52; 19.4; 29.22
Vindir = Wends
Vindland (= Slavia) 14.20
Wends 24.t., 12–19, 35–38
Þjálfahellir, N 7.31; 10.5
Þjórsárdalr, in Iceland 12.18
Þrándheimr (and people of), N 15.48–49; 19.2, 5
Qlfus, in Iceland 12.18

3. AUTHORS AND BOOKS

Augustine, St 18.111; 26.46
Bede 20.21, 24
Boethius Prol. 23
Book about the birth of the blessed Mary 26.51
Book of the infancy of Jesus 26.50–51
Chronicle of Hugh of St Victor Prol. 28 (cf. n. 9); 20.29 (cf. n. 210)
Chronicle of Sigebert of Gembloux Prol. 34
Chrysippus 17.4
Eusebius 20.13, 17, 22
Gelasius 26.42, 48
Genesis 17.8
Gospel of St Bartholomew 26.53
Gospel of St Thomas 26.52
History of the Normans (by William of Jumièges) 13.18–19
History of Pannonia, see Paul the Deacon
Hugh of St Victor Prol. 26; 20.25, 30; cf. Chronicle of Hugh of St Victor
Isidore, St 20.20
Itinerary of Clement 26.52
Jerome, St 8.20; 13.35; 18.91, 100–107; 20.28, 30
Jornandes (his history) 17.26
Lucan 4.6 (cf. n. 36); 14.38; 18.56; 23.27; 26.24; 27.28; 31.19; 34.24
Natural History, see Pliny

On the exaltation of the Holy Cross 26.38–39, 55–56
Origen 18.84–89
Ovid (= the satirist) 34.18
Passion of St Andrew 26.50
Passions of apostles 26.49
Paul ('the apostle'), his first epistle to Timothy 1.15
Paul the Deacon 17.9–12
περὶ ἀρχῶν ('Concerning first things'), see Origen
Plato 18.69, 75
Pliny the Elder 17.2–3; 18.47, 53; 26.27; his Natural History 17.3; 18.48
Psalmist 17.53, 18.95
Register of Norwegian kings 20.53–54
Remigius of Auxerre 20.23
The Roman History 5.19; 26.37, 56–57
Septuagint (translators) 20.18
Sigebert, monk of Gembloux, see Chronicle
Virgil 27.21 (cf. n. 265)

4. CHURCHES & MONASTERIES

St Benedict and St Laurence's monastery (Niðarhólmr) 31.31–35
Holy Trinity church, Niðaróss 29.15, 23–24
St Mary's church, Niðaróss 29.18
St Michael's monastery, Bergen 32.31–32
Monte Cassino monastery 17.10
St Peter's church, Skálaholt 12.15–16
St Victor's monastery, Paris Prol. 27 (cf. 20.25–26)

5. MISCELLANEOUS

Alþing 12.31
Apollo, image of 18.110
Christ's cross, relic of 33.16
seiðmenn 11.22